Nowhere Bound

Nowhere Bound

A SPUD'S REFLECTIONS ON CLIMBING
AND CAVING—AND OTHER USELESS TOILS

David A. Ek

Published by:
Badwater Books
Catlett, Virginia

Editing: Kristy Phillips
Cover Photograph: David A. Ek
Cover Art and Design: Delaney-Designs
Interior Design: Creative Publishing Book Design

ISBN Paperback: 979-8-9876517-4-2
ISBN eBook: 979-8-9876517-5-9

Printed in the United States of America.

Dedicated to all the climbing and caving souls I've shared adventures with, especially Rick, Dan, Roger, Mike, Andrew, Ronal, Larry, and Ken.

Contents

All Things Green

The image of the lone alpinist is inaccurate, for even the solo climber ascends with, and their climb is enriched by, a community of the past and present.

Dimensions. I've always loved dimensions. I grew up in a world where horizons compelled us not to look just out, but also up. Later, upon pushing forward into the vertical realm, I began noticing footprints and enticing clues leading back. Over time, landscape riches grew with each step forward *and* back. The expanding horizon became a page-turning mystery that demanded exploration in four full dimensions.

For me, an interest in mountainscapes naturally extended to the past. Legends and lore are essential elements of any human construct—even for an aspiring mountaineer. Images of the Eiger flash through my mind. If it weren't for human dimensions, the Eiger's infamous North Face would merely be a scenic photo op of a steep and crumbling wall of ice and rock. However, within the realm of interconnected dimensions, the legend of the Eiger was born.

Ah, the Eiger. This neophyte bows not only to your mighty presence, but out of ominous respect and fear, I speak your name in quiet and hushed undertones. You don't need a second name or qualifier. It's not Eiger Mountain, Mount Eiger, or Eiger Peak, but simply the Eiger. John, Paul, George, and Ringo don't require further introductions. Why would the Eiger?

There were repeated attempts, failures, disasters, and deaths on the Eiger's mighty North Face before the first ascent on July 6, 1938, by Anderl Heckmair, Ludwig Vörg, Heinrich Harrer, and Fritz Kasparek. Place names such as White Spider, Ice Hose, Difficult Crack, Swallow's Nest, Hinterstoisser Traverse, Traverse of the Gods, and Death Bivouac send shivers over sane climbers contemplating ascending the Eigerwand because the climber must face both the mountain *and* the legend. Even Clint Eastwood joined the foray in his murder mystery adventure film *The Eiger Sanction*. As a stark reminder that the legends weren't baseless, a falling rock killed a camera operator during filming on the actual North Face. In a twisted quirk of human nature, the Eiger's notoriety and degree of risk contributed greatly to climbers' desire to test their mettle and step into the legend by stepping out on this crumbling face. Have we eaten the insane breadfruit that took reason prisoner?

As in all legends, the dimension of time both fades and softens harsh edges. An ascent of the Eiger's North Face now has lost some of the mystique it once had, but it's still a difficult, challenging, and dangerous climb. However, the North Face has forever transcended into the sacred realm that gives birth to magical dreams. From a young age, I mentally entered that realm, both day and night. It sustained and nurtured me—and life was good. Only much later did I understand that to climb challenging dream mountains requires planning, preparation, and training.

When I first started climbing, it seemed odd or incongruent to physically train for a climb. As a youth, I practiced techniques all the time, ranging from aid-climbing in trees and rappelling off basketball backboards, to experiencing the thrill of jumping out of trees while tethered to a rope. However, physical training never crossed my mind. In hindsight, this lack of training may very well have contributed to my perpetual mediocracy—always being on the cusp of being a good climber. At the cusp, but never crossing that magical line. In the end, the cusp means squat.

During those naïve days, I prescribed to Don Whillans's theory of physical training. Don's fame came from not only his outstanding technical abilities on climbs from the 1950s to the 1970s but also his stamina, bold ascents, gruff exterior and witty working-class humor—and his pub belly. He theorized that physical conditioning only lasted for a finite duration, so why waste it? Therefore, if someone exercised before a climb, the body's peak performance period would pass and then fade while still on the approach hike. Consequently, his logic dictated it's best to condition on the approach hike, on the climb, or not at all.

From my understanding, his theory also extended to harder climbs requiring starting from an even lower level of physical depravity. From what other starting point could a climber demonstrate the greatest range of improvement? Before long approaches in the Himalayas, he "conditioned" by drinking vast quantities of alcohol, sleeping little, eating junk food, and lounging in pool halls for extended periods. This may sound odd at first, but I have no doubt that it worked for Don Whillans.

Well, I may never have been *that* bad, but then again, I was never *that* good.

Intensive training for climbing didn't become the rage until much later. Pioneer mountaineers didn't need to spend time honing their technical climbing skills to meet the biggest challenges of the day. Their biggest obstacles ranged from endurance and mental control to boldness. As climbs became more technically demanding, it became harder to easily transition from being a TV-watching slug into doing one-finger pull-ups on overhanging cliffs.

In the 1980s, we praised and revered John Bachar as a rock god. He performed his heroic and otherworldly ascents through intense physical and technical training—all the while honing his craft and toning his muscles specifically for climbing. John Bachar's gut profile probably had few comparisons to Don Whillans's.

John introduced the Bachar ladder, a rope-and-PVC ladder used for arm and shoulder training. The Bachar ladder isn't much more than monkey bars made of rope—the type of plaything children used to play on before helicopter parents and our litigious society replaced them with nothing. Even *I* began accepting the need for training. For me to climb the Eiger and other bold classics, Don Whillans's philosophy might not have been the best model.

When assured no one was watching, I flailed on the lower rungs of the Bachar ladder until my unconditioned arms gave way—or my fear of falling kicked in once I got beyond eighteen inches off the ground. I quickly learned I was no Don Whillans and no John Bachar. I also learned there were far too many people watching me train in such open areas. Training is hard, but finding a hidden mock-free place is even harder. While my training and conditioning didn't take me far, still, my well-exercised dreams and aspirations lifted me to countless summits and beyond. It became painfully obvious, even at a tender age, that my climbing passion and desires exceeded my body, skills, and abilities, as well as the training regimen needed to successfully execute.

In other words, I failed a lot.

In the Cascades of my youth, it seemed most of my failures occurred on, in, or below the green-book mountains. By that, I mean the green-covered Volume II of Beckey's Bible. The first edition of Volume I had a brown cover, while Volume III stood out in dark red. Technically, none of these volumes were Beckey's Bible. The real Beckey's Bible, an informal name given to a small one-volume, pocket-sized climbing guide Fred Beckey wrote in 1949, had long been out of print. This booklet became the area's standard (hence the Bible moniker) until Fred replaced it with his much improved, expanded, and glorious *Cascade Alpine Guide: Climbing and High Routes, Columbia River to Stevens Pass.*

As I came back home from the store in 1973, this newly minted, brown-covered godsend in my hand so captivated me that I didn't catch the part that said, "Columbia River to Stevens Pass." At ten times the mass of the original Beckey's Bible, why wouldn't it cover all of Washington's Cascade Range? I had to wait a painstakingly long four years for the last volume to come out. In the meanwhile, I studied each photograph of the brown volume under a magnifying glass, thumbprinted and caressed every word and letter, and salivated over every one of the ample footnote references.

Finally, the last volume came out in 1977. Once again, I couldn't wait to return home from the REI store (only one in the nation at the time). Only then did I realize this blessed green volume didn't extend from Stevens Pass to the Canadian border as expected. It truncated the range at Rainy Pass.

Will I be an old man before Fred Beckey completes the entirety of my beloved North Cascades so that I, too, may explore their depths? I wondered. Volume III, the *real* last, came out in 1981. I waited eight long years. At that stage, nearly half my life! The wait was worth it. I could now explore the extent of the range to my heart's content from the comforts of my bedroom and hearth.

The brown peaks are the most accessible and snow free, the red peaks more remote, with mythical, trailless expanses. But as a book, the green volume had the greatest heft and greatest lure. The green-book mountains were taller and more glacier clad. The green book held the greatest legendary mystique. All were wonderful, but each color-coded part of the range had its defining personality and mood. And since 1981, these colors came to hold deeper meaning and significance.

I had climbing successes and failures on brown and red peaks, but for the longest time, most of my failures were bounded by green. I began wondering if there was a green volume curse. Maybe green mocked and reminded me that mastery of the green eluded me. Maybe it told me that my training and conditioning rose to only the browns and an occasional red but weren't worthy of a green. I failed on dozens of greens—lost, dejected, repulsed, stormed, iced, avalanched, darkness-befallen, time-stolen, and overall befuddled. The unforgiving greens.

To further deflate and mock me, my failures weren't on the grand and storied green classics. This would have been more palatable. I could boast of powerful mountain forces repulsing us off a winter ascent of Johannesburg Mountain's North Face or of raking rockfall on Bonanza Peak's Company Headwall. Masters and neophytes alike would accept bold failures on dramatic peaks. This would even be grand. But no, the woefully less fabled kind tortured me, including the diminutive Peak 5,335. Peak 5,335—too insignificant and lowly to even rank a name.

Beckey's green god said this diminutive peak is "very rocky on the N," and the mountain's core is composed of quartz diorite—a rock climbers prefer for its soundness. These were good indications that the shadowy northern flank could hold technical challenges and new discoveries. New climbs seemed ripe for picking, ripe for exploration, and ripe for potentially new technical climbing routes. It was as if Fred Beckey laid the trail of breadcrumb clues directly for me as a personal gift—all wrapped in green. Even though it was winter, my palms sweated, and my soul turned green with envy and anticipation.

I couldn't wait for winter's white to melt so I could explore this uncharted green jewel. I talked the unsuspecting and naïve Randy into coming along. We attempted a circuitous approach. Snow still covered everything. We didn't get far before we were wallowing and flailing in deep whiteness. We came back the next time with snowshoes. The avalanche danger soon grew too high, and prudence dictated another retreat. I waited until the snow had melted. I waited too long. The avalanche slope that repulsed us earlier held no snow, but the horrible nightmare of green tangled brush and green biodefenses slowed us even more. We never got close to the mountain. The cursed green!

In the following year, I timed it just right: late enough in the year for the white not to avalanche or require snowshoes, but early enough that hardened snow covered the hateful greenery. That part worked. We made good time, considering neither of us was in good shape. I began to doubt the wisdom of the Don Whillans training plan. While our good time might have been enough for a brown, green refused me to pass that easily. We ran out of time. We got above the repulsive slope and reached the saddle leading to 5,335's summit. We finally gazed at the peak's northern flank—just a slice. Through fading light and swirling mist and upwelling clouds, we caught glimpses of what looked like a climber's dream—a grayish granite buttress jutting from the mountain's stark and sepia-toned base like a dagger slicing upward into the enchanted, mist-swirled heavens. My conjured image might have been wishful thinking, but that fleeting image is all I've got.

Touching this buttress with boots and adrenaline-pumping and fear-induced sweating fingers would have to wait. With the last glimmer of light, we scrambled as fast as we could up the nearby easy gully to the summit. The clouds were too thick to let us catch any further view of the northern rampart. We headed back, regaling ourselves with wild tales of our anticipated return and glories of new routes on Peak 5,335. This never happened. We never returned, but not from a lack of want or desire. Randy drifted off in his direction, and I drifted off toward mine. For me, this included a move to the blue-skied, red-rock canyon country of northeastern Arizona.

From that glorious moment on, that mist-shrouded image moved with me. From Washington to Arizona, to Colorado, Wyoming, New Mexico, Puerto Rico, Kentucky, Oregon, Georgia, California, Nevada, and eventually Virginia. While it might have continued to feed inner fires, it lifted me no closer to touching a hand to rock. In my mind, a whole new cultural construct had developed. The mountain took on a mythical distinction all its own.

I may never know. Perhaps the swirling mist deceived us—the untrodden buttress might not have been as glorious as it seemed to tired minds under fading light. Perhaps it *was* just as glorious as it looked, but we weren't up for the task. Maybe the climb's technical needs required a team with green-level technical abilities, more boldness, and a greater willingness to stick brown necks out. Perhaps there's a reason I failed on many greens.

❦

My green failures were often the result of weather and conditions beyond my control since, after all, these were alpine mountains in a region known for its horrific rainy and stormy weather. However, a little rain, snow, storm, and avalanche never stopped the early climbing legends. Weather rarely dampened Hermann Ulrichs's drive and determination. So why should it stop me?

Hermann Ulrichs's prolific storm blew into the Californian, Cascadian, and Canadian climbing scene in the 1920s and raged furiously throughout the 1930s. However, not even the mightiest hurricane can sustain itself forever. Hermann's storm dissipated by World War II, as if the clouds could no longer hold enough moisture to satisfy his thirst. Despite the storm's brevity, the aftermath of Hermann's path through the Cascades forever reshaped the landscape and, for me, gave the peaks their vivid green distinction. My internal storm produced no wind, only puffy and diminutive clouds that released no moisture. Like Peak 5,335, I, too, have no name. I must have spent a lot of time under other people's clouds because it seemed to rain on me a lot—and I repeat, *a lot*. I experienced unmeasurable rain in green-book attempts, but never as much as when failing to retrace Hermann Ulrichs's route up Silver Eagle Peak.

Rick and I began the approach up the Foss River Valley in a flood. Despite the atrocious weather, we had the time off and itched to head into the mountains. It had been a long and dreary winter, even by Pacific Northwest standards, and we were anxious for summer to arrive. Our chances remained slim, due both to it being too early in the spring and my unrelenting green-book curse. Snow blanketed the higher mountains, and the recent torrential rainstorm swelled river valleys. Disregarding these green-book defenses, Rick and I hiked up the Foss River late in the afternoon, during a heavy squall, with the hope of finding a reasonably dry spot to camp. We planned to climb Silver Eagle Peak early the next morning.

The Cascades were usually wet. If it wasn't currently raining, it soon would be. But this trip was wetter than I'd ever experienced—*ever*. The rain came heavy and steady, and it was unrelenting. Hiking in such conditions was absurd—and humorous. Rivulets on the "ground" merged into one continuous and swirling maelstrom. The high water obscured the stream channels. All streams merged into one continuous Noah-level sheet-flow. Our eyes could discern no higher "ground" from the depths of stream channels, so while wading, our feet routinely plunged unexpectedly into deeper water, knocking us off balance and each time nearly tipping us into the flood. I can't remember why we continued in such conditions. We must have been desperate for an adventure. Maybe we were making light of the green.

No place seemed conducive to set up camp, so we continued well past dark, proceeding into the storm by headlamp. After wading in this fashion for another hour, through the splatters of rain bouncing off our headlamps, we saw an unusual glow far in the blackened distance. We couldn't identify the apparition, so we approached cautiously. Laughter and human merriment accompanied this mysterious phenomenon.

After approaching to within a few feet, we gazed at an absurdly surreal scene. There in front of us were two redneck-looking fellows in their forties who'd set up an elaborate camp, complete with family-sized tent, a separate large frame with rainproof awning, Coleman lanterns, tables, large ice chests full of beer, a crate of Wild Turkey whiskey, and what looked like a month's supply of food and supplies. They were drinking Wild Turkey, were well inebriated, and kept laughing at their stupid antics. Unobserved, we stood in amazement at the farthest extent of the lantern's glow, wondering how in the world they'd packed all their supplies several miles up the Foss River.

What are they doing here? we wondered. *Are they dangerous?*

Eventually, we called out, hoping not to startle them or give an indication we'd been watching them for the last few minutes. Upon hearing disembodied voices, they dropped and knocked things over while darting their eyes left and right, up and down. They almost fell off their chairs from both surprise and inebriation. After gaining as much control as people in such conditions could muster and discovering we were living, corporeal beings, they invited us into their camp and under a dry awning. They offered us Wild Turkey. We accepted the awning but declined the drink.

During a long and slurred conversation, they told their story of having arranged with a horse packer to drop them and their supplies off several days before our arrival. They'd remained there ever since. They'd arrived before the rain and flood came, and now the storm had them trapped. They'd made the best of it. To them, this meant Wild Turkey—lots of it. They were enjoying both the solitude and being uninhibited. We chatted with them for about an hour before continuing our pointless hike through the continuing storm, thick brush, and darkness. Both parties probably thought to themselves, *While in the green woods, you meet the strangest people.*

We never made it even close to Silver Eagle Peak. While my boots have graced green summits, they never made it up Pirate Peak, Mount Maude, Mount Cleator, Chiwawa Mountain, Mount Higgins, Sentinel Peak, East Wilmans Spire, Mount Chaval, or Peak 5,335's northern untrod ramparts. I also never made it up the north face of the Eiger. Sometimes, late at night from the comforts of home, I wonder why I never rose to the challenge of climbing the Eiger—either *the* Eiger or the many *my* Eigers. Whatever the reason, they remain forever green peaks to me. These enchanted summits have grown beyond a mere high promontory or a primary color. They've transcended into the realm of another dimension—the fifth or green dimension.

Beyond the Sunless Cleft

*F*amed sports-medicine doctor and triathlon coach John Hellemans claims there are three progressive stages of athletic development: trainee, maturity, and champion. Similarly, I've read that chefs have ten development stages. However, what these classification experts fail to recognize is that the lower and moderate levels contain hidden off-ramps that lose a significant number of aspiring masters down one-way cul-de-sacs mired in endless construction detours. For these people, neophytes don't turn into experts, and experts into champions. And masters don't expand into new dimensions. These pitiful wannabe champions will never taste the sweet dish that comes only when body, soul, mind, and masterful experience transcend individual ingredients contained in an otherwise common recipe. There will be no master chef turning potatoes into toròz, crocchè, or even pommes Anna with Gruyère, for the potatoes that reside within these one-way cul-de-sacs will forever remain no more than a mere spud.

❧

Plodding and stumbling along in a weariness-induced stupor, I wondered how long it would be before my next dry heave. Suddenly a snowshoe-shod boot slipped off the icy log, and my foot plunged into the underlying stream—the first vestige of an early spring melt. I privately cursed my sloppiness. How long could I keep the misery hidden from my climbing partners? The fact that I cared indicated I must not have been as tired as I felt. This kept me going for a few more steps. Human bodies, especially mine, weren't made for such abuse.

I was in the beginning stages of a multiday early spring snowshoe and climbing trip in the Enchantment Lakes region of Washington's Cascade Range, so I had no time to dwindle, peak, or pine. *How could I endure the strain for days?* I worried, *If I can't hold food or water down or stop my nearly endless convulsive dry heaves?* I somehow managed to make it to the end of the day after miles of subconscious and delirious effort. In times such as these, miles and minutes, even hours, are abstract and meaningless.

The boot heels in front of me stopped. I stopped. When the heels began moving, I strained under both the pack's weight and the Earth's gravity field by once again began moving. All movement and thoughts were joyless and fully automated. Finally, after what seemed like a lifetime, Don, Kurt, or whosever heels I'd been following for hours, days, lifetimes reached a place that must have seemed a good place to settle in for the night. Subconsciously, I listened to disembodied voices as they pondered the relative merits of the site. I no longer cared where to throw up the tent. For me, it became just another dry heave. I only wanted to crawl inside and end what had been a long day.

While the disembodied voices debated protection from wind, storm, and avalanches, I gazed into what probably was an enchanting winter landscape, complete with magical ice crystals dancing on little hummocks and raising their upstretched arms toward the sky as if trying to pull snow-laden fir branches down so they could touch and converse in a unified subalpine harmony. Fairies dancing in circles around magical shining crystals and sparkling sun dabs only added to the enchantment. Suddenly, I realized the crystal dancers weren't magical fairies. They were Don and Kurt tamping down snow so the tent could have a firm base. I interrupted my delirium long enough to pretend to help. After someone or something tamped the snow and set up camp, I undressed, tossed my wet clothes into the tent's far corner, and, as quickly as I could, drunkenly fell into the chilled and damp sleeping bag.

By the middle of a long and fitful night, I regained enough clarity of mind to tend to my wet clothing—items essential to climbers in harsh environments. In the dark, I groped for the frozen lumps that previously had been my socks and placed them inside the sleeping bag and against my cold and clammy skin. I'd regained enough mental discipline to endure a short-term discomfort with the knowledge it would pay off in the end—giving me warm and dry socks in the morning. Small comforts and pleasures are few when winter moun-taineering. Sometimes it's the little things that are most appreciated while passing through high and primitive mountains in the depths of a terrain humans weren't meant to trod.

For the rest of the fitful night, bent in a fetal position around frozen socks, I caressed them next to my frigid body. Although the frozen bricks drained me of precious heat and energy, for the next day's sake, I *had* to persevere so my socks would be tolerable by morning. I became single-mindedly focused upon this one task. It became my sole purpose in life.

At last, first light's crescent called an end to the miserable year-long night. I'd survived the ordeal. Survival is always the mark of a successful trip! The frozen socks episode that I so painfully endured had transitioned into the dry and toasty realm of survival—even hope. Unfortunately for me, the dry and toasty realm was not to be, because the socks turned out to be Kurt's. Mine were still frozen lumps lying in the tent's corner. With failing energy and strength, and a coldly indifferent ice ax, I pummeled and chipped *my* socks into submission. I planned to continue the beating until either the socks were pliable enough to stuff feet inside or my anger dissipated. Kurt smugly thanked me and said his socks were "perfect." No amount of pummeling would have dissipated anything coursing through my spudly blue-blood veins, but the bricks finally gave way to the axe, so I stuffed groaning feet inside, gulped a cup of white-gas-contaminated oatmeal, sipped some water, and immediately rushed off to dry heave. This must have been Don and Kurt's signal to go, since their boot heels forged ahead. I donned my one-half-body-weight pack enough to overcome Earth's gravitational pull and started the day's tortuous ritual all over again.

Non-climbers often wonder why mountaineers willingly and repeatedly place themselves in pain, discomfort, misery, and sometimes life-or-death epics. It's one of those situations in which if you have to ask, you'll likely not understand the answer. In any case, climbers usually have strong willpower, inner strength, and the ability to derive something mentally or spiritually from climbing that's of greater value than the costs. This is the only way to overcome overpowering urges to quit and the only way to explain such otherwise irrational behavior. Going home usually involves just as much discomfort as continuing; therefore, the only painless alternative is to simply give up. To continue despite short-term pain is a sign of character. At least that was what I told myself.

One strength I drew upon was my deep-seated bond with alpine mountains. Mountainscapes, even non-Eigers, are more than mere rock, ice, snow, and physical features. They're the stage on which intrepid souls find the alpine god's timeless interplay of body, spirit, cosmic forces, and Earth's past and present, all converging at the experiential point. It was far from being just exercise or a hobby. It was life. It was joy—at least after fully recovering from the last ordeal. This enchanting bond motivated me enough to endure one more step, one more move, one more rappel, one more dry heave—all to progress one step closer to nirvana.

With or without dry heaves, pioneer climbers had it much worse, and they kept at it despite mere physical discomfort. Famous modern-day climbers likely suffer even more than I ever did, so who am I to complain? Kurt was the epitome of strength and endurance, but he must have been as weary as I'd been since he, too, carelessly left his socks in the corner to freeze. Even on lonely, wild mountains, I found I wasn't as alone as I originally thought. Other climbers, past and present, formed a standard by which I not only gauged my mettle but formed an image to aspire to with each passing step.

Besides, one of the beauties of wilderness is it strips away all pretenses and exposes the meaninglessness of petty human complaints. Sacrificing a little comfort was worth it to grovel at the feet of grand cathedrals, whether under the sublime glow of sun-warmed granite or bent into the stinging wind of winter's mighty fury. How was it *not* worth it? Was my lowly comfort so important in the grand scheme of things? Who was I compared to the mountain gods or pioneering alpine masters? I wasn't, after all, a mountain god, or a climbing god—or even a talented and accomplished climber. I was but a spud. We can't all be John Roskelleys, can we? To transcend my spudness,

I thought I must endure physical discomfort and take it in stride if I ever hoped to make it to the top.

When I entered alpine cathedrals, I was never alone, even without Kurt's or Don's boots to follow. I also followed the boots of all pioneering climbers who passed through the same hallowed cathedrals. Their boots and presence left an indelible image on the same terrain my boots and socks trod. It therefore provided me strength to have relatable life experiences.

I have deep respect for pioneer climbers, since they endured even greater discomfort as they plowed deeper into the magical cathedral—and *they* continued despite discomforts. They carried heavy and primitive equipment, and they lacked even a rudimentary understanding of the terrain or impending dangers that awaited them. They must have had tremendous perseverance and an indomitable spirit. How can you not feel more alive by walking, crawling, or dry heaving in their footsteps?

Near the highest of these pinnacled motivational summits sits pioneer climber Hermann Ulrichs. Hermann experienced some of the same mountains I have, but he experienced them in much more difficult conditions and with primitive equipment. He also had farther to travel just to get to the mountain's base. Pioneer climbers like Hermann Ulrichs had to contend with mapless and uncharted terrain. In addition, there was no chance of rescue if problems arose. Self-sufficiency was a necessity. My feeble and mere discomforts and tribulations paled in comparison. It would insult Hermann's monumental efforts and exploratory contributions if I complained. Why was I so important that I needed shielding from the harsh realities of such a magnificent landscape? Would I have been a better person for not experiencing the world's alpine cathedrals or exploring their physical and spiritual realms? I think not. Such experiences breathed life into normality. I would have gladly followed Hermann's boots into any wild frontier.

Hermann Ulrichs climbed into exalted realms beginning in the 1920s and continued intensely throughout the 1930s. Most of his explorations were in the Sierra Nevada of California, the Cascades of Washington, and various ranges in western Canada. Initially, my interest and fascination lay in Hermann's North Cascades adventures, for the North Cascades have been, are, and always will be my favorite place on earth.

In Hermann Ulrichs's time, not only were many North Cascades summits unclimbed, but many weren't even on maps. This step into unknown blank regions, with no chance of a rescue, presented a level of challenge and difficulty that modern climbers can scarcely fathom or comprehend. Intrepid climbers from the 1920s and 1930s carried with them intense psychological burdens as they stepped into trackless unknowns. Why would they do this? They were as ill-prepared to solve this mystery as we are today. However, mysteries and burdens aren't unique to pioneering generations. Each climbing generation has its own burdens and challenges. The remaining constant, across generations, is this unifying quest for the mysterious unknown. Mysterious enchantments have pulled in not only pioneers, legends, and masters, but, like a cosmic black hole that sucks in all matter, they've even tugged on the hapless, neophyte, dreamer, misfit, and eccentric. Being part of a unifying cosmic force connecting both legend and spud—is this not motivation enough to continue, one step, and even one dry heave, at a time?

The Nerv of Perv

I admit it—climbing attracts misfits. No one accused me of being a typical teenager. My obsession with climbing and the North Cascades became acute and all-consuming. It went well beyond a mere interest or hobby. It was on par with Richard Dreyfuss's fixation on Devils Tower in the movie *Close Encounters of the Third Kind*. Library books taught me climbing moves that I practiced in backyard trees. I aid-climbed up maples, rappelled from branches, and even willingly jumped from sylvan perches to test climbing ropes and knots and to practice lessons learned page by page and in rock-remembered dreams as I reenacted my foliage fantasies.

Later, the North Cascades became my iron lung, dialysis machine, and Jarvik 7 all rolled into one. However, there was nothing artificial about the range. Just like Richard Dreyfuss in the movie, while at home, I made a precise to-scale clay model. Instead of Devils Tower, the North Cascades' Mount Shuksan served as my model. The carving accurately depicted lateral moraines and erosional features on my spiritual mountain. Mostly, I just constantly dreamt of mountains and wanted to learn everything I could about alpine landscapes. Climbing and the North Cascades gave me a purpose—gave me focus.

In a college geology class, I wrote a paper on the geology of the North Cascades. In a park management class, I presented a paper on the administrative history and the creation of North Cascades National Park. For a planning course, I investigated and discussed the controversy over adding a higher segment to Ross Dam located on the North Cascades' Skagit River. Instead of studying for subjects related to my University of Washington degree, I spent most of my nonclass time holed up in the university archives located in the basement of Suzzallo Library, reading about the North Cascades, their biology, their physical processes, and their history. Still, I had the sense enough to understand life demanded a *real* job, and for me, that meant persevering through college. I hoped to pursue a career with the National Park Service to be closer to my beloved mountains. I could then climb every day and every night—or so I thought.

This fixation led me to work seasonally in a state park containing no North Cascades, no mountains, and no climbs. Seasonal work became a necessary challenge one must endure to make it to the employment summit. However, to be farther away from climbing and the mountains seemed incomprehensible. This also meant having a non-climbing boss, doing non-climbing tasks, and interacting with non-climbers. While Harry Potter, in the magical world created by J. K. Rowling, had Muggles, I, in my world, had non-climbers. Fortunately for me, I met Pete. Although he had graying hair, he was no wizard. However, I found it magical working for Pete, despite him being a non-climber.

Besides being one of my better supervisors in my forty-year career, Pete remains one of the most unique and charismatic characters I ever met. For my second year of working with Pete, I moved to Crow Butte State Park. It occupied one-half of an island in the Columbia River west of the Umatilla Chemical Weapons Depot, where the US military stored and disposed of chemical weapons and nerve gas. It was also north of the Boardman coal-fired power plant, south of Chateau Ste. Michelle's vineyard, and east of the empty cheatgrass expanse of the Horse Heaven Hills. This isn't even remotely near any quality climbing. Why did I move to this desolate cheatgrassed island in the first place? Pete's charisma, my youth, and foolishness. Also, Pete asked.

The previous summer, I worked for Pete in a state park not far from Washington's Leavenworth climbing area. I soon discovered the fact that dawned on Hermann Ulrichs in the 1920s. He, too, naïvely chose to work seasonally in a mountain-festooned national park, thinking it would afford him infinite climbing opportunities. He and I were both wrong. Hermann, in Yosemite National Park, and I, near Leavenworth, learned our lessons the hard way. Living far removed from other climbers leaves park-bound climbers partner-less. Also, park schedules, including weekends, leave little time for climbing—least of all on rocks.

To compensate for these deficiencies, while working in the park near Leavenworth, I repeatedly climbed all the doorframes, door hinges, garage door track mechanisms, and everything that would hold my weight on the inside of the park's maintenance shop. This became my intensive training area, so much so that my soft rubber climbing shoes left black smears on all white-painted surfaces on all walls and even the ceiling. Pete, always easygoing, had his limits by the end of the season. He demanded I scrub off and repaint all surfaces. One day of painting removed all recorded evidence of my first ascents.

Pete knew of, but never understood, my climbing obsession. He used that knowledge for evil ends—to lure me to Crow Butte. He wanted me to follow him to his new park assignment. I told him I had no interest in Crow Butte. I wanted to live closer to worthwhile climbing. He boasted excitedly that there were several unclimbed cliffs on the island. He said I could climb on these cliffs to my heart's content and that, "I wouldn't even make you scrub the walls at the end of the year." I wanted to work with Pete, the supervisor, again, but I was hesitant to go to Crow Butte based on his, the non-climber's, recommendation. However, when the lure of first ascents and the opening of a new climbing area became too much for me to resist, he sold me. I signed on and moved to Crow Butte.

The park's reality didn't match the scene Pete painted, or fabricated. He'd white-washed its many blemishes. As I'd originally imagined, the island consisted of a cheatgrass lump far from anywhere and nowhere. In passionate exasperation and youthful shrillness, I shouted, "Where are the climbing cliffs?"

Grinning like a teenager who'd just snuck into an R-rated movie, he whispered, "Hop in." We then sped off toward my grail. No mountain walls, no matter how grand, could contain my excitement—David's cup runneth over. However, my short-lived euphoria and overflowing elixirs suddenly froze. After we came to a stop and stepped out of the car, Pete turned to me, sheepishly grinned, and pointed to a hideous crumbling and disintegrating old rock quarry. Explosives had shattered it so much that it looked like the whole grotesque thing could implode any second. I grimaced and then hesitantly approached.

Not unlike an Indiana Jones movie, there were rattlesnakes every-where—on the ground, on rocks, under rocks, and slithering up rocks. Like in a game of Twister, I maneuvered and contorted myself around snakes as I approached the cliff to test its climbing potential. As soon as I touched the cliff, a huge block rumbled, fell, and disintegrated into powder at my feet. I moved a few feet to the left and tried again. More of the same. Eventually, one narrow section sent only small, rumbling pieces to the ground. Testing this potential new route while disregarding the yawning two-foot void below my feet, I stood and balanced on my right foothold—and suddenly stared into rattlesnake eyes and a quivering tail. It became incumbent versus usurper, Rocky versus Apollo Creed. I was eyeball to eyeball, mano a mano—or rather mano a repto—with an angry rattlesnake rattling at head height—*my* head.

My recoiling action caused the rock I stood on to shatter, and gravity threw me in a heap at the bottom of the quarry. Fortunately, no snakes fell with me. I yelled at the uncontrollably laughing Pete, "You enticed me to come here for that hideous pile of crumbling rock!"

He renewed his laughter and said, "What do I know? I'm not a climber!"

I couldn't wait to leave this hideous disappointment of an assignment. In hindsight, I can't fully explain why I held Pete in such high regard as a boss. He made even tedious assignments fun. But if anyone else treated people like he did, any human resources department would have taken them to task for being cruel and mean-spirited. However, he had the magical ability to have it come off as good-natured ribbing.

"Perv" was a perfect example.

Pete introduced me to coworker Perv on my first day, and from that point on, I always called him Perv. He never corrected me or said anything about it, despite our working together closely for most of the summer. Being a young and naïve tater tot, I took it at face value that his parents had named him Perv.

Pete paired Perv and me on many projects that summer, including painting the outside of the campground restroom. They were big restrooms, and I had no knack for speed painting. This meant we had time to talk—lots of time. In those days, I couldn't let a moment pass in silence. After having worked with him for a month already, my curiosity got the better of me. As we dipped paintbrushes into the park-like green exterior paint, I said, "I've never heard the name Perv before. Where did it come from?"

With an annoyed look that didn't come from the tedium of painting, he explained that Pete had, years earlier, given him that nickname as a joke. It stood for *pervert*. Despite the two apparently being close friends for years, Pete's perverse sense of humor made him think such a name would get under Perv's skin, especially in front of the public. Apparently, it did, because Perv once made the mistake of showing his displeasure to Pete. This only caused Pete to double down and use the name Perv exclusively. Perv gave up objecting and settled into the fact that his name for all time would be Perv. I can't even recall Perv's real name now. He must have had one.

While painting that restroom with Perv, far removed from any mountain, cliff, machine shop, or maple to climb, I overcame the tedium by training my mind on mountains. I talked to Perv about climbing—to an extent that, at the time, I never imagined could be to excess. Painting the restrooms took nearly the entire day. As the last of the fishing boats returned to the marina and the sun moved toward the Horse Heaven Hills, we were still painting that blasted restroom. While I painted the trim on the left and Perv handled the vertical boards on my right, I proudly beamed upon the thought that I alone had made the day's tedium fly by so fast by efficiently vanquishing every moment of silence.

We were nearly finished painting when Perv threw his paintbrush into the cheatgrass and doubled over in convulsions. Out of concern, I rushed in to help and find out the cause of his affliction.

"Are you dry heaving?" I asked.

While still convulsing, Perv screamed at a volume sufficient to scare every rattlesnake from there to the sewer lagoon, "I like mountains just as much as the next guy, but goddamn it, Dave, you haven't shut up once about climbing in the last seven hours! It's mountain this, mountain that. You've recited the precise elevations of every named mountain on the planet, who climbed it, and when they climbed it. And then, by God, I think you started the whole goddamn climbing talk all over again. I like you well enough, but do you *ever* shut up about mountains?"

After his convulsions quieted, I, for the first time, stood motionless and dumbfounded. In the awkward silence, my stunned and motionless paintbrush slowly dripped green paint onto the brown and desiccated cheatgrass. It had never occurred to me that one could have too much climbing talk. Despite not being able to relate, I had enough social graces to understand that I *might* have contributed to Perv's convulsing affliction. I needed to make amends, since Perv was a friend and decent human being, despite being a non-climber.

Perv did me a huge favor that day. I started the slow process of becoming self-aware on the side of that partially painted green restroom on that cheatgrass-lumped, rattlesnake-festooned island that day. Reflecting on that summer and my Crow Butte life, I realized I had indeed talked nonstop the whole summer about mountains, climbing, mountaineers, mountain landforms, mountain history, and mountain aspirations. I just assumed everyone shared my interest in mountain minutiae. *Why wouldn't they?* I wondered. My stunned mind ascended toward knowing and becalming words from Emily Dickinson:

The Mountain sat upon the Plain

In his tremendous Chair

His observation omnifold,

His inquest, everywhere …

Since ancient Greek, Roman, and Viking eras, have not gods strolled among the hills? Apparently, Perv was too uncultured to know or appreciate such historical mountain legends. I decided I would have to teach him. However, until then, I apologized. As a gesture of goodwill, I asked him his real name. Out of respect and my newfound self-awareness and understanding of proper social graces, I vowed to use his real name from that point on.

In hindsight, I never used his real name again. His nickname, however rude and insensitive it was for me to do so, had become far too ingrained in my conscious and subconscious.

Besides, I pushed such trivial matters aside because I'd just remembered I hadn't asked Perv if he gave more credence to the 1951 or 1957 first ascent claim of the beautiful Alpamayo—the exquisite 19,511-foot conical mountain in Peru's Cordillera Blanca.

"Hey, Perv. Do you think Alpamayo is more beautiful than Chopicalqui but you have to admit Leigh Ortenburger's 1954 photograph of Chopicalqui perfectly captured the mountain's graceful beauty Perv I bet you would not have guessed Chopicalqui is higher than Alpamayo it is really Chopicalqui is 20,998 feet while Alpamayo is only 19,511 by the way, Perv, this reminds me of Hermann Buhl's first ascent of Pakistan's Nanga Parbat oh Perv did you know Hermann Buhl spelled his name with two *n*'s just like Hermann Ulrichs well you probably know on Nanga Parbat ..."

For some reason, I saw little of Perv for the rest of the season.

The Face, the Fiend, and the Ascent of Mount Bad

When not spending my teenage years in the mountains, I thought, talked, and dreamt incessantly of climbing big mountains with the famous, larger-than-life leading climbers. I wanted to follow in their footsteps—and then step out front. I had the drive, and I wanted that spark to push distant horizons.

During the summer, I worked for a local state park near the foot of a well-known mountain range and near a famed rock-climbing area with enticing and intriguing names that whetted my appetite for epic adventures. Surely, greatness would prevail simply through proximity. My future greatness only required a like-minded climbing partner. History had Terray and Lachenal, Kor and Dalke, and Fred Beckey and anyone who would hold his rope and pay for his gas. I could vividly see it—Ek and his partner, *the team*. Fate would surely shine on me. As the devout may say, providence will see me through! Oftentimes, after having such lofty notions, I would run home and reread Gaston Rébuffat's *Starlight and Storm*.

I perused the bulletin board at the local climbing shop. A note pinned to the cork asked for climbing partners for intermediate-level climbs. Ah, the holy grail! My mountain fantasies would soon begin. I called the number immediately.

Duane and I forged plans to climb one of the nearby rock pinnacles within a nearby rock-climbing area that consisted of mostly short routes on gritty and crumbling sandstone towers and slabs. What more could one ask?

Duane called the following morning to cancel our trip due to a recent injury he'd suffered. I suspected his pain had more to do with his injury interfering with my destiny than his sprained ankle, but I left that assumption unconfirmed. Oh, what an unfortunate fate had befallen me—and the impediments I must endure! Before he hung up the telephone, he suggested that I give his friend Derek a call instead. So, for this higher purpose, I overcame my natural shyness, and I called Derek. Well, I called Derek's mother. Apparently, Derek was spending that day climbing on the Liberty Bell massif. For me, it was yet another disappointment.

The following week, my call made its way past his mother and directly to Derek. We spoke for an hour about the only subject worth talking about. We made plans for a climb of the nearby north ridge of Mount Bad. We first agreed to climb a shorter rock route together to see if we were compatible as a team—and to gauge if we were up to challenging Mount Bad.

Warm early-morning heat waves were already rising into a deep-blue sky as I anxiously awaited Derek's arrival for a climb of a rock dome in a nearby canyon. He rolled up in his beat-up pickup truck as sounds of "Layla" wafted off canyon walls. We had the whole day for this relatively short climb, so I was in complete shock when

Derek, without a word, grabbed his pack and climbing rope, jogged up the trail, and disappeared into a pine forest. Not wanting to give the impression of weakness, I ran into the dust cloud.

I occasionally caught filtered glimpses of him up higher. He pressed on as if possessed. My body strained under the load as I feebly hauled my rope and hardware higher and higher—the best I could muster. Somehow, I finally caught up. Although we were nearing the start of the climb, I knew I couldn't keep up the maddening pace *and* hide the sheer agony my legs and lungs were enduring. However, my ego wouldn't allow me to ask for a break. Instead, looking out at a group of rock pinnacles within the Thorntree Crags, which were visible on the skyline, I asked a question that required Derek to momentarily stop to answer.

"Boy," I managed to get out. "It's sure a good [gasp] view of the [gasp] Domino Creek Group. Which one [gasp] is which?"

It was the first question that popped into my throbbing head, but as soon as I asked it, I knew I could have thought of a less lame question. *The answer is obvious, idiot*, I scolded myself. *Everyone knows the Domino Creek Group consists of ten uniquely shaped rock spires with such names as The Rat, The Leper, and The Snafflehound. Anyone can name them. He's gonna think I'm a clueless idiot.* I inwardly cursed myself for not thinking of a more intelligent question as a ruse to let me catch my breath.

It didn't take Derek long to rattle off all the names of the Domino Creek Group and begin once more his merciless attack of the steep and dusty slope. I sensed he wasn't the type for thoughtful and philosophical discussions. I followed in both mute frustration *and* admiration.

We reached the start of the climb and quickly roped together. I'd barely thrown the belay before he cruised up the main crack splitting the dome, and I meekly followed his lead. Where Derek flashed, I labored. Where Derek cruised, I thrashed. Nonetheless, I reached the top, content with the belief that my awkward gyrations were well concealed and I instead projected an image of experience, confidence, and control. Yes, *that* is the image I chose to carry with me. Apparently, my deception worked, since, as we coiled the rope, he asked if I wanted to tackle Mount Bad the next week.

We careened down the slope in a race to the car, leaving the dust to settle on anything not moving. I tried to keep up and not pitch headfirst down the pine-studded hillside. I soon forgot my leg and lung pain to live in the moment—and to immerse myself in dreams of Mount Bad and my rise in climbing greatness, which would surely come soon.

Next week couldn't come soon enough. I left work early in the afternoon to meet Derek at our prearranged roadside pullout. My car broke down farther along the road, interrupting our carpool. So we didn't arrive at the trailhead until four in the afternoon.

Like he had the previous week, as soon as Derek stepped out of the car, he grabbed his pack and dashed up the trail, leaving behind an all-to-familiar dust cloud. I grabbed my shiny new equipment-laden pack and ran into the billows, all the while wondering if he could keep up this insane pace the whole way. *Could it be possible Derek only knows one speed? Or is this his warming-up pace?* I asked myself. To the torment of my lungs, legs, and ego, I quickly learned it was the latter.

After a mile up the trail, I suggested we slow our pace, not as an admission of my poor conditioning but, undoubtedly, as a reflection of my greater alpine wisdom. "We should save our energy [gasp]," I calmly [gasp] explained [gasp], "so we may dash up the climb in the morning. This will ensure a greater chance of success."

I didn't think he would buy it, since I didn't. But I could think of no better excuse. Surprisingly, he bought it. He said it sounded wise. But from that point forward, I detected no deviation in speed.

As he cruised along, he filled the fresh air with stories of his many climbing exploits and adventures. He said he often climbed solo (or "so low," as he recorded in climbing registers) so he wouldn't have to "Creep along at this paltry pace!"

After passing the flanks of Mount Good, we arrived at the destination meadows just as the sun fell behind the horizon. I ate my nauseating freeze-dried dinner, which appeared to have a faint white-gas odor, before I settled in for the night in my new bivouac bag. The faint alpenglow on Mount Bad's northern flank contrasted sharply with the ever-expanding Milky Way's star-filled spectacle. As an even greater omen, I held my food down—no wet or dry heaves tonight! I drifted off into the painless and idealized world that exists only in youthful alpine dreams.

I woke Derek at three thirty in the morning. After I gulped down a quick cup of hot, white-gas-flavored Cup O' Noodles, we slipped into the dark talus cone at the foot of the mountain at four.

Could this be real? I wondered. *I'm actually on the hallowed Mount Bad!* I remained silent so as not to offend the mountain gods. Mount Bad hadn't gotten its name for nothing!

We donned crampons and crossed the Nasty Glacier just as the sun's first rays graced the beautiful and elegant summit. The morning's alpenglow beckoned and gave a welcoming gesture, but I knew this, too, was an illusion. Alpine landscapes operate on a scale that a human life is too brief to even register. I knew that if we treat the mountain with respect, at best, the mountain tolerates human intrusions. Mountains treat disrespect more severely. In either case, there are occasional random acts of rage regardless of intent, reverence, social standing, or economic condition. If unleashed, the alpine god's wrath in all its fury isn't evil. It's merely indifferent and often severe. Alpine landscapes grant no quarters or favors.

The darkening sky touched upon something deep inside me. The clouds grew ominous and descended. *This may be a bad sign,* I thought. *The color has a pall-like feel and smell ...* Perhaps the darkened clouds touched upon nerves. Perhaps I felt intimidated. Perhaps I tasted the lingering remnants of my white-gas-infused breakfast nausea.

Fifteen minutes after crossing the glacier, we heard a deafening roar. Behind us, a rockfall swept the entire glacial slope. It barely missed us. The mountain god let us go—this time. The glacier's crevasses swallowed every rock from the avalanche, leaving not a trace of its passing, as if it had all been a wondrous dream. The stark contrast between the booming roar one moment and the magical alpine silence the next exhilarated every bone, fiber, and synapse in my body. Nature's defibrillator. Adrenaline coursed through my body as I realized I'd just had a Rébuffat moment.

We reached the notch in the ridge just as rays cast their warming glow on us through the otherwise monotonous gray ceiling. I quickly grabbed my camera and snapped a photo of the upper Gnarly Glacier on Mount Bad's precipitous eastern flank. I transcended from a Rébuffat to a nirvana moment.

Derek shattered my imagery by scolding, "We stopped too many times already. There will be *no* more stops until we reach the summit!" Although this forty-second camera stop was our first since strapping on crampons on the glacier's toe far below, I thought, *Oh well, that's just Derek's way!*

We charged up the upper north ridge by repeatedly climbing up and down the many intervening towers located along the ridge crest. They stood like gendarmes baring the summit from unworthy souls. In a rappel from one lone sentry, the rope stuck, preventing us from easily retrieving this critical piece of equipment. We lost precious time extracting the rope from menacing rock protuberances as the mountain gods played with us.

The gods also played with the weather. Mountains not only influence prevailing weather patterns. They also generate their own localized weather. Every morning, the sun warms a mountain's flanks. This in turn warms local air mass. And since warm air rises, upslope winds develop. Conversely, after the sun sets, air begins to cool—at first in the higher elevations, and then progressively lower. This cooling air begins to flow downhill. On Mount Bad's craggy and complex northern flank, there can be several of these localized and regional processes happening simultaneously, thereby creating unpredictable and sometimes violent weather.

During the time it took to free our stuck rope, the weather on Mount Bad turned worse, the storm clouds circled in, and it started to rain. The surreal sky both menaced and generated awe. The mountain lived up to its name.

We made a mad dash for the summit, managing to reach the top before the mountain gods decided our fate for themselves. We located and signed the summit register. While Derek perused notes left by past climbers, I gazed into the whole world that lay before my feet. I took deep breaths, hoping the air would forever linger in lungs and heart—a remembrance of my first significant alpine summit and one of the highest peaks in the state. The exhilarating feeling of contentment I derived upon standing on what seemed the top of the world formed my definition of purity and truth. I drifted into a quasi-religious experience after finding my emotional and spiritual home.

"We need to get going. Time's a wastin'!" Derek's retort instantaneously dashed all magical, esoteric ponderings.

We collectively decided to go down by a different route. We descended the upper ice chute that led to the Heinous Glacier, passing through an ominously dark cirque nestled amongst colossal walls towering on three sides. We descended the Heinous's magnificent cathedral without incident.

We came upon a double bergschrund and searched for a safe crossing of the icy pits. I climbed down into the bowels of one, and then, using a combination of classic and less orthodox ice-climbing moves (the ignorant may call them clumsy), I quickly climbed the nearly vertical ice of the opposite bergschrund's wall. To my amazement, Derek took much longer to cross, as if he was less familiar with ice climbing. I wondered, *Could it be that Derek has a climbing weakness, and I a superior ability?* I grinned upon the fanciful possibilities.

This momentary delay offered me an opportunity to take a photograph and gaze at the grand alpine cirque walls from which we'd just emerged. It also gave me time to ponder the massive Pleistocene glacier and the mighty forces that had excavated the basin from inside the granitic monolith. However, the present glacier is a mere laughing remnant of its former glory. *Have no fear, glacier. Someday your time will come again—the ice wall cometh!* A glacier must have incredible patience, not only to wait out interglacial periods but also to put up with my momentary intrusion and incessant ponderings.

In a matter of seconds, Derek's arrival ended my thoughtful and peaceful reflection, and it reminded me of the witch's question in

Shakespeare's *Macbeth*: "Shall he dwindle, peak and pine?" Derek, on Mount Bad's northern flank, answered that question definitely: "No."

Instead, we focused on the task of getting down.

While descending the glacier-scoured and denuded slabs and rocks approximately seven hundred feet below the glacier's snout, it started to rain—again. Intellectually, I knew rain works in conspiratorial cooperation with gravity to loosen rocks precariously strewn about since the last rain and propel them to the foot of the mountain. Knowledge, however, is no use if not applied. For some reason, I didn't heed the warning even though it was the perfect place to have applied this knowledge. We were in a large denuded gully directly below the snout of an active glacier—such places are Mother Nature's garbage chute, and we were deep within her funnel.

I felt strong, confident, and fit. I thought, *Nothing could happen to me!* We were almost down the gully and moving fast and strong. As Derek trailed fifty feet behind, a strange feeling compelled me to look up. I saw a massive boulder careening faster than the speed of sound off the snout of the glacier and heading directly toward me. Instinctively, in the interest of survival, I ran as fast as my little legs could carry me in a desperate attempt to get free of the gully. When I traversed out to safety, I turned to witness the house-sized granite block crash into the slabs where I'd been just seconds before. With a deafening roar, its impact with the slabs split the block into two Volkswagen-sized chucks. The unimaginable volume and magnitude of the explosion drew awe and respect. I gazed in humbled and stupefied amazement.

The whirring of a grapefruit-sized missile sailing a foot over my left shoulder shattered my daze. I suddenly found myself deep inside the path of a secondary volley of smaller rocks. While I was running for cover, a baseball-sized rock missed my ear by millimeters and struck the ice ax strapped on the outside of my treasured Sacs Millet backpack. The impact tore the nylon straps off my pack and flung my axe carelessly downslope. I abandoned all lost equipment and ran as if my life depended on it—and it did. I ran, and ran, and ran across the boulder field, hopping from one rock to the next. While I was still running and hopping, another grapefruit-sized rock struck my uplifted heavy leather boot as it searched for its next boulder-hop landing. The rock hitting my boot knocked me off balance, and I missed the landing. I careened into a heap between slabs, talus, and boulders—literally between a rock and a hard place. As best as I could, I protected my skull as rocks continued to smash all around me. I felt as if an oversized shotgun loaded with baseball-sized buckshot had shot me. Amazingly, after the rock volley subsided, I appeared to have received no more direct hits. Lingering rock dust and an intense acrid smell punctuated the surreal scene.

Still in my between-a-rock-and-a-hard-place hollow, I reached for my foot to inspect the damage. Sudden panic swept over me in another massive adrenaline rush. *Where's "Derek?* I wondered. I sweated as my eyes frantically scanned the impact zone. It had just occurred to me, from the moment I saw the rock avalanche until that sudden realization, that I'd only thought of myself. I'd made no customary warning call of "Rock!" to warn Derek, and despite frantic efforts, my eyes only saw boulders and the lingering drift of pulverized rock dust. *Derek is gone, and I have a broken foot*, I realized. *Damn it. I made some whopping mistakes!*

Just then, I heard Derek's voice. "Are you okay?" he called to me as he casually strolled within sight.

Apparently, when he'd seen me look up and start running, he needed no further motivation to start running himself. Only he chose to run to the near side of the gully while I'd crossed at the longest stretch.

"I may have broken my foot," I replied.

"Oh," he said as he found, retrieved, and handed me my bent ice ax. From that point on, my ice ax's aluminum shaft has had a distinctive sharp bend in it where the rock struck. War wounds on me are one thing, but not on my ice ax—poor thing!

"Can you walk?" Derek asked.

I used the disfigured ice ax as a crutch to test my foot. I told him perhaps I could move if I took weight off my foot by leaning on the ice ax. Before I finished my sentence, he said, "Good. Let's get moving!"

Off he charged. Miffed, I had little choice but to hobble after him while trying not to lag too far behind. To make matters worse, it had started to get dark, and we had no flashlights. *What more could go wrong?* I thought. Just then, the darkening rain clouds hurled a volley of stinging hail directly at us. I should never have asked the mountain gods *that* question. While silently cursing my unsympathetic and callous "partner," I wretchedly hobbled in the direction Derek had disappeared in.

When I caught up with him, he gave me a choice: head out today by going directly down the trailless Miseries, or climb up the thousand-foot-high divide, and then drop down another thousand feet to where we'd stashed our bivouac gear. If we chose that option, we would rest up by spending the night there and head out on the trail in the morning.

I didn't relish the thousand-foot intervening ridge climb, but I thought it preferable to the Miseries—a trailless bushwack through downed logs and brush. With no flashlights and my energy level nearly spent, getting to our bivouac gear and resting up so we could head out on a trail by daylight seemed the most sensible course of action. We both agreed.

The painful struggle over the ridge took a lifetime, but with persistence and sheer force of will, I made it to the top in the height of the storm. Wind-driven hail lashed and bit into exposed skin, causing a curious sensation of simultaneously being hot from the climb and cold from the storm. Darkness had fully encased us as I stumbled into our inviting bivouac site.

No sooner had I arrived than Derek quipped, "Let's hike out tonight."

I wasn't given to complaining, but I pleaded with him. "You're crazy. With your rushing the whole time, we haven't had a bite to eat or anything to drink since three thirty this morning. My foot is swollen and in pain. It's dark and storming. We don't have flashlights. And you want to hike out tonight? Are you crazy? To spend the night here was the reason we chose to climb over the ridge and not head out by the Miseries."

"Yeah, I agreed to it," he admitted. "But I changed my mind."

Despite continued efforts, I discovered the futility of trying to make Derek change his mind. I silently cursed both of us—him for being demanding and insensitive, and me for not bringing a headlamp. I usually did, but right before leaving the car, Derek had talked me out of carrying it in the interest of being lighter and faster. Rationalizations and silent cursing meant nothing, for we packed up and began the six-mile hike out in the dark, in the rain, and amid the storm's fury.

We covered approximately three miles by waiting for lightning flashes to light enough of the route to give us a glimpse of the layout of the next thirty or so feet of trail. As soon as lightning flashed, we made a mad dash based on this illuminated mental image. I traveled from thirty to fifty feet at a time until my memory faltered, causing me to fall over unseen rocks and logs, bruising myself in the process. Each time, I got up and waited for the next lightning flash. I repeated this ordeal over and over, each time despite my deepening injuries and fraying nerves. Derek did the same, but he could see better in the darkness than I could, so he fell less frequently. He grew impatient with me. But I couldn't help it. Between the night's darkness, the dark storm clouds, and the obscuring forest canopy, I could see nothing between lightning flashes. Just absolute cave-dark blackness.

The epic had exhausted and thoroughly banged me up. *There has to be a better way!* I inwardly cursed. While in the darkness between flashes, I groped in my pack and pulled out my trusty Primus stove. I primed it with white gas and lit the stove by feel. I welcomed its warmth and the purring of its insipid but growing flame.

I began hiking in a severely crouched and stooped position, holding the stove as close to the ground as I could. The Primus lit only a two-foot section of trail at a time, but it was sufficient for the desperate to navigate by, despite being extremely slow. It also proved painful to walk with a heavy pack while stooped over. Graceful it was not.

We covered one mile in this fashion until the sputtering Primus ran out of gas. Trying to refill my stove in pitch-dark blackness proved futile. We then gathered a few dry twigs found underneath large logs and lit the bundle with match-lit candles. By carrying bundles of smoldering twigs, again in a crouched position, we could see well enough to descend a bit farther down the trail. However, each bundle would stay lit for only a minute or less. We needed to constantly seek dry twigs. Matches alone wouldn't light the damp twigs. We eventually ran out of candles, matches, and hope.

The storm finally abated, and a little starlight filtered through the trees, just enough that we could follow the trail unaided and with only minimal falling mishaps. I was too numb to notice if I suffered any further damage.

In an endless series of falls, I thought, *what's one more?*

For one brief moment, I fell asleep while still standing. Losing my balance and beginning to fall down woke me. It took another second or two for me to understand and get reoriented. I sat out of weariness and apathy. Seconds later, Derek frantically shook me as he shouted, "You can't go to sleep here!"

I mumbled, "Why not? And if not here, where?"

Off he charged down the trail. I got up and lamely followed.

We eventually reached the car, twenty-six hours after leaving our bivouac site. Except for the brief stay on the summit and the taking of a couple of photos, we were constantly on the move without a single bite to eat or sip of water. I was well beyond exhausted and worn out. Derek showing no signs of tiredness made matters worse. *Does he not require sleep? And is there no draining his stamina?* I wondered. I'd just turned twenty years old, but Derek was seventeen. The nerve of him!

Derek left for home. I drove to Denny's, the only food place open twenty-four hours. When I attempted to get out of the car, all muscles in my injured leg contracted, locked, and seized tight, as if made of wood. I couldn't bend my leg or move my foot. They were rigid as a board. *Does rigor mortis affect the living?* I wondered. *Am I still alive?* If I were to stay among the living, I thought, I needed food. So I hobbled into Denny's.

Upon the first sight of me, the waitress shrieked. "Are you alright? Do you want me to call the doctor?"

I laconically replied, "No, I just want food, and lots of it."

I went into the bathroom to clean up and realized why the waitress had shrieked. Upon looking in the mirror, I, too, gasped. Bloody cuts and gashes covered my face. My frequent brow wiping had the additional effect of smearing blood around. *What bloody man is that?*

I wondered. Apparently, sharp rock fragments had hit me during the rockfall. Or I'd injured myself more than I thought during my many falls off the trail.

While staring into the mirror, I imagined that, hobbling into the restaurant on one leg, covered with wet and torn clothing, all cut up, and having blood smeared over all exposed skin, I must have been quite the sight. I cleaned up the best I could and then returned to the table, where I consumed three large helpings of Grand Slam pancakes. I savored every bite.

For a while after the epic, I thought I would never go on another climb with *him*. A year passed, during which I occasionally told stories of this madman on Mount Bad. Perhaps at the same time, Derek wildly complained about this fool who'd slowed the whole team and endangered everyone. In his mind, if he thought of himself as Terray, I, clearly, was no Lachenal.

Upon further reflection, with the advantage of time and wisdom, it occurred to me that to be successful on bigger mountains, one must move fast. Derek, with his not-too-subtle scolding, had likely attempted to teach me that vital lesson. Over time, I no longer saw him as a madman. Instead, I held him in a deepening level of respect.

Nearly a year after the swelling went down in my foot and scar tissue replaced former wounds, I called Derek to gauge his interest in another challenging climb. Apparently, I hadn't scared him off. We completed this climb without it turning into a disaster, without it turning into an epic, and without us turning on each other.

On this climb and all the many other successful climbs together, we formed a reasonably good climbing team. At least I thought so. (I would never have dared ask him.) He turned out to be a good climbing partner, and I enjoyed every climb, whether successful or not. We never made it into any book as a legendary climbing partnership. He had the capabilities for it, but I didn't. And I settled into that fact. Good climbing partners are hard to find.

When non-climbers hear of the experiences we had on Mount Bad, they often ask, "Why do you still climb?" The answer was varied and convoluted. It was simply unacceptable to stay away from the mountains. Like spawning salmon entering their prenatal birth waters or the unknown force that draws moths to flames, for some people, there's an irresistible urge and calling to climb the mountain's crest. Once one hears the calling, one must obey.

I now experience the world differently, as ruminations, thoughtful reflections, and time has passed. But one thing remains clear and focused: pushing my limits on Mount Bad left an indelible impression. I stepped through a doorway—just not the one I'd expected. This epic experience whetted my appetite for new adventures and gave me the confidence and willingness to push beyond my comfort zone. From that point forward, there was no turning back.

The Dagger
I See before Thee

It's quite easy, even glorious, to exalt successes on difficult summits despite inconceivable obstacles and daring challenges. One rarely hears of failures, although this is the norm for the pathetically average alpinist. Failures are par for the course. There's little danger of others exposing this truth because they fear reciprocation—like teenagers who never speak of others' inflamed pimples erupting as protruding placards for fear that their own blemishes be the next topic of embarrassment. It's the suffrage of the spud—the code of the coccyx.

I may grudgingly admit to green-book failures among close friends, but it's much easier to admit to failures on Yosemite's fabled walls. A climber earns bragging rights by merely dragging a rope across Yosemite's sacred ground or bleeding on its hallowed, sun-warmed granite.

For the rock climber, there's nothing comparable to Yosemite Valley, or The Valley. Chris Jones, in his otherworldly *Climbing in North America*, calls The Valley the "granite crucible." Any climber worth their salt, or climbing chalk, partakes in at least one Valley pilgrimage. It's a crucible that the afflicted enter, but only a few exit unchanged by the experience. It's the climbing bum's version of The Eagles' *Hotel California*. Climbing zen masters forge their legends in Yosemite, complete with storied adventures told over and over to aspiring neophytes, wannabe climbers, and an occasional spud. Masters put up new routes reminiscent of Rembrandt or Picasso that are hailed by the masses, underlings, and the far less exalted.

The Pacific Northwest has few ramparts, walls, or stony buttresses comparable to Yosemite, and absent of global climate change, it certainly has no sun-warmed rock. However, it does, and did, contain Northwest-born Yosemite-trained climbing zen masters. Foremost exalted among these rock gods was James Thomas Madsen. Although Jim died in the crucible eight years before I began climbing, I couldn't escape his presence or the lingering vortex left with his untimely passing. I spoke his name in hushed and reverent tones. Compared with Jim Madsen, we're all spuds.

Jim Madsen came from the Pacific Northwest. I came from the Pacific Northwest. Jim Madsen went to the University of Washington. I went to the University of Washington. This is where comparisons end. Jim Madsen climbed, while I dreamt of climbing. Jim Madsen climbed the university's Suzzallo Library. I holed up in Suzzallo Library's basement archives, reading about Hermann Ulrichs's and Jim Madsen's exploits. I have a photo of the library's exterior where Madsen's feet once levitated. During these many Suzzallo-, Cascades-, and Yosemite-inspired dreams, I fell under the spell of Jim Madsen— both the person and the legend.

I've been to The Valley a few times, mostly during college spring breaks. Spring 1982 soaked into my morale, causing everything to turn wet, snowy, and dreary. Mountain gods draped the classic climbs in snow. Spindrifts wafted across the steeper cliffs, and slushy avalanches rolled down the Glacier Point Apron. I saw not the sun-warmed walls of legend. For all of us non-Madsens, nothing was climbable. We spent long hours waiting for the weather to break while lounging in a sagging tent or warming chilled bones by the Ahwahnee Hotel's beckoning fireplace. If no respectable person witnessed, we dried clammy clothes and warmed stiff limbs by the hand dryers in the hotel's bathroom.

The rock never warmed, and the Ahwahnee's bathroom hand dryers could do nothing about that. We became restless and couldn't wait. During a lull in the snowstorm, we ventured into the surreal white crucible, hoping to at least do *something*. Under the mocking glare of snow-draped big walls, we struggled on climbs more our size and more suited to our abilities, but at a fundamental level, it didn't matter—I was at long last climbing in the fabled Valley.

Perhaps due to the draping ice, alpine-esque swirling gray clouds, or numbing fingers and toes, our climb didn't hold the allure I expected. However, that didn't diminish my excitement. As spindrift sloughed inside my collar and my eyes scanned across the grimness, I saw flashing images of Madsen and Ron Burgner on *their* first Valley trip. While they made a name for themselves on impressive climbs of sheer and imposing walls, Eric and I flailed on the diminutive Manure Pile Buttress. Not exactly an exalted climb of legend. After we topped out, we returned to the Ahwahnee's bathroom blowers to warm shaking bones and frozen spirits. The next day, we packed wet gear and escaped to warmer and more hospitable climes.

❧

Not all climbing failures are of a technical, logistical, or weather-related matter. Some are legal and ethical, and some even occur in warm, hospitable regions. By all definitions, Navajo land—the red-rocked,

Four-Cornered sandstone towers, cliffs, and canyons—held an almost magical, mythical, and haunting allure for generations of climbers. Given that, wouldn't this enchanting land be an enticing land to climb, play in, and fill with climbing successes? On the red-rocked surface, one would think so. However, there are other matters of concern.

No matter how many times I looked at the Totem Pole, Moses, Shiprock, or Spider Rock, they gave me pause, and I took a moment to stare. Thoughts of climbing the classic and alluring desert spires also gave me pause, since the Navajo tribal government deemed climbing on their reservation illegal.

I would hope that the thought of climbing something illegally would give any person pause, at least any with a sense of ethics and right and wrong. However, in my case, when I lived in the Four Corners, I worked as a law enforcement ranger with the National Park Service. It wouldn't be good optics for a National Park Service ranger working in partnership with the Navajo tribal government to be arrested by the Navajo police for violating a tribal climbing ban. I like to think my integrity level is high enough not to get into such a bind. However, living among so many mesmerizing climbs that were routinely calling and beckoning constantly put me in ethical dilemmas.

For nine months, I looked at Spider Rock daily and felt pangs of regret and a longing to stand among the bleached bones of the bad little boys and girls Spider Woman had discarded on the summit. True to my conviction, I never stepped foot on Spider Rock. However, wayward children weren't the only people who graced Spider Rock's summit. Some climbers were unencumbered by moral dilemmas despite Spider Woman's threats and watchful eyes.

While on duty over the Memorial Day weekend, I received a call on my National Park Service Motorola that visitors had spotted climbers near Spider Rock's summit. Chief Ranger Reed Detring dispatched me to investigate and catch the offending climbers if I could. The light faded fast as I put the park's law enforcement cruiser at top speed. It could go from zero to fifty in 3.2 minutes. Slower if going uphill.

Upon arriving at the overlook, I scanned the summit and peered into the canyon bottom along Spider Rock's base. I couldn't see a soul. I almost closed the investigation and called it a day. However, I felt adventuresome, fit, and non-spudsy. On foot, I dashed for an unadvertised trail that descended to the canyon's bottom not far from Spider Rock. The sun's crescent had long since fallen below the canyon rim when I reached Spider Rock's base. Nothing found—only Spider Woman's enticing fang slashed into the deepening ruddy sky. Suddenly, I thought I heard distant talking. I dashed off in silent pursuit.

After ten minutes of chase, I caught a brief glimmer of unnatural movement in far pinyon and juniper branches. With full leg and lung power, I silently surged toward any subtle branch movement. My chase had begun. No matter how fast I powered ahead, the pinyon and juniper vibrations remained a constant distance away—the speed of hunter and prey perfectly matched. I barked orders to Scotty for more power, but he said, "I'm giving you all she's got, Captain!"

Reluctantly, I stopped the chase. Logistical realities filled my head. I had no flashlight or headlamp. While not quite fully dark, it would be soon. I would find it hard to reach the canyon's ramparts under only a dim, moonless night, despite knowing the route well. I turned around and made it back to the cruiser just as the last of any usable light faded in western skies. On the way home, the cruiser had no problem maintaining fifty miles per hour on the long coast downhill. I stated in my shift report that I'd seen the climbers and pursued chase, but they got away. I didn't put in my report that instead of chasing them, I would have preferred joining them. I still have pangs of regret over never standing on Spider Rock's blanched-bone summit—another climbing loss, another climbing failure.

Six years later, while I was chatting with cavers preparing for a weeklong Lechuguilla Cave expedition within New Mexico's Carlsbad Caverns National Park, the conversation turned to the Jones brothers—Dave and Peter. Peter had been caving for decades. While an exceptionally gifted climber, Dave had never been in a cave before. Lechuguilla would be his first.

I spent two hours talking with Dave that evening. For years, I've read about Dave's first ascents on big walls in Zion National Park and elsewhere. He gave me the impression of a person I would enjoy climbing with. During this chat in the park's research cabin bunkhouse, the other cavers in the once crowded conversation had long since drifted off, leaving Dave and me alone, discussing climb after climb. Unlike Perv, Dave didn't mind a climbing obsession. During our talk, I casually mentioned some of the other parks I'd worked in, including Canyon de Chelly. David suddenly became animated.

"Canyon de Chelly. That's a fine canyon. I climbed Spider Rock on a Memorial Day weekend several years back. Everything went fine until some ranger began chasing us. We thought, *How hard could it be to shake a law enforcement ranger?*"

I interjected, "Was this in the mid-1980s?"

"Yeah, yeah. Eighty-four or eighty-five. Anyway, he kept coming and coming," he said as his arms almost knocked over the pile of caving gear precariously set on the nearby shelf. "We were only able to escape by diving and hiding under a thickly set juniper." With even more wild gyrations, David sputtered, "We stayed there for a *long* time to be sure the ranger had left. By that time, it was too dark.

We had no idea how to get out of the canyon. That damned ranger caused us to spend a cold and miserable night under a tree with no food or warm clothing!"

"That was me!" I proudly proclaimed. "I was that ranger."

Beyond the need for words, I could tell from his smiles that he forgave me for the cold bivouac. I proudly beamed because I'd given *the* hardman Dave a run for his money. *Take that—Derek!*

Maybe some climbing losses are sweeter than others after all.

৩৬

Even when it's legal to do so, sometimes spuds can fail on a climb even when they reach the top, since reaching the end point isn't often the mark of success. It certainly isn't when low-angled spuds venture into the fabled vertical walls of Colorado's Eldorado Canyon. Before this moral defeat, I filled Eldorado Canyon with ghosts, haunts, legends, fables, and mythologies surrounding Layton Kor (Colorado's Jim Madsen). Chris Jones, in *Climbing in North America*, calls him, "Layton the Great 'Un." Eldorado became Layton's early climbing playground.

Energized with the thought of belaying in the same airspace where Layton had once belayed, I soaked in the ambiance. However, esoteric soaking seemed out of the question due to the constant stream of climbers, hikers, strollers, and other ambiance killers passing below, followed by their ever-faithful din and rabble. Still, Layton's magic filled the air—enough for me to retain my smiles as I belayed Ken on the ever-steepening wall. As with most of my climbing partners, Ken, was a far better climber than I'd been or ever expected to be regardless of how much I wanted and dreamt it to be different.

Ken chose to lead Redguard, a moderately easy route by both Eldorado's and Ken's standards. That's why his hesitation intrigued me. Ken didn't hesitate on easy or moderate climbs. Being a fine

51

climber, he also carried a dignified grace and style that I hoped one day would rub off on the spud. I soon would find out if it had, since Ken arrived at the belay station and motioned for me to follow.

Although I'd climbed many harder routes than this, for some reason, Redguard seemed more difficult than its rating or reputation implied. Holds on the ever-steepening wall were becoming slicker the higher I went. *What do you call a hold if you can't hold on to it?* I pondered while struggling directly above and within plain sight of strolling pedestrians. While my eyes focused on where my sweating hands could lunge for, the pedestrian noise became inescapable. Having an audience didn't diminish my muscle fatigue or make it less intense. It did nothing for my shaking hands, throbbing forearms, or growing panic. I was out of my element.

I mostly climbed rock that was less than vertical. Vertical and overhanging rock required more upper-body strength and boldness than spuds could usually muster, and it required different techniques.

Commentary from the growing trail-bound pedestrian non-climbing cabal didn't help. The steep walls amplified and reverberated comments—made even more intense by atmospheric conditions and my self-conscious spudness. Instead of climbing a wondrous route in the hallowed steps of Layton Kor, this became like climbing inside a crowded fishbowl. Every passerby gazed at the spectacle of the flopping fish gasping for air.

One apparently naïve person said to her walking companion, "That guy up there must be climbing something hard."

"No, not really," her companion replied. "He's making it look harder than it really is."

Just then, an anonymous passerby overhearing the ridicule chimed in, "Well, he *is* off route."

Perhaps he heard the insult, ridicule, speculation, worry, and scorn. Perhaps he saw the growing crowd and worried there had been an accident. Or perhaps he thought one would soon occur. Regardless, out of nowhere, a rope-less and partner-less middle-aged climber bounded, quite adroitly, from somewhere higher and off to the side. Perhaps he had been *on* route. Worried for my safety and fearful that I was in over my head, he gently spoke to me in a way an adult would speak to a child. While pointing to obvious handholds on the vertical rock face, he instructed, "You can put your left hand here, and over here, your right hand can ..."

Less gently, and perhaps less kindly, I might have replied, "Thanks, but I got it handled!"

"I was just trying to help," he retorted indignantly.

"Again, thanks. But I would rather climb it myself."

I might have insulted him, but I had more pressing worries. His effortless bounding back across the vertical cliff face with total grace and skill made me loathe him and the mocking crowd even more intensely.

Since I hadn't fallen yet or provided sufficient afternoon entertainment, the cabal began dissipating. Apparently, watching a struggling climber *not* fall grows tedious fast. Only a few remained as I inched closer and closer to the belay and out of the fishbowl. I longed for a cave to crawl into. Right before arriving at the belay and seeing Ken's annoyed expression, I heard one last comment from below.

"Did that guy know he was off route?"

☙❧

If the definition of a climbing failure is a measure of tangible feet ascended compared with the level of effort expended, then the trip I took with Dan to Utah's Henry Mountains would surely rank at the top of the list. The Henrys are the lost and only recently named mountains

53

located between the Dirty Devil River and the Waterpocket Fold. Butch Cassidy could see the Henrys on the horizon from his infamous Robbers Roost hideout. One would likely not suspect that I hatched this failed climb from a hideout of sorts deep within the cockroached and odorous urban streets of Old Town San Juan, Puerto Rico.

For a person born and bred for the mountain and desert wilds, inner-city San Juan felt especially confining. Derek once wrote, "Puerto Rico, eh? My, how some people change ..."

Yeah, well, what can I say? I went for a career move. To work in the National Park Service on a permanent basis usually required many years of short-term seasonal assignments combined with a park willing to grant someone official permanent status within the federal workforce. Once a person worked at one of these entry-level permanent positions, they received lifetime permanent status and could apply to any qualifying federal position. Open competitive positions were highly coveted back then. For the sake of this employment designation, I worked 462 days at San Juan National Historic Site, located on the Caribbean island of Puerto Rico—far removed from Yosemite's walls and alpine glaciers.

While I had my permanent status, the position required that I take an annual thirty-day unpaid furlough. My long-awaited furlough finally came in May. I longed for the wilds—real wilds. Not the nightly storm-sewer-emanating, clockwork-like cockroach mass migrations. Not the lawless Wild-West-like walks down Calle del Sol past drug dealers or the passed-out drunks along La Casa Rosa. I longed for real wilds and real landscapes. I wanted to travel west, continental west. However, winter's grip still held firm to western summits, complete with snow, ice, and green impenetrables. Even Yosemite's Manure Pile Buttress would be out of condition. I therefore flew to Seattle to gather my truck and climbing gear stored at my parents' place and drove to the wilds of the American Southwest.

I met Cucamonga Dan in Flagstaff, Arizona—the Dan in his youthful post-herbal medicine business phase but before his eventual life in acupuncture. This Dan worked with computers in a government office in Flag, and he, too, needed to stretch his legs in the wilds. Dan held fond teenage memories of southern Utah's Henry Mountains. This is where he learned to climb. Back then, you couldn't get much more isolated and wilder than the Henry Mountains.

The Henrys are isolated and off the beaten track—the last mountain range in the lower forty-eight named by the Board of Geographic Names Committee. Curiously enough, the Navajo name for the Henry Mountains translates to "Mountain whose name is missing." The Henrys were far removed from the urban San Juan cockroaches and depravity. Besides seeing them on maps for years, I'd only experienced the Henrys from a distance. I planned to change that perspective.

In the mid-1980s, there weren't many climbing routes on the scattered Henry Mountains cliffs and walls. There still aren't. Dan recalled one especially beautiful crack splitting the east face of The Horn. He knew intrepid explorers had climbed the crack using aid-climbing techniques—meaning climbers ascended the route by standing or holding on to pieces of protection they placed in the rock, not by the naturally occurring holds. The highest and purest climbing style is free-climbing. This is where the artist climbs only what nature provides. Cucamonga Dan wanted to make the first free ascent of this soon-to-be classic. I needed no further encouragement.

The drive up the long dirt road provided no practical metric within this rugged and isolated landscape. The lower scrub and creosote bush habitat slowly faded as we ascended to the mid and upper slopes dominated by clumpy ponderosa pine, Gambel oak, and pinyon pine. We camped near a boulder field below The Horn's jutting outline, not far north of Mount Pennell.

Despite the isolation and wildness, we weren't alone. Hunters were nearby, and we stopped by to say hello. We soon learned this group of friends routinely hunted mountain lions in the Henrys. As we sat on logs circling their robust cowboy fire, our chatter segued into them proudly showcasing their overflowing bounty. Stretched across a makeshift A-frame were eight cougar skins curing in the juniper-scented Utah desert air. My memory recalls that the drunken hunters claimed they usually killed many more cougars than that year's paltry take. I was less impressed, for I would rather have had seen or known the creatures were still roaming free within the Henrys, but that's just me. The hunters held a different mindset and had different life experiences and perspectives.

Amid pondering such matters and perspectives, Dan and I noticed the lateness of the hour. We needed to head back to our camp and worldview. Us saying goodbye while still sober might have marked us as outsiders, so we simply said, "Hey." With our anonymity now secured, we retreated to our dry camp among the boulders. Two groups—six people—in the entirety of the northern Henrys at the same time. The Henry Mountains weren't as isolated as I'd imagined.

I hardly slept. My mind was too filled with cougars, climbs, and anticipation. To get to this point, I'd flown from the Caribbean to Miami, and then flown across the continent's east-west breadth, only to drive across the country's north-south spine before I snaked up the Henrys' long, dusty roads, my destination now close at hand.

I must have slept some because the morning's first light caught me off guard. We rustled our things together by the dawn's faint glow.

We were soon shrinking the distance to The Horn. As we ascended the crisp slope, I looked down toward the hunters' distant camp. Their tents and fire ring were as still as the splayed pelts tightly bound to frames and cordage.

Unbounded, Dan and I made good time to The Horn. As in the past, difficult climbs meant Dan led. He led flawlessly up the first pitch's obvious crack. The fissure began finger width, slowly expanded to hand shaped, and then grew to fist size. Dan finished this fine lead at expansion bolts left by the original aid climbers. They used the bolts for a hanging belay, and we did as well. A hanging belay is where the climber's stance consists of hanging from the bolts connected to a climbing harness. Dan belayed me up to the bolts. I clipped into the bolts and began setting up the next belay for Dan's lead. Each pitch is one rope length closer to the top and one rope length closer to completing the first free ascent. It's also one pitch closer to rising out of the spud realm—never into the rarified air of a Jim Madsen, but at least not grubbing in the spud-filled subsoil.

As expected, Dan offered to lead the second, and even harder, pitch. Hanging by bolts and my harness, I belayed Dan and scanned the horizon. There are free-roaming bison in the Henrys, but I saw none from my lofty perch. However, I could plainly see Dan as he struggled only twenty feet immediately above me. He hadn't moved in quite a while. He was never one to talk excessively, but when climbs got hard, Dan became quieter than normal. His cougar-pelt stillness hinted that the climb provided no safe placements to catch him if he should fall. I immediately doubted my ability to ascend into the real climber realm—at least this day. If Dan struggled, what hope had I?

Without warning, gravity spat Dan into the air, and he plummeted straight for me. With my waist tied to bolts and feet dangling uselessly in the air, I could go nowhere. I braced for the impact. Instinctively, I knew above all else to protect my belaying hand. If not, Dan would fall even farther. His hurdling body impacted me squarely on my outstretched and dangling legs, but my belay held.

After regaining our airy perches and composure on vertical igneous rock, we contemplated our next move. Bedraggled from the fall, Dan felt less inclined to try again—at least that day. Besides, the gritty rock surface would likely take some cleaning before we could climb the crux. While still hanging from the bolts, I wondered if, during the fall, Dan had hit his head, since he asked me if I wanted to take a shot at the lead. If fright hadn't prevented me, I would have laughed at the prospect. I did not, could not climb at Cucamonga Dan's level. I thought, *If it spit him off...* He might have only asked out of kindness. Regardless, I politely declined. Besides, my hand, arm, and leg were still numb from the fall. I was in no shape for *any* lead.

We rappelled to the bottom of The Horn and returned to our boulder-strewn camp. Later, we briefly poked around the Henrys before going back past the cougar camp, the long, dusty road leading back to pavement, and the shimmering black ribbon leading into Flag.

That was the extent of the technical climbing on my monthlong furlough. I returned from another climbing failure, back to Puerto Rico, back to nightly cockroach mass migrations, back to Calle del Sol drug dealers, back to stepping over passed-out drunks along La Casa Rosa, and back to my life as a climbing spud.

Is a career worth such sacrifices? I wondered. *Like on Eldorado Canyon's Redguard, did I go off route in the Henrys as well? I'll never climb Yosemite's fabled walls, and I'll never be an exalted climbing master at this rate.*

As I lay sweating in the humid heat of the three-in-the-morning-car-alarm-blaring, rum-scented tropical blur, my mind frequently wandered back to the Henrys, back to the mountains, back to the wilds, back to fading dreams, and back to the thrill of chasing western winds.

Bow to the Wind

Wind is the aggressor. It blows in storm and fury. It bites, ravages, erodes, sinks, grinds, scours, and levels everything ranging from mountains and sandstone arches to Great Lakes pig-iron ships. More personally, it can topple or tear roof shingles, trailer parks, and upright walking bipeds. Wind is destruction—and more.

However, this isn't universal. In caves, wind can be a welcoming and benevolent friend. In caves, people seek wind—both its source and destination. To cavers, wind represents promise, hope, excitement, and new beginnings. In every cave cardinal direction, wind is worth salivating over and cherishing.

Unless we talk metaphysically, wind within stone requires a void. Underground wind needs space. This means in caves, wind needs more cave—and lots of it. "Where the cave blows, it goes," is the popular saying.

Cave winds have flirted with me on more than a few occasions. Wind has lured, baited, and mocked me. It has toyed with me. And then, when I no longer amused it, the wind blew into distant quarters, seeking fresh playthings. Only later did I discover the ruse. When it comes to wind, I seldom learn. Like an addict, I keep coming back for more.

The first time I entertained the wind, I was in the bottom of a nondescript twenty-foot-deep pit that smelled of stale dust and dried goat excrement. Hantavirus and histoplasmosis came to mind. I unhooked from the rappel rope to take a few photographs of the decrepit dust covering the rarely visited flat-bottomed floor. I noticed a lone cave beetle clambering up a sandy hummock pressed against the wall on the far side of the dust- and poop-coated floor. Leaning in to take a close-up beetle photo, I shifted my weight onto one knee. Suddenly, the sand hummock gave way, and a small black hole opened and began sucking sand, dust, guano, fungal spore, and beetle down into its inky maw.

High-velocity wind rushed through this ever-widening hole, consuming more sand and more floor. The venturi force's roar brought instant thoughts of a massive new cave and the wondrous nirvana of discovery literally opening at my feet. It also brought instant fear that the entire floor might give way and sweep me into beetle oblivion.

Is there enough solid floor to support my weight? I wondered. Is this the throat of a giant Tatooine sandworm? With cave wind moments like this, there's no time for wonderment or fanciful reflection. Survival instincts take over. I rushed for the safety of the still dangling rope securely tied to an anchor outside the sandworm's throat. By the time I tied into the rope, the hole stopped enlarging, but the rushing air continued sounding like a Hoover. Safely fixed to the rope, I gave a push on the hole's sandy collar. Three more pushes widened the hole and sent all loosened grains into the mysterious gullet.

Still attached to the rope, I offered my entire body, headfirst, to the unknown. A short distance later, where the epiglottis should have been, I landed on a safe, solid, and horizontal cave passage surrounded by darkness and silence. However, I sensed less than total darkness. Ahead, behind, I couldn't be sure, but a single point of light beckoned me. Could Jules Verne have been right all along? Is there a lit world hidden below the Earth's crust? Had I passed through a spatial dilation that turned me around, reshaped the cave, and removed the rope and my grasp on reality? No explanation seemed rational. I could find out only by untethering from my rope, my safety, and my reality, then heading toward the light and an uncertain fate.

Eighty feet of stooped-over waddling brought me into the light and the end of my adrenaline surge. I left the cave's reality and returned to normal surface space—an air-filled, goat-feces-lined dejection. What had happened? I neither knew of nor recognized this cave. The cave I entered had been high on a ridge overlooking a large valley. The cave I exited was formed in this same ridge, but it wasn't as high, and it overlooked a different valley. My newly discovered cave provided a shortcut from one valley to another. It passed through the entire ridge.

Wind can be deceptive. That's the nature of wind—you can never trust it. Apparently, this wasn't the sign of big winds whistling through deeper and unknown miles of yet-to-be-discovered cave. Cavers, physicists, and the inflicted source this wind to the chimney effect. Nature creates this wind when there's more than one cave entrance located at different elevations. When a weather front moves across multiple entrances, there's a slightly different air pressure hovering over each cave portal. This slight difference is enough to cause air to flow through the cave from the high-pressure entrance to the low-pressure exit.

This is yet another example of nature rebalancing itself. Nature rebalances this way for both pressure and temperature. While air flows from high pressure to low pressure, warm and cold temperatures seek each other to form a happy medium. As morning sun warms lowland mountain slopes, warmer air rises—just like it did on Mount Bad. In steep mountains, upwelling air currents can be severe. It becomes a daily cycle.

The opposite effect occurs when the sun sets. Cold air near the summit sinks and blends with warmer air below. Nature rebalances. Mountain protuberances may alter the air mass flow path, but the same basic principles apply. As cold air flowing down a mountain slope encounters a cave's upper entrance, the cave acts as a shortcut for the air to rebalance itself with the warmer air below. This was likely the scenario that elicited my adrenaline rush in the goat-feces-festooned cave high in the Guadalupe Mountains.

Wind knows the effect it can have on cavers, and we so easily fall for its ruse. Tricking, mocking, and flirting with cavers must bring wind much joy and satisfaction. However, cavers, being the creatures we are, keep falling for the deceptions, since the thought of new cave discoveries is hard to resist.

Most cave digs turn out to be busts, but there are enough successes to keep digs going and the diggers hopeful. Arguably the most wondrous successful cave dig happened when dedicated souls, after years of half-hearted efforts, finally dug and broke through from old Misery Hole into the newly minted Lechuguilla Cave. This cave set the world on end, with not only its spectacular beauty but also its scientific marvels. The cavers sifting through old bat guano followed the wind in that situation. Cavers worldwide have since flocked to peer into Lechuguilla's wind-filled depths.

❦

Shortly before the breakup of the Soviet Union, I hosted a group of the Union of Soviet Socialist Republics' leading karst researchers on a multiday trip into Lechuguilla Cave's deepest known point. Wind had carried news of the cave's uniqueness all the way to Moscow and the premier National Academy of Sciences of Ukraine.

There were a couple of their cavers, such as Alexander Klimchouk, who spoke English, but neither I nor the others from the United States spoke Russian. One of the Soviet cavers spoke no English at all. I have a vague memory that he called himself Dimitri, but my memory is much too foggy on this unwritten detail. The detail that stands out in vivid particulars, not unlike the cave's many gravity-defying helictites, was Dimitri's taste in music. He knew only two English words. Both, as translated for me, were words used to express both wonderment and pleasure. Also, according to the translator, Dimitri was a huge fan of American rock 'n' roll.

When Dimitri became excited, he turned to me with a big grin and a dramatic thumbs-up sign, then exclaimed in a thick, drawn-out Ukrainian (I presumed) accent one of his two known words—*F-O-G-E-R-T-Y* or *P-R-E-S-L-E-Y*. These, of course, honored rock 'n' roll legends Elvis Presley and John Fogerty of Creedence Clearwater Revival.

John Fogerty was the singer, songwriter, and lead guitarist for the band Creedence Clearwater Revival, also known as "Creedence" and "CCR." Bruce Springsteen, when he introduced CCR to the Rock and Roll Hall of Fame, said they weren't the hippest band of the time, but they were the best. CCR's infectious rock-and-roll songs dominated American airwaves in the late '60s and early '70s. Working-class stiffs, preppy college kids, bikers, long-haired hippies, and soldiers belly-deep in Vietnam rice paddies all related to Creedence's socio-conscious lyrics and working-class sentiments. Like few bands before them, or since, they received both popular and critical appeal. Their music and style would later become the definition of classic rock and the Americana genre. It is little wonder that CCR's music also reached out to youth behind the Soviet-era Iron Curtain—and formed a relatable platform for West-and-East dialogue and communication. The translator had informed Dimitri that I was a huge Creedence fan. So apparently, Dimitri loved to share with me fifty percent of his American vocabulary.

Despite knowing only two English words, Dimitri, with his childlike grin and Fonzi-style thumbs-up gestures, made wondrous progress in the otherwise frosty Cold War diplomacy between these two cultures—at least as far as my limited involvement in international geopolitical affairs can tell.

After we exited the cave, Dimitri gave me one last grin, thumbs-up, and *F-O-G-E-R-T-Y*. I smiled and gave him a *F-O-G-E-R-T-Y* back; however, I left never knowing the relative ranking of a *P-R-E-S-L-E-Y* versus a *F-O-G-E-R-T-Y*. What's the exchange rate between these two rock icons? From my estimation, in our American-Soviet de-escalation efforts, both were priceless.

A few weeks after the Soviets returned home, I received an unexpected package in the mail from Ukraine addressed to me. I opened it and discovered a lone cassette tape of Paul McCartney's 1988 *CHOBA B CCCP* album, at the time, released only in the Soviet Union. No note accompanied it; however, I knew it had to have been from Dimitri in thanks for the many F-O-G-E-R-T-Y cave experiences we shared while following Lechuguilla's winds. I made a cassette tape of a selection of solo John Fogerty music and mailed it to the return address listed on the McCartney tape.

Dimitri might have taken a little of Lechuguilla's winds back with him, since soon after returning home, winds of change swept throughout the republic. While there may be a little matter of correlation versus causation, for me, it remains an inescapable fact that shortly after Dimitri returned to the USSR, the entire Soviet system collapsed under the winds of change. One point for Dimitri, F-O-G-E-R-T-Y, and David, zero points for the politburo. Eat that, Khrushchev! Cave winds are indeed powerful.

⚬❦⚬

Caving provides one of the last remaining opportunities for true exploration. Global Positioning Systems (GPS) and precisely drawn satellite maps have removed the mystery and excitement of most true exploration. Since satellites, drones, and remote sensing equipment don't work well underground, firsthand human experience and boots on the ground while following the wind remain state of the art in the subsurface world.

We can aid our search for caves by using computer models, geologic mapping, and lidar analysis. But once at the entrance, where does the cave go? To a caver, poking their head into unknown darkness to see if it goes or not is often one of life's most exhilarating experiences. Most caves go nowhere, but enough contain mysterious cave winds to keep hope running high and adrenaline surging as cavers continue following the wind. It indeed had for Tom for quite some time. But then again, if one hears of a crazy cave-related idea that originated from the Guadalupe Mountains of Texas, chances are that wind would lead to Tom.

It might have been my naïvety that caught Tom's attention. Regardless, I'm sure it helped. I easily fell for his ruse to help him with a cave dig. Tom knew of a blowing and sucking hole, and he kept pleading for help to dig deeper. He was sure a bigger cave lay below and beyond.

Tom's small, miserable cave had a tiny round entrance located not far from the edge of a road. The known cave held only four thin people if they huddled together in the "room." This "room" consisted of an enlarged fissure created from the disintegration of friable, partially balanced boulders held up by dried, packed, lung-choking porcupine poop. Tom jokingly referred to them as "cave walls." While that image alone might have been enough to entice Tom to enter, even more so, the strong winds in this misery hole blew strongly and blew consistently. However, the winds also blew strongly enough to erode the powdery porcupine poop bond, which in turn would topple a portion of the "wall" and enlarge the "room," by incremental collapse. Tom wanted me to help him dig into the porcupine poop adhesive so we could accelerate the cave's collapse.

No, really—this was Tom's plan. Have I mentioned that Tom singled me out because of my addiction to cave wind and my youthful naïvety?

The cave had undersized passages but oversized airflow. Air rushed from the narrow spaces between boulder, dried mud, and friable bedrock. There *had* to be more cave beyond. To get to any real cave beyond required digging into the rubble. Every rock or plastered mud chunk removed seemed to shift the entire cave passage above and below, filling us with fear of a total cave collapse. No sane person would dig into such unstable caves. That's why Tom led this effort. Others knew better. Tom and I did too, but the wind's beckoning roar became too compelling. If cave wind helped topple the former USSR, what chance would Tom or I have to resist?

To safeguard his dig, Tom deployed carefully cut lumber to shore up weaker wall segments. However, all walls were weak and needed shoring. So, with so many shoring timbers already in place, it made the small passages even more cramped. This meant any movement would likely knock one or more shoring timbers out of place and cause the whole shoring system to implode. Therefore, when passing by any shoring, we exhaled and held our breath, all so we might continue with our Ahab-like dig obsession.

Working into the wee hours of the night also created complications. For one, cold air raked across our dust-plastered but sweaty skin. We soon discovered that the right airflow rate provided wondrously fun games for feeble minds on the verge of hypothermia.

We found if we released a stuff sack full of clothing anywhere near the inside of the cave entrance, the strong outflowing air would attempt to expel it. But if we stuffed the sack sufficiently, it would get stuck in the small entrance, thus forming a cork that calmed the chilling wind—as long as the air pressure remained in a blowing phase. It took experimentation to find the right stuffing material to fill an entrance-plugging stuff sack. This is the type of experimentation problem that Tom excelled in. It provided me much amusement as I watched (and avoided any further digging). If Tom had placed too few contents into the stuff sack, it would sail out of the cave and hang up on nearby creosote bushes. A too-stuffed stuff sack would simply fall to the floor since its buoyancy insufficiently matched the airflow. This is exactly (well, not *exactly*) the design struggle nautical engineers have in new boat hull design.

We had no business being there. My newly married wife hated our trips to this hole. I made the mistake of taking her there once.

Days of toil produced no new cave, and it gave us no opportunity to come to our senses. Cave winds and their pull on us remained just as strong. After several futile digs with Tom, I eventually moved out of state. Tom remained behind, always on the lookout for suitably stupid and naïve new diggers.

I discovered upon a check-in with him more than thirty-two years later that he never found the source of that wind—at least not yet. Perhaps he realized it's folly to chase *all* winds. Wise souls know that some winds are best left alone. However, it also could be that in the age of information overload in an interconnected world, he has found a diminishing pool of equally obsessed, ignorant, gullible, and naïve assistants. However, I have faith in Tom, the cave, and the innate gullibility hardwired into humanity, since, as P. T. Barnum once famously said, "There's a sucker born every minute."

⚬❦⚬

In all my travels across this wide country, from the fiery desert to the bluest glacier, and from the profundity of ancient canyons to the mountain's apogee, I had a constant and unforgettable companion—wind. At times, I battled forces head-on, while on other occasions, I found solace in giving myself willingly to the current. Due to its ubiquitous nature, humbling power, and uneven temperament, wind has often been used as a metaphor for everything ranging from spirituality to blunt-force trauma. However, in all my time with wind, I can never say it provided comfort. At its worst, wind is struggle and resistance; at its best, it's invigorating joy and haunting serenity. Comfort is a soft lounge chair on a warm beach. Invigorating joy is a ship's prow cleaving a storm surge in the height of a gale. Such are the many faces of wind—friendly or otherwise.

Various cultures speak of internal winds. *Pranas* is the Hindi term for winds that circulate through a human's mind and body. Different pranas serve specific purposes, including ones that guide vital internal currents leading toward the center of the heart and mind in ways that provide balance and enable a spirit to soar.

Once, while cross-country skiing through the wintery chills of Rocky Mountain National Park, I chanced upon a frozen lake amid a windstorm. With outstretched arms as a sail, I embraced and caught the wind. However, I created little friction and collected no detritus. Without effort, stride, or will of mind, the wind took me where the wind chose. I was light as the wind—in powerless flight. The lightness, joyousness, and freedom of that timeless moment provided solace and comfort for many winds yet to come.

I can't state one way or the other if I was able to attain any plane of existence beyond that one flat, frozen lake surface, but Visoba Khechara, the noted Hindi poet, philosopher, and yogi guru, claimed there are six lower levels of consciousness that one must pass through to attain the highest state. At this highest, seventh level, the body merges with the wind, and the person becomes a Walker of the Sky, an entity that treads the winds and whose feet never touch the ground.

Path of Elders

Alone and naïve, I scurried to the base of Mexican Hat Rock. This is *the* Mexican Hat, the quizzical, unnatural-looking sandstone oddity located north of Utah's San Juan River and northeast of the namesake town. I was making good time, but not fast enough. This is a knee-jarring red-ocher and bare-rocked ancient land. With all its legend, lore, and history, I needed to move fast to catch up. Sagebrush wafting from high and soil crunching from low, I could smell the Four Corners even if blindfolded and lost in a dream.

I scurried to see, smell, and hear—or exploit, if you will—this corner of dreamland. I came to scrutinize Mexican Hat Rock up close. Mexican Hat is an approximate forty-foot-wide pancaked disc balanced on an eroding minute sandstone pedestal. From afar, the disc does indeed resemble the brim of a wide sombrero sitting on top of a diminutive head. Up close, the ensemble defies the laws of gravity. Erosion, gravity, and time will eventually win, and the sombrero will fall off and break into pieces, the discarded chunks coming to lie to the side, along with the boulders and other remnants of other sombreros, towers, spires, and freaks of nature. Those still standing erect in bold defiance to the hot, hazy blue sky will one day lie humbled and prostrate, for, in the end, gravity and time always win. In the meanwhile, Mexican Hat draws me like a fly to dung.

I also came to follow the path of the larger-than-life climbing master Royal Robbins. Perhaps due to the oversized legend of the mighty Royal Robbins, I'd expected a grander behemoth. A few minutes of scrambling brought me to the shoulder and head. I had a good, up-close view of the sombrero's brim and undersides. It was much smaller and less impressive than I'd imagined. I couldn't readily discern Robbins's first ascent route, but on the opposite side of the squashed pancaked disc, the bolt ladder stood out like the Liberty Bell's crack. I later learned that the Los Banditos, the mysterious and clandestine climbing clan, had drilled the bolt ladder just a few years previously. I'd heard of the Banditos by that time because I enjoyed following legends. Hey, if you can't be a legend yourself, then let a little of their allure rub off on you by following in their hallowed footsteps.

The Banditos's bolt ladder visibly and boldly taunted me to continue to the sombrero's actual top. For me, the summit of Mexican Hat Rock is the heart and soul of San Juan River country. If I were a fly, I could alight on the top with no effort at all. But where's the sport or respect in that? Flies know nothing of respect. So, I pulled my rope, hardware, and sundry other climbing paraphernalia out of the rucksack, all the while imagining climbing the bolt ladder. The climbing fever firmly held me in its grip in those days, and the fever was always more virulent when I was standing just a few bolts short of a summit. However, I began to have doubts, even worries. I was unaccustomed to climbing alone and self-belaying, so the severity of the overhanging sombrero brim made the thought even more daunting.

While my fever ran high, I avoided recklessness. I also wondered if there was a bolt on top to rappel from, since downclimbing the overhanging bolt ladder seemed next to impossible. If I obeyed, I imagined the fever stranding me on the summit. No one knew where I'd gone off to, and it would be days before anyone would see the weathered, desiccated, and prostrate lump defiling the sombrero's top. Neither Royal Robbins nor the Banditos were likely to come back soon to mount a rescue. The first to notice would be vultures. They were already pungently close by, egging me on and stoking my fever. They wanted me to attempt fate. Vultures, in all their forms, are never far off in flyover land.

After several false starts, I defied the fever and defied the vultures. I simply sat. I sat in the shade of the sombrero, sat on the Mexican's shoulders, and sat gazing at the illustrious San Juan River country lying in wide, lazy expanse beyond the brim, beyond my outstretched arms, and well beyond my dangling and protruding feet.

I lost all sense of time while scanning the San Juan River country. Earth and water shaped this eloquent land, but other deeper and magical forces must also have contributed deft brushstrokes. The view, far too busy to be sublime or beautiful, stood out in its starkly denuded, rilled, and scoured convolutions. Far too many upheavals and eroded flanks to take in. As I said, too busy. I closed my eyes to reboot processors and then slowly opened them to see if I could perceive the landscape differently. Still too busy. It was as if I'd awoken to find archangels greeting me at the gates of ascension. However, with perfection and eloquence such as this, why ascend?

Returning from slumber, I found myself still free from the vultures' gullets and firmly earthbound on the shoulders of Mexican Hat Rock. I gave one more feigned thought of ascending beyond the brim, but it came and went. That gate opened and shut. Prudence and perseverance overcame my fever that day. Besides, one doesn't treat or leave scuff marks on a Michelangelo masterpiece. Sorry, vultures. Perhaps another day! The river now beckoned.

As I turned, the only sound was sand pelting the ever-thinning pedestal. Beyond that, silence. Before descending, I turned my eyes once more to the river. From that moment on, I intuitively knew this wild and desolate landscape had activated a switch deep in my circuitry that no reboot could ever erase. With still too much to take in and process, I knew that one, two, or even a dozen looks would never suffice.

If I knew then what I know now, I would also have cast my eyes toward less esoteric and more human-scaled elements, such as the nearby abandoned uranium mill. No one had yet mitigated or reclaimed the site, so the old uranium settling ponds would have been plainly visible in those days—evaporating in the sun and cast about by the wind. However, I was too naïve, too uninformed, too young, too protected, and too suburban in those days to know anything about the region's dark secrets and less-than-glorious history. I was too caught up in legends, mystiques, and the broader view. However, views always change when looked upon at different scales.

Before the drive back into the heart of Navajo land and my temporary home, I pulled into Bluff, Utah. My hunger prompted me to taste and savor the local culture. By all appearances, it was a true flyover or drive-by hamlet and a collection of buildings that might never have had better days. I suppose if it were my home, I would have viewed it differently. Despite my hunger, I stopped first along the San Juan River, near where the murky waters slowly rolled past the town's shoreline. It was less glorious up close. Perhaps I can better appreciate an artisan and their work from afar, where I can place the art and artisan in proper context. The San Juan River is a master sculptor, and for all such works of art, it's better to appreciate the entire artwork in view at a time. One better appreciates a Michelangelo statue by looking at the entire statue, not by zooming in on only the details contained on a single finger.

I finally strolled into a nearby restaurant—a hole-in-the-wall dive. Over the years, the specifics of the site and name now elude me. It has long since evaporated, much like the nearby San Juan River waters will dissipate before reaching the Pacific Ocean—evaporated, irrigated, or pooled in some stagnant mosquito-infested backwater. I chose a booth against the far wall to maximize my view of people strolling in and out to eat, talk, or kill a few hours. What else is there to do in Bluff? I ate slowly—and watched.

The lively conversation in the booth next to me was hard to ignore. From their conversation, it appeared the two men, in either their late twenties or early thirties, had known each other for years. They shouted out and greeted by name each person who stepped in from outside. The eatery must have been Bluff's community hub. Without being too obvious or rude, I listened.

The two spoke loudly and openly, so I needed no refined eavesdropping skill or effort. They were debating which archeological site to loot in the coming week. I don't recall any site names, but the larger man dismissed the smaller man's first suggestion. He casually explained that a mutual friend of theirs had recently looted that site, so there was little reason to revisit. The larger man suggested another antiquity, but as it turned out, the smaller man had already looted that ruin. They crossed off many sites from their potential looting list. They eventually settled on one pre-Puebloan ruin. They'd begun looting it together two years previously, but they'd run out of time.

The site, they believed, still held potential for exciting and valuable finds. With so much to exploit and so little time, it seems a looter's life is never idle.

I scanned the crowded diner for shock and disbelief. I found none. Everyone continued eating, talking, and greeting one another as if it were a church picnic. I never imagined God-fearing church-picnic types would loot archeological sites. However, this overheard conversation occurred right after the first two Indiana Jones movies had come out, and the greater public's interest in archeology had produced a corresponding surge in archeological looting. As my jaw remained agape, everyone else continued eating. It was as if looting topics were as common as drought or the weather.

Well, I'd wanted to observe the local culture.

I imagined if the sheriff were there, he wouldn't have paused chewing his sandwich and filling his gullet. I guess each culture stomachs things differently. It's little wonder the various tribes with ancestral roots in the area—such as the Ute, Navajo, Hopi, and Zuni—don't trust local jurisdictions to protect Native American sacred cultural sites. If they knew and objected, would the sheriff have intervened? Or would it have been simply dust in the wind?

I had no discernable or identifiable proof of a crime about to be committed, so I passed no warnings or reports to either the county sheriff, the Bureau of Land Management, or the tribal office. I therefore became just another part of the problem. I guess I conformed to societal pressure. I remained silent.

Winds are ubiquitous in arid lands, and they carry a lot of dust. You simply learn to shake the dust off at doorways before stepping inside. The smell and taste of my food changed. The time for people-watching had ended.

In the end, like with the San Juan River, I better appreciated Bluff from afar. It's rarely easy to free oneself from past burdens—for individuals or entire communities. It's much easier to look the other way and strip our minds and consciousness of distractions and nuances. Perhaps, then we may have some peace. However, such temporary peace is never sustainable, so it's not true peace. Decisions continue to haunt us like a hypnotic dirge we can't get out of our heads. My mind drifted beyond Bluff and into the swirling enchantment of the San Juan River. In true flyover fashion, I turned my car away from Bluff and toward home—deeper into the Navajo Nation.

⚬❦⚬

For two years, I worked at Canyon de Chelly National Monument, a wondrously wild land of imposing spires, bold mesas, sweeping canyons, and haunting mysteries. I didn't go there for enchantment, enrichment, or desolate loveliness. I also didn't go there for its rich cultural heritage. I went there simply for a job. Back in those days, to get a permanent job with the National Park Service, a person had to spend several years as a seasonal, paying dues and learning the ropes. I wanted to pay all my dues in western mountains. However, seasonal jobs in the Cascades, Sierra Nevada, and Rocky Mountains typically lasted only for the three or so snow-free months. I'd graduated from college by then, and I didn't see how I could live and climb for a whole year on only three months' pay. That would be a long, cold, and hungry winter.

Unlike at mountain parks, seasonal positions in the desert Southwest extended to six months. The Canyon de Chelly position lasted nine. So, for the lure of money, job, and security, I reluctantly headed out of the mountains and pointed my car south. I felt like such a bourgeois sellout. Knowledge that Fred Beckey, Layton Kor, and other famous climbers spent time among desert sandstones helped soften my bourgeois blues. If the red-rock canyon country was good enough for Fred, it would have to be good enough for me.

It didn't take long for the red-rock canyon country to cast its spell on me. Like a barbed and irretractable cactus spine lodged in my flesh, the Four Corners country has been a part of me since. This affliction happened somewhere after the first lightning storm, after discovering green-splashed mini pools and patina-stained mega alcoves, after getting stuck in my first two-track rut, after experiencing its wild isolation, and after the very first glimpse of a hidden and previously unknown adobe wall. The canyon country didn't grow on me instantly, but its gestation developed organically.

While I still call mountains home and my first love, I began seeing a future as a desert rat—at least the canyon country high-desert variety. Mountainscapes have lush and beautiful coverings and outer garments, but nature splayed the desert inside out—exposed for all to see and experience its raw innards. Although the flesh is long gone, this wild landscape still pulsates with life and is filled with antiquities that lie far below the obvious. It's a land of subtleness, it's a land of contrasts, and it's a land that has experienced a lot of footfalls. However, despite a hundred years of abusive modern exploitation, hundreds of years of Navajo occupation, and then millions of ancestral Puebloan footfalls, a desert rat can *still* make modern discoveries and rediscoveries.

In modern times, Canyon de Chelly lies in the center of the Navajo Reservation. This remains a unique national monument—in more ways than one. For starters, the National Park Service doesn't own the land. The Navajo do, along with all the surrounding canyons and rimrock. The National Park Service only manages park operations. There were nearly fifty Navajo families living deep within the monument's canyons—without electricity, water, or other amenities other than what can fit inside a traditional Navajo hogan or in the back of the ubiquitous pickup truck.

Besides Navajo homes and families, Canyon de Chelly National Monument contains deeply incised sandstone canyons. The namesake canyon, Canyon de Chelly, may not even be the largest. By some measures, that honor belongs to Canyon del Muerto, or Canyon of the Dead.

Big and small alike, all the monument's canyons begin their grandeur within the pinyon and juniper forests of the Defiance Plateau and the Chuska Mountains' lower western slopes. At mid-distance, the canyons reach their grandest spectacle in both depth and steepness. All canyons eventually converge and gradually diminish in height and impressiveness as the inflated uplift dissipates into flanking valley plains. By the time the unified canyon reaches its mouth, the once mighty incision becomes just another sandstone wash. At this point, there's no hint of the countless deep vertical slots or perpetual shadows hiding and haunting the ancestral ruins that lie upslope. At this point, the canyon's labyrinth lies beyond unknowing eyes and is shrouded in obscurity.

The obvious way into the canyon is from its mouth—from the sandy wash. If you're traveling east, the walls slowly rise before your eyes. However, a trek on foot from the canyon's mouth to its upper reaches would take days. When the canyon isn't in flood, there's a four-wheeler path of sorts that goes as far as Spider Rock in Canyon de Chelly and Mummy Cave ruins in Canyon del Muerto. Beyond that, canyon travel is by foot or horseback. To deal with the canyon's inaccessibility, the ancients constructed bypasses. Using stone tools, they chipped handholds and footholds up the canyon walls in convenient locations. These lines of hand-and-toe holds allowed canyon occupants to climb out of the canyon in a hurry—sometimes in minutes (or whatever units of time ancients used).

After the ancestral Puebloan climbers left the canyon for good, the Navajo moved in and continued to maintain the hand-and-toe-hold trails—at least most. I suspect outside an inner circle of family, friends, and clan members, the earliest Navajos wanted to keep trail locations secret. Trails provided an emergency exit route—ones the US military forced them to use on more than one occasion. No one wanted to get trapped in a dead-end canyon.

While modern-day Navajos may have less of a need for secrecy, they have little incentive to share trail locations widely. From my observations, the Navajos living in the canyon intimately know of all trails near their home, even the obscure, but often know little to nothing of other trails throughout the canyon. While working in the park, I took on as a project of my own to inventory and document every hand-and-toe-hold trail in the entire system of canyons within the park. I interviewed many Navajos, but many weren't overly willing to share such culturally important details with a non-Navajo stranger who had formed no personal bond or trust. Therefore, I had more success by systematically field-checking every canyon wall, alcove, buttress, slope, and bastion.

This inspection required many footfalls, many false starts, and many abrupt endings. Sandwiched between these two extremes, like a zone located between patina streaks, lies the canyon's most tantalizing, subtle surprises. The more I climbed ancient climbing routes, the more my respect grew for the original climbing artistry. By modern climbing standards, many hand-and-toe-hold trails were technical rock climbs, and nearly all offered their own mystifying and even frightening moments.

A few of the hand-and-toe-hold trails I explored and mapped—such as Slim Canyon, Blade, Ya-ba-chai, Ladder, Wild Nut, Woman, Man, Bad, Baby Pee, Crack-in-the-Rock, Many Ladder, and Hanging Ladder Trails—already had names. For other trails I found, no one claimed previous knowledge or awareness of their existence, so I bestowed my own names, such as Talus, Ruin, Obscurity, and Gnat Trails. I climbed thirty-three different hand-and-toe-hold trails during the two summers I lived in the park. I heard rumors of a possible nineteen additional trails that neither I nor anyone else could locate. My forty-year-old notes reveal additional confusions that hint at both additional mysteries and highlight my poor note-taking abilities back then. My notes mention that I climbed White Cave Trail and Whiskey Creek Trail, but I have no recollection of ever hearing of these trails, let alone any memory of climbing them or where they're located. They're not on my inventory map. Canyon de Chelly, then or now, doesn't give up its secrets easily.

Many of the carved holds are now old and worn smooth from use and age. Navajos keep some of the trails in shape, including sharpening edges, because it's scary to use rounded and worn holds. Throughout a trail's entire length, there usually is no potential for climbing protection, so a fall is unthinkable. While you may have heard of the National Park Service's deferred maintenance problem, within Canyon de Chelly, the trails modern Navajos don't maintain are now smooth, rounded dimples, the handiwork of wind, time, and neglect. That's what you get when the last maintenance stopped in the thirteenth century.

I knew of only one dimpled antiquity that I didn't climb—one I discovered and no one else had reported. In an obscure, out-of-way location, if the light shone at the right angle, a person could barely make out a line of minute dimpled shadows. A close inspection uncovered it to be a well-worn hand-and-toe-hold trail—one much too unnerving to venture on alone.

I invited Roger, the park's superintendent. He was *always* up for adventures, the more unnerving and unprotected, the better. He, too, reveled in the insane. We made a good team. What he lacked in technical skill, he made up for in nerves and a casual disregard for personal safety—the perfect combination.

Since the rock offered no place for protection, we kept the rope coiled. If one were to fall, there's no use in pulling the other down too. We both crept higher on the ancient climber's handiwork. It got steeper and steeper. While still no place for protection, we roped up nonetheless since it provided a false sense of security. Although this mental trick fooled neither Roger nor me, we both knew what would happen if anyone slipped on the route's first ascent in a thousand years.

We made fast time over the moderately sloped first section. Besides, I convinced myself that any fall less than one hundred feet, while it would break bones, would be survivable. As we climbed higher, the route grew more puzzling. It led to a vertical and blank headwall with overhangs on either side. I scanned the canyon walls, wondering where I'd gotten off route. Unlike at Eldorado Canyon, I lacked any obtuse comments from spectators to inform me of the direction I should have gone or guide me to safety. Roger and I only had ourselves. Getting off route is easy both in Eldorado Canyon and when following faint, dimpled hand-and-toe holds in Navajo land. Natural depressions can easily appear carved when you're looking from afar or in desperate straits, but they can turn out to be "never in my lifetime" when inspected up close. I kept backtracking to see where I'd veered off. Being a perfect partner, Roger never chafed at my delays and hesitations in such situations. He knew better. Besides, he rarely wanted to lead, so he patiently waited as I pondered and studied the mystery, scrutinized each dimple, and made many false attempts that kept leading me back to the same blank cliff and the same overhang.

I shouted at Roger to carefully watch me and prepare for a fall, although he could have done nothing if I had fallen other than let go of the rope and watch me bounce to the canyon bottom or allow the rope to pull both of us down. At least I gave him time to decide. In situations like this, while I got nervous, Roger grew more alive and attentive to the canyon's spiritual vibe.

I had no time for vibeness. I focused my entire concentration on traversing left of the overhang, looking for more dimpled trail. None existed. I climbed gingerly to the right. Again, no sign. My curiosity grew with each repeated attempt. I sensed Roger's vibe was growing as fast as my anticipation and apprehension.

Maybe the ancient climber fell, and everyone else left the unfinished trail as a tribute to the fallen, I thought. *Maybe the climber got too unnerved and never came back*. I considered the possibility that maybe the ancient didn't want to get out of the canyon *that* badly. I never found out, since neither Roger nor I spiritually connected with any ancient on that topic.

I was less inclined than the ancient to give up. As Roger basked in the canyon's aura, an absurd Tom-like whim overcame me like a Chinook wind's first seasonal burst. I climbed under the overhang as high as my body permitted. With our lives hanging on two small depressions for my feet and whatever friction hold I could get by palming the rough sandstone with my left hand, I extended my right hand and arm as far as they articulated. Blindly, I probed the slope above the overhanging lip, looking for something—anything. My hand finally came upon a dimple-like sandstone depression. Worn, but unmistakably an ancient handhold.

Simultaneously placing both hands on this blind, sloping surface and pressing down as hard as I could to maximize friction, I hoped it would be enough to hold my weight. I called out to Roger to watch for a fall as I raised my head high enough to peer over the overhanging lip. Sure enough, a faint line of alternating and staggered dimples continued up the wall above the overhang.

Although the ancient route continued, I'd already reached a precarious position with just my eyeballs above the overhang. Attempting to haul my entire body over the overhang using only this one shallow dimple was, to put it mildly, beyond crazy—even by Roger's standards. With fading arm strength, I couldn't come up with sufficient words to describe how much this ancestral Puebloan climber impressed me. I had no idea how they chipped holds above the overhang without hanging on to nonexistent ropes. Even more mysterious was why. Why would the climber use such a dangerous trail when safer alternatives were located nearby? I wondered if this ancestral Puebloan's neighbors constantly asked why they climbed. If asked, the response might have been, "If you have to ask, you wouldn't understand."

After the ancestral Puebloan climbers left Canyon de Chelly, the Navajos moved in. It's been now five centuries. Navajos today live in the canyon, along the rim, in the town of Chinle, and elsewhere throughout the expansive reservation. During my Navajo Reservation wanderings, most Navajos acted as if they ascribed no real emotional or antiquity value to the hand-and-toe-hold trails. They only served a practical use. Navajos used some of the ancient trails to travel in and out of their canyon home, but otherwise, they appeared disinterested.

In all my canyon travels, most of the Navajos I saw on the hand-and-toe-hold trails were women and children. Many young Navajo men had pickup trucks, but the women either lacked access to the vehicles or chose to perform their many errands by foot. Mothers often had a baby strapped to their back as they casually negotiated the hand-and-toe holds as if they'd traversed them hundreds of times. Perhaps they had. Adults appeared to leave children from age four on up to fend for themselves on the trails. Perhaps canyon-living Navajo mothers taught their children the fine art of safe hand-and-toe-hold canyon travel.

The few Navajo teenage boys I saw on the trails were often using the route to escape capture as they plundered visitors' cars or indulged in other forms of idle mischief. At least in those days, there were many Navajo boys who ransacked visitors' cars as the lawful owners enjoyed the park's many canyon overlooks. These were popular activities—canyon viewing and car clouting. Between riffling through unlocked vehicles, teenagers hid under nearby juniper trees, waiting for the next car and their next victim. If a park ranger patrol came near, the kids scurried down nearby hand-and-toe-hold trails and disappeared into the desert as fast as water in an Arizona afternoon sun.

Navajo sheepherders used the trails as shortcuts to tending their sheep. They might have penned sheep on the canyon rim to protect them from coyotes when the herders couldn't be around to watch them. Sheep herding was a job for women, the elderly, and pre-car-clouting-aged boys. Once boys reached the age to drive pickups, it seemed they never got on their feet again until they became ancient and were once again relegated to sheepherding and getting places on foot.

I had a magical time searching for and exploring these hand-and-toe-hold trails. It involved the perfect blend of true exploration, the allure and mystery of the past, and the testing of boldness and technical and physical skills. Few non-Navajos are afforded this opportunity. As such, I respected the privilege and took full advantage of the opportunity. I made the canyon walls my home. I seemed to have the entire canyon edges to myself, save for the occasional Navajo mother with children in tow or a teenager running from a fresh car break-in.

Throughout those two years in the mid-1980s, I climbed and explored as many nooks and crannies as possible throughout the canyons. Through these wanderings, all areas, even steep canyon walls, showed at least some signs of previous human use. Rarely was any canyon-scape left untouched. It's a land that easily conjures the noncorporeal presence of people, places, and antiquities—for the ghosts of previous generations continue to haunt the canyon depths, walls, and recesses.

Bill the Pill

*P*once de León and the Spanish conquistadors sought the Fountain of Youth. Spoiler alert: they never found it. Conversely, we have Bill. In all his cave wanderings around the globe, Bill must have come across the Fountain of Old. This allusion has not anything to do with his age, since I don't begrudge anyone for succumbing to the passing of years. Instead, it has more to do with his curmudgeoness.

I first heard of Bill decades before I met him. I grew up in the 1960s and 1970s, reading his many caving books and articles. By the time I began caving with him in the 1980s, he acted as if he were in his eighties. In our multigenerational crossroads, I was physically fit and in my ascendency, while his had passed. It mattered little to me, since those things were of lesser importance than him being a legend. As such, I cut him slack and put up with his crotchetiness, his cutting and frequent insults and put-downs, and his overall Billness. Who am I to speak ill of a legend? We must be patient with those who first trod our chosen paths.

I worked at Carlsbad Caverns National Park as a cave specialist shortly after project cavers discovered Lechuguilla Cave and during the height of its political craziness. The cave turned out to be not only immense but unlike any other cave experienced on earth. Its existence upended everything we thought we knew of desert caves. Lechuguilla Cave drew attention from cavers the world over, scientists, crazies, politicians, and exploiters from all walks of life. My job had me managing the cave and the crazies, and, if appropriate, taking people into the cave to show them around. Because of the cave's bigness and technical complications, the powers that be didn't allow duffers. If noteworthy, skilled cave managers or cave scientists came around, then I escorted them into, and hopefully out of, the cave.

The National Speleological Society's Board of Governors wanted a firsthand look at the much-talked-about Lechuguilla Cave. Park managers agreed to let them in, and they volunteered me to escort them to keep the cave safe from them and to keep them safe from themselves.

There were five of them, and in hindsight, few of them had any business being there. And Bill should not have been on that list. The cave was simply too technical and too physically demanding for most of them. Bill could have handled it years, or even decades, earlier, back before the Fountain of Old took hold. If only he'd found the Fountain of Old in his youth, so it could have locked in his age during his youthful stage—back when he was fit and had vigor.

Two other group members could handle the technical and physical challenges reasonably well, but for one, his high degree of arseness should have ruled him out from any team selection culling. Consequently, with this lack of proper screening and culling, I rappelled the first of Lechuguilla's drops with one competent and trustworthy caver, two reasonably competent cavers who lacked experience and needed some watching over to keep them safe, the arse, and Bill.

I found it obvious from the first encounter with photon-limited space that Bill needed 100 percent of my attention to keep him safe, keep the cave safe, and deflect or absorb his excruciatingly biting insults and accusations. I assessed that the two wonderfully nice but technically less-experienced team members might also need some looking after. I, as team lead, couldn't watch both groups simultaneously. Fortunately for me and the team, the competent caver, in wordless understanding, sensed the situation and focused his full attention on keeping an eye on the two nice but less experienced cavers. That freed me to focus on Bill. The arse chose to wander between the two factions, spreading equally his ample arseness and useless complaining.

In short order, Bill seemed to lose all bodily energy, motivation, and, at times, will to live. He appeared to want only to curl in a fetal position so his aged body would turn to dust and blow away into the timeless void of Lechuguilla's wind-filled nothingness. Apparently, the magical power of the Fountain of Old doesn't easily transmit through fossilized Permian reefs. The Billness needed kind, motivating confidence. I provided gentle words of encouragement.

Bill's response: "What do you know, you stupid, insipid, ignorant nobody?"

I answered, "I don't claim to be anyone." (For I am but a spud.) "Other than I'm the person who knows you need to get up and take a few more steps. Each step is one bit closer to the surface and the end of the trip."

Despite continued barrages from him that I was nothing but a stupid and ignorant nobody, I offered more soothing words of encouragement. Something eventually worked, since Bill rose to his feet as if he planned to move. That ended when the arse came by to grace us with his presence. The arse looked at Bill and said loudly for everyone to hear, "Look at him. He's pasty white, and he's dying, if he's not dead already. Just leave him here to die, 'cause if not, he'll surely be the death to us all!" Several times, he blurted out for all to hear, "We're all going to die."

After many soul-crippling, unhelpful bursts, I quietly pulled the arse aside and firmly told him, "What Bill and the team need is patient encouragement, understanding, and help. We don't need insults, put-downs, and screams that we're all going to die. Get a grip on yourself so that we may all come out in one piece."

Finally, after hours of coaxing, prodding, and absorbing Bill's bite and the arse's arseness, we arrived at the base of Boulder Falls, not far from the entrance and the escape from the nightmare. Boulder Falls is a one-hundred-and-eighty-foot vertical cliff that's the only way out—one must climb the fixed rope to get out. On top of Boulder Falls, there's only a few hundred feet of reasonably mild caving passage to reach the bottom of the entrance rope. A vertical climb up this ninety-foot rope takes a person back to the surface's normal world and the gentle trail leading back to the escape cars.

After another of the arse's put-downs to Bill, Bill responded, "He's right. I can't make it. You go back and call for a rescue, then haul me out on a Stokes litter."

After hours of calmly absorbing his severe insults and endless verbal abuse, I took a different tack. With conviction, I pointed in his face and scolded, "I am NOT going to call for a rescue simply because you're tired or exhausted or gave up. You need to get off your ass and up the rope. I don't care if you need to stop on the rope every inch to rest or if it takes us twenty-four hours to get out, but you *will* be getting out under your own power. I'll be there with you every step of the way, but we *are* all getting out together! Understood?"

The arse blurted some dire warning involving us all dying. However, much to Bill's credit, he placed his jumar ascenders on the rope, hoisted his pack, and slowly but silently climbed Boulder Falls. He negotiated the intervening cave, and then slowly and quietly—without curse, insult, or condescension—climbed the entrance rope. We were out!

Months later, I saw Bill in a cave management meeting. He pulled me aside and offered me a deep and sincere apology for his verbal abuse during the Lech trip and thanked me for patiently helping him throughout his ordeal. He presented me with an autographed copy of one of his early caving books—the one that inspired me as a youth.

From that point on, the few times our paths crossed, he demonstrated to me the epitome of grace, respect, and endearing kindness. However, from stories picked up elsewhere, I knew that he remained Bill to most everyone else. While his Lechuguilla Cave epic might have smoothed out one rough edge, one cave trip alone can't offset the magical powers of the Fountain of Old.

The last I heard, he was still going strong. His longevity is impressive. How does he do it? Perhaps some things, like quantum theory, aren't supposed to make sense or don't reside in the logical realm. There are some things in this world that nature intended to hold in suspended animation, and Bill is clearly one of them. Upon further reflection, it appears Bill has an uncanny resemblance to Ponce de León. No wonder Bill is such a legend.

A Dose of Vadose

Nature creates caves in myriad ways, but many form by acid solutions working and dissolving soluble bedrock, like limestone. Lechuguilla, and others in the Guadalupe Mountains, and a few scattering ones elsewhere—primarily in the West—are atypical. Acid solutions still form these atypical caves, but the acid comes from brines within deep petroleum deposits. Conversely, the dissolving acid for typical caves—atmospheric carbon dioxide—comes from above. That's right, normal rainwater is slightly acidic. Over time, even weak acids dissolve bedrock to form stupendous voids big enough to drive a car through (and, in some parts of the nation, large enough to dispose of decades worth of discarded appliances, used oil, and carcasses of slaughtered farm animals). They're clearly big enough for water to continue flowing through and enlarging cave passages.

Although there are infinite varieties of cave forms, those that develop close to the local groundwater surface are one common category. While cave passages may wind around and follow wherever the rock was easier to dissolve, this category of cave passages tends to be reasonably flat or level at the water table. Kentucky's Mammoth

Cave, the world's longest cave, is a classic example. Park visitors may take boat tours on the underground Echo River. Mammoth Cave's Echo River is no more than the gently flowing groundwater surface making its way toward daylight to emerge as a spring that feeds surface streams.

Another cave category is vadose caves. While many caves form by slightly acidic water gently flowing at the groundwater surface, acid rainwater must reach the water table somehow. In mountains and plateaus, gravity may plunge that acid water steeply through cracks and weaknesses in the bedrock in its search for the more stable water table level. This plunging groundwater—also called the vadose, or meteoric water—is simply behaving as nature intended. One of nature's well-known rules is water takes the path of least resistance on its path to the ocean. (Think of the oceans as the world's ultimate water table.) If a stream hits a mountain, the path of least resistance will likely be to flow around the mountain. However, if that mountain is soluble rock, such as limestone, the path of least resistance may be for the water to flow along ever-enlarging cracks that go through the mountain. If that stream originated near a summit, the path of least resistance for rain and snowmelt may be to plunge deep under the mountain and eventually flow back to the surface at a groundwater spring located far in the distance. While vadose water remains in contact with soluble rocks, caves continue to grow, enlarge, and form new water shortcuts. Plunging vadose waters form plunging cave passages that require cavers to have specialized techniques and equipment if they want to explore their vertical depths.

❧

Cavers place a certain distinction on being a vertical caver. This term refers not to cavers with good posture but rather to those who enter caves oriented vertically—the cavern, not the caver. Horizontal caves force the inflicted into crawls, stoops, squats, and waddles, whereas vertical caves allow them to pose upright in glorious hero photos while adorned not in mud but in technical gadgetry that would make Tim the Toolman proud.

There are downsides to vertical caving. For one, rarely is the entire cave vertical, so for those in-between sections, cavers must push, pull, and scream at the beastly, leviathan bags holding their metal vertical tactical gear, including the additional eight pounds of dry-weighted rope—or thirty-six pounds when mud-saturated. It's all worth it though, since once we've dragged the beached whales through tortuous belly crawls, the vertical sections allow gravity and open air to rearticulate spines, unstick packs, and dangle bloody and bruised legs freely and far above the dark and twisty labyrinths—and to briefly remind us that cavers *can* be more than blind primordial grubs slithering in earthen burrows.

There are few things as graceful and lovely as a rappel down a deep, cavernous shaft when body and headlamp are far from surrounding walls and free from rockfalls, waterfalls, or caver falls. It's these rarified moments that uplift the vertical caver's soul to otherworldly sublimity.

The rarity of such moments is also because subterranean pits don't abound everywhere; vertical cavers must search them out. For the vertical caver, there's a region of the world considered sacred and hallowed—a place where pits predominate. Cavers refer to this vertical paradise as TAG. TAG stands for Tennessee-Alabama-Georgia, the hallowed and hollowed patch of landscape clustered near these states' shared border.

Although horizontal caves abound in TAG, when cavers think of this region, they think of vertical caves. It almost seems as if you can't toss a dead possum without hitting one—at least of paltry or pittance size. It's this abundance of vertical pits that contributed to TAG being the birthplace of American vertical caving, for TAG is to vertical cavers what Yosemite is to rock climbers. While many climbers feel compelled to make pilgrimages to Yosemite, vertical cavers find themselves pulled to experience rappelling into classic TAG pits.

❧

At the end of an August a few decades ago, during one of my pilgrimages, I found myself belaying Jim, the Jim of Mexico's Huatla Cave fame, as he drilled bolts high in a vadose dome in Alabama's Russell Cave. Huatla is a hard-man and hard-woman cave in the depths of Mexico's Yucatán Peninsula. It's as close to the caver's version of the Eiger as one could possibly find. It should go without saying that Jim is no spud. Our Russell Cave destination for this August spud-free day had us traversing a vertical shaft to a ledge on the far side. A dome is simply an in-cave pit when looking up from bottom—especially when that pit has no readily apparent top-side exit.

On this Russell Cave dome, Jim made quick progress. After all, he'd spent a big chunk of his adult life in the vertical and, if rumors were true, a share of his youngling years as well. Jim flowed across the shaft as gracefully as cave wind. If he hadn't been such a large man, I would have sworn I'd just witnessed a hobbit stealthily stealing the jewel right from under Smaug's nose. Beyond belaying, there was nothing for me to do other than watch and learn. As soon as the wind reached the far side, he called back that someone had preceded him.

Jim figured it had to have been the equally legendary Bill (a different Bill, so for clarity's sake, I'll refer to this one as Bill T.) during one of his many undocumented early Russell Cave explorations. Hard cavers and spuds alike know Bill T. for his bold, often solo, and unprotected climbs and cave explorations. I'm amazed that he must have made it up the dome solo. Bill T. also was no spud.

Later that day, Jim found an in-cave pit that he believed no one had ever descended, not even Bill T., but we were out of rope and time. This pit, on the edge of the known map, would have to wait for another day and another belayer.

⚭

Later in the same TAG pilgrimage, Larry and I donned waterproof suits for one of the nation's most stunning pits—Green's Well. The pit's smooth and round borehole shape elicits imagery of rappelling into a vertically oriented gun barrel. As I peered down the shaft, I witnessed an unusually high volume of water plunging its way toward the water table located far below. Upon watching and listening to the falls, my imagery changed from being shot down a gun barrel to being sprayed out an immense fire hose. The couple of recent squalls had changed the nature of the pit considerably.

I was the first down the rope. The waterfall's fury effortlessly coalesced with gravity's pull to create a wholly new unified force. Both Newton and Einstein would have been impressed. I felt like an astronaut experiencing negative g-force for the first time. Blind as a cave-adapted crayfish, I rappelled into the middle of the waterfall. I could see nothing beyond water and spray, felt nothing but pounding and joy, and heard nothing beyond my laughter's wild merriment and the thunderous roar.

With no visual bearing to assess my descent speed or spatial positioning, I couldn't gauge how close I was to cratering on the rocky bottom. No mission control guided my descent. Impact waves coursing up my skeletal network indicated I had made touchdown on something solid.

"Houston, the Ek has landed."

At the bottom of the 227-foot rappel, I could hardly stand under the force of the waterfall, but for some odd reason, the experience prompted more laughing and merriment. Not just a snicker but a full belly laugh. This remains one of my all-time favorite rappels—classic TAG.

❧

Since I was in TAG, I hungered for multiple-drop pits and vertical superlatives. For a single rappel from the surface, such as Green's Well, one long rope suffices. At the end of the trip, intrepid souls simply climb back up the rope, then either go home or on to the next pit. However, some vadose waters plunge multiple times on their way to base level. Cavers on these multiple-drop pits must carry enough rope to leave one behind on each successive pit they plan rappelling down. As they descend deeper underground, the mass of ropes they must carry through horizontal sections of the cave becomes less burdensome until they run out of pits or ropes—and then they must retrieve all ropes as they climb back out the way they came in.

There are a few vertical caves that have multiple entrances located at different elevations on the mountain or plateau. On these, instead of leaving a succession of fixed ropes on each pit they rappel, brave cavers may choose to do a through trip. On through trips, cavers don't leave ropes behind on the pits they descend; instead, they pull down their rope after each rappel with the plan to exit the cave from a lower entrance. Planned one-way trips out a different entrance have serious consequences if, for any reason, the lower entrance is blocked or can't be found. In such situations, the caver can't go up, or down. They're truly between a rock and a hard place. Bold cavers do through trips. Rarely do spuds.

Since I was on a TAG pilgrimage, I wanted to experience a challenging multiple drop. Shakespeare must have been thinking of vertical caving when he wrote in *A Midsummer Night's Dream*, "Lord, what fools these mortals be!"

I longed to have Ellison's Cave humble me into submission. When it comes to big pits, Ellison's is THE classic. At 510 feet, Ellison's also contains the longest in-cave rappel in the continental US.

Ellison's would likely be more popular than it already is if it weren't for logistical challenges. The cave requires too much rope for Larry and one wimpy companion to carry. So instead, we turned our eyes to a cave more suitable for a party of two. The multiple-drop Thunder Hole fit the bill to a T.

In hindsight, the fifty-foot difference between carrying 460 feet of rope versus 510 wouldn't have made much difference. It was still brutal pushing a mass and tangle of rope through tight belly crawls. Regardless, Thunder Hole turned out to be a near-perfect cave. We couldn't have chosen better.

The approach found us carrying full vertical gear, four ropes, and two wet suits across an immense soybean field, then up a steep hillside of overly cut eastern deciduous forests. I was glad I no longer ascribed to Don Whillans's conditioning theory. A front carrying ninety-degree temperatures and 100 percent relative humidity lingered behind but fast approached. The heavy metal equipment strain, as well as nearly forty pounds of rope, allowed the front to catch up, beat us at its game, and leave us far behind.

As we toiled past soybean fields, I thought, *While this weather does nothing for cavers carrying heavy loads, it must be great for soybeans, for they seem especially lush.* The happy soybeans and oppressive humidity must have been better companions than I thought, since we arrived at the cave's small entrance sooner than anticipated.

The first two rappels, Thunder Hole and Flash Flood Drop, went straight down active waterfalls. After that, we, but not the water, entered Constrictor Crawl. After many lost moments of pushing snagging packs and soggy ropes, I wondered if it would've been any worse with the extra gear required for Ellison's. Doubts were quickly cleansed upon rejoining the water at the top of a wonderfully miserable waterfall rappel. Leaving that rope dangling in the spray, a short and steep down-climb, under the watchless presence of eyeless, translucent crayfish, brought us to Neptune Well.

As my headlamp's beam scanned the well's frothy tempest, I thought of Thomas Fuller's reassuring words: "Bacchus hath drowned more men than Neptune." Neither Bacchus nor Neptune got the better part of us on this beautifully classic waterfall rappel. There was no use in bringing wet suits if not planning on being wetted.

After our Neptune Well wetting, we passed by more blind aquatic creatures as we approached the Winding Cleft. This aptly named sinuous passage teemed with troglobitic crayfish, probably *Orconectes pellucidu*. They seemed to prefer plunge pools. If left up to me, I probably would as well.

Later, Fossil Canyon's long passage ended on the top of Maelstrom Shaft—another wet one. More wet passages and rappels would have brought us to the watery sump that marked the cave's terminus—at least for air-breathing humans. However, we were one short rope short. Instead, we had to be satisfied with only shining our beams down upon the swirling sump that blocked all further access without diving equipment. While flicking our beams about within the depths of the cave's lower enchantment, and still within earshot of Maelstrom Shaft's roar, my mind slipped back into *A Midsummer Night's Dream*: "The skies, the fountains, every region near seemed all one mutual cry. I never heard so musical a discord, such sweet thunder."

❧

After Thunder Hole, it took me hours to clean all mud and former vadose water from my vertical equipment and clothing. While clean gear hung drying in the sun, I talked a reluctant Larry into going into a cave that didn't need the impediments of ropes, ascenders, rappel rack, slings, metal protection, and the typical vertical caving tonnage.

"What's the point of horizontal caves?" he grumbled.

Larry, like many other TAG-born, would much rather drop long free rappels into deep pits than walk upright on two feet within a horizontal cave. A few years previously, after Larry and I had rappelled a classic TAG pit, I commented upon the huge volume of water pouring from the pit's bottom into a frothy, inky abyss. As Larry climbed up the rope to return to the surface, I shouted, "Hey, whatcha doin'? It looks like the cave continues, and continues big!"

While stepping higher on the rope, he replied, "There's no cave beyond the entrance pit."

"It certainly looks like a cave," I said in astonishment. *Is he blind as a crayfish?*

Farther up the rope (since Larry has always been quick on rope), he blurted, "Yeah, but it's horizontal. So what's the point."

Therefore, given Larry's horizontal reluctance and that he'd already humored me with one horizontal cave that week, it surprised me that I so easily talked him into another horizontal cave—Dancing Fern Cave, reported to be a nice horizontal stream cave.

As Larry's well-worn and well-TAGed Toyota crept past a run-down house far down a remote four-wheel-drive road, Larry finally concluded we weren't in the right place. This is always an avocational hazard while finding privately owned TAG caves. All along the well-rutted road, we passed numerous hand-scrawled warnings, including blood-red Do Not Enter and No Trespassing signs. Even TAG native Larry had an uneasy feeling about the place. Suddenly, he turned to me and, with a straight face and in all seriousness, said, "Have you seen the movie *Deliverance*?"

We knocked on the door of a nearby modest home in the center of a plethora of hand-strewn trash, abandoned equipment, and derelict pickup trucks. We knocked again and called out. I was grateful that no one answered. I'd wondered if our knocking would only provide them with a known point at which to aim.

"They're probably inside ignoring us," Larry whispered.

We gladly abided by their wish for privacy by hopping into the Toyota and driving back over the ruts and back into known territory. We headed to Owens Spring Cave instead.

At the cave's parking lot, as we geared up to enter, a man sat nearby in his pickup, doing nothing but intensely staring at us as we changed into wet suits. His glare and scrutiny grew more intense as we donned wet suit parts, cave lights, and other soon-to-be-wet caving gear. His stare continued as we passed from light into darkness. Perhaps he, too, thought of Shakespeare: "Lord, what fools these mortals be!"

The beautiful stream passage got my mind off thoughts that the staring man might soon vandalize Larry's Toyota. Larry didn't worry about it despite it being his truck. It wasn't as if vandals hadn't visited Larry's truck on more than one occasion. If Larry had no worries, why should I? So, I turned my full attention on this beautiful, classic example of a water-table-type horizontal stream cave.

A sternwheel could make its way up Owens Spring Cave's trunk passage. The broad and bubbling stream covered the entire cave's floor with the clearest water I'd seen in a long time outside the Caribbean and Florida's blue holes. Despite it being easy wading, cavers were surprisingly late in exploring Owens Spring Cave. In the days before wet suits, wading long distances through four feet of cold water was more of a deterrent than a five-hundred-foot vertical shaft.

The invention of wet suits made stream caves, such as Owens Spring Cave, accessible to all—all who could afford wet suits and gear. Using the wet suit's buoyancy, I found it much less tiring to just float and propel myself through the cave with gentle arm strokes rather than thrash about by attempting crawl strokes burdened with boots, helmet, and pack. I felt peace and serenity by silently floating on my back through the darkened stream passage. Well, I was feeling peace and serenity. Larry chafed, cursed, and thrashed with the thought of having to move horizontally.

Eventually, we called an end to our float. As we drifted out of the cave like discarded flotsam, we noticed two obviously poor country folk cooling themselves at the entrance. I instantly recognized a glaring contrast between the poor and ragged farmer's clothing and our expensive high-tech wet suits, helmets, packs, lights, and other necessary implements. I'm sure we supplied them later with a chuckle or two and marked ourselves clearly as outsiders.

My weeklong vacation neared its end. Regretfully, I declined an offer to join a large group of rope-carrying strangers headed toward Ellison's Cave. I also declined Jim's offer of another crack at the Russell Cave dome climb. I ended up spending the day scraping mud off climbing gear and hosing down what had once served as clothing. I then headed home—at the time, non-TAG Georgia.

◈

In my many dreamlike states, I often ponder the contrasts, differences, and similarities between caving and climbing. Some mountain climbers seek intricate technical challenges that push their gymnastic skills. Some prefer lofty heights, ascending above the clouds and pushing the limits of physical and mental endurance. The non-caving public can often understand and relate to climbing summits more than they can understand or appreciate caves.

Former South African Prime Minister Jan Smuts once stated, "We place the seat of our highest religious ideal in heaven and consign all that is morally base to hell ... We may truly say that the highest religion is the religion of the mountain."

It's true that when we ascend into the heights, we leave all the weariness and troubles of our normal existence behind and feel, however momentarily, as if we're at one with heaven.

If so, how does this philosophical thought jibe with desires to descend to the lower realms of our deepest chasms? The lure of caves is clearly different than that of summits because we rarely associate heavenly pursuits with crawling into the Earth's darkened bowels. However, caves allow us a momentary respite where we can leave normal life and troubles behind. It's an otherworldly experience outside the norms of everyday existence. Perhaps, in our wide, diverse, and stressful world, there's solace for everyone, whether they seek the world's heights or depths, or simply a cool and shady place to spend a lazy afternoon.

Once, while caving in rural Alabama, I spoke with a landowner busily planting okra outside a cave on his farm. Shaking his head at the ridiculous thought of anyone wanting to go into the hole, he retorted, "Don't have no use goin' deeper 'n grubbin' potatoes nor higher 'n picking peaches."

Well enough and well said. However, for me, I'd rather seek both the highs and lows as well as all that lies along our unsettled and troubled margins.

Willi and the Winkettes

*I*n the 1980s, Washington colleges and universities started a tradition of having their outdoor clubs gather during spring break for a shared outing. In my last year at Green River Community College, before transferring to the University of Washington, I joined this shared outing for a three-day adventure in Leavenworth, one of the state's premier rock-climbing areas.

Mark and I were the only ones attending from Green River. Ten people from a university I can't recall now came for a whitewater rafting trip on the Wenatchee River. The only other college representation came from Evergreen College, an infamously free-spirited and free-programmed institute in the southern Puget Sound area. I rarely saw the rafters, since they kept together as a group. Mark and I hung out with the ten from Evergreen and camped together in Icicle Canyon.

Evergreen's most celebrated faculty member was Willi Unsoeld—a noted Teton climber and the first American to climb Mount Everest. Three weeks after Jim Whittaker and Nawang Gombu reached the summit by the standard route, Willi Unsoeld and Tom Hornbein reached the top by the previously unclimbed West Ridge. After reaching the top, they traversed over the mountain and descended the South Col route. Their daring climb went into the history books and firmly placed Willi Unsoeld on the walls of the mountain-climbing hall of fame. After Everest, Willi became one of the leaders and organizers of the Peace Corps. Friends, followers, students, and faculty also knew him for his unconventional and trippy beliefs and lifestyle.

While he was climbing in India, Nanda Devi instantly captivated him. It was the most beautiful mountain he'd ever seen. He vowed at that moment to head back to the States and find a woman who would bear his daughter so he could name her Nanda Devi. He did just that. He began asking strangers on campus if they would bear his child so he could name the baby Nanda Devi.

I imagine most young women recoiled. However, someone took him up on the offer and said, "Sure." (Well, this was a trippy, hippie college in the 1960s.) They had a daughter together, and, as per his vow, Willi named her Nanda Devi. When Nanda Devi became old enough to climb, Willi invited her on an expedition to climb her namesake mountain. While on the climb, Nanda Devi died of altitude complications, and Willi buried Nanda Devi, his daughter, by pushing her off the slopes of her namesake mountain. There she still lies in her icy tomb. From that point onward, by some accounts, Willi Unsoeld was only a shell of his former self.

However, the students at Evergreen, where Willi taught, looked upon him as nothing short of a demigod. Students who climbed worshiped him. Only a couple of years before our Leavenworth outing, Willi Unsoeld and several Evergreen students died in an avalanche on Mount Rainier. All the Evergreen students I camped with along Icicle Creek had known and worshiped Willi. For most of the evening, the students told reverential Willi stories by the flickering firelight.

While their stories were entertaining, the students were a bit too trippy for my staid and reserved demeanor. Not only were they practitioners of the one-unifying-life-force belief, but they firmly believed Willi personified that one all-powerful life force. In addition, although they all came from wealthy families, they staunchly believed that to be true and pure, they must eschew all comforts and symbols of wealth for the duration of the three-day vacation. Therefore, they brought no food. Instead, they made daily pilgrimages to Leavenworth's Safeway for a dose of dumpster diving. They ravaged the dumpster and garbage cans, looking for whatever edible scraps had been tossed aside.

I quivered with the thought of eating dumpster food—not because it came from the dumpster but because of the students' pretentiousness and that they didn't do it out of need. They weren't rummaging through the dumpster out of economic need or the desire to pursue the noble art of being a climbing bum. No, they were dumpster posers. They had the perverse notion that dumpster diving led them to the purity of spiritual realism. Again, posers. However, their antics provided impromptu entertainment.

Back at the Icicle camp, they assembled scrap metal they'd collected from the town's dumpster, then forged the metalware into pots to place on the fire to cook their dumpster bounty. They held up rotting meat as they would an Olympic gold medal. The least offending parts were carefully placed in the improvised pots, along with dumpster celery and carrots. Although it was highly tainted, they ordained their resulting stew as ethically pure. They graciously offered me a taste of their spiritually pure bounty, but I drew the line on meat from a garbage can. Hiding my stove-cooked Cup O' Noodles from disapproving eyes, I thanked them but declined the stew. Well into the night, they continued with more Willi stories, beyond what I could stomach. So I went to bed while they were still deep in reverent Willi-isms.

In the morning, I hopped in an empty space in one of the two Evergreens vans, and we headed to the Peshastin Pinnacles climbing area. I still had no idea who I would climb with; I hoped to decide while sorting gear in the Peshastin parking lot. However, as soon as we arrived, the Evergreen climbers departed on foot up the sandy slopes so fast, Mark and I didn't see which way they went. Having a long history of being ditched, I knew what being ditched looked like, and this Evergreen group, by all appearances, were good at ditching. I guess their hope of attaining spiritual purity from their dumpster stew didn't work.

The Peshastin Pinnacle area isn't *that* big, so I wandered about, looking for the Evergreen crowd to see if I could find anyone. Not far from Martian Slab, Mark and I came across Stewart, one of the Evergreen students. After asking to join him, we sensed his displeasure at having to climb with both spiritual heretics *and* people not tuned to Willi's aura. However, Stewart must have been desperate to climb that day, since he relented.

As we traversed over to Sunset Slab, Stewart talked about nothing but his superior climbing abilities and how he'd breathed the same air as Willi Unsoeld. Yadda yadda. Fortunately, our arrival at Sunset Slab ended his Willi-fixation conversation.

For our first climb, Stewart chose a diminutive and easy slab route. Considering how bad-assed superior he made himself out to be, I assumed he would have chosen something harder. Stewart asked to take the lead. Mark and I followed. Stewart then suggested we head over to Grand Central Tower. Mark took off to find something else to do while Stewart and I headed to the tower. He talked more about his superior climbing skills as I dutifully followed and listened. Stewart stopped at the foot of Shady Lane, a climb several grades over anything I'd ever climbed before, but he insisted this should be our next climb.

He proclaimed that since he'd led the last climb, I should lead this next pitch. Not only had I not climbed anything as hard as Shady Lane, its technical challenges far exceeded my abilities or anything I'd ever attempted—especially at the sharp end of the rope. Normally, I'm not easily goaded into doing things I don't want to do, but this time seemed different. Stewart seemed so experienced, and I felt inadequate by comparison. I didn't want to admit my failings and inexperience, especially considering Stewart had personally known the mighty Willi. I swallowed hard and sheepishly said, "Belay on, climbing."

The climb followed a flaring groove that proved to be impossible to protect. In a typical climb, the lead climber wedges pieces of metal hardware of various shapes into cracks in the rock. This was well before the easy and sophisticated camming devices that modern-day climbers have available to them. Before cams came to be, each metal piece (a chock) contained a sling that the leader clipped into the climbing rope using a snap-link carabiner. This way, the rope between the leader and the belay could slide through the carabiner attached to the protection. If the lead climber fell, the belayer held the rope fast against the highest or last piece of protection. If that wedged protection failed, then the next lower piece hopefully held. If there was more rope between the lead climber and his last protection piece than there was distance to the ground, then the protection and rope wouldn't serve any benefit. In this case, the lead climber would crater into the ground into a pile of mashed potatoes. The same lead climbing and belaying principle still holds true with modern cam devices. But climbing with the older-style solid-metal chocks was more awkward, encumbered, and dangerous.

On my shaky Shady Lane climb, I couldn't get any protection to stay wedged in the flaring groove. The first dubious piece wobbled out and spun around the rope as it fell defiantly to the ground. So did the next one. I eventually placed one that held. As I climbed past it, it looked wobblier than I cared to admit. I dared not trust it. I climbed far beyond my ability and far beyond the height of a survivable fall. With my legs, arms, and mind violently shaking, a fall felt imminent, but with only one dubious protection in, fall I must not.

My mind flashed with bouts of panic and fear of death or serious maiming. I attempted to shed any thought that didn't focus my staying on the rock. Zen-like, I managed total control over distracting thoughts. My entire world consisted of where each hand and toe would go and how I would move. Eventually, after what seemed like days, I arrived safely at the belay ring. After I securely clipped into the anchor, waves of pent-up shakes swept over me like a Cape Horn tempest. For five minutes, I continued spewing heat into the already shimmering heat waves emanating from the tower's western slope. After sufficiently calming myself, I set up Stewart's belay and looked forward to witnessing how a true master would climb the route.

Following climbers are always infinitely safer, since the belay rope comes from above, so if following climbers fall, they don't go anywhere. However, Stewart appeared to be struggling more than even I had, and he seemed shakier. As he arrived at my belay station, he wildly exclaimed, "Wow, that was a fabulously great lead! I could never have climbed it if it weren't for the spirit of Willi showing me the way."

I said, "What's this about Willi?"

"You didn't see him? He was right there beside me on the whole climb. He showed me the way. Are you sure you didn't see him? He was right there."

"You mean thinking of Willi gave you moral strength?"

"No, no, I say. He was right there in visible form, showing me right where to place my hands and feet. How could you miss him?"

I couldn't wrap my head around either his thoughts or apparitions. Apparently, I truly was *not* tuned to Willi's frequency. I was dialed into reality. I kept my concerns to myself as I looked up toward the next lead. It looked easy. I called out, "The next lead is yours."

He said, "No, Willi says you should take the next lead too."

"Willi said that?" I asked.

"Yes, he's tied into the same belay ring we're clipped to. Are you going to take the next lead or not?"

While long-dead Willi might have comforted Stewart while tied into our shared belay ring, I gained nothing. The belay ring seemed too crowded for me. I wanted nothing more than to get off the rock and place feet firmly on the ground—well away from Stewart and any incorporeal Willi. I couldn't feel safe placing my life in Stewart's or Willi's hands despite the live version of Willi being a notoriously excellent belayer. I envisioned that Willi might say to Stewart, "Let go of the rope, or clobber the spud. Don't let it breed." While choosing my words carefully, in the least threatening tone I could muster, I said, "If it's alright with Willi, I think we should just rappel down and head back to our Icicle Canyon campsite."

Both Stewart and Willi agreed.

Back at camp, as the Evergreen crowd ate more of the purity-infused dumpster meat stew they'd left un-iced throughout the heat of the day, they told stories of how Willi had been with them, showing the way. Apparently, Willi has the power—like quantum physics or Schrödinger's cat—to be in more than one place at a time. I chalked the experience up to mass hallucination brought on by tainted meat. I ate another Cup O' Noodles and retired early for the evening. In the morning, I left for home, and I left Leavenworth to Willi and his Winkettes—real, corporeal, or otherwise.

❧

During my college years, I did much more than converse with spiritual avatars. After having transferred to the University of Washington, I had to contend with spiritual beings operating on an entirely different wavelength.

The University of Washington's Climbing Club had a richer history and tradition than that of Green River Community College, so I couldn't wait to join. However, the Climbing Club had waxed and waned over the years. The club had remained strong and active during Jim Madsen's time and continued throughout the time of Creedence, but it languished for a few years afterward. When I transferred to the university, the Climbing Club existed, but it was neither active, visible, nor engaging.

A couple of other students and I sought to change that dynamic. As officers, we hosted prominent climber presentations, ranging from Jim Bridwell to Mugs Stump. We also hosted talks on lesser-known climbing areas, including the little-known Christmas Tree Pass. We sponsored and organized club trips, ranging from Yosemite Valley to Smith Rocks, Oregon.

Soon, membership climbed, and people began hanging out in the club's office after we posted regular office hours. Although we were the university's largest sports club, rumor had it that university managers didn't look kindly on the Climbing Club. I believe they saw us as having less-than-ideal school spirit. We were a different breed than, say, the Tennis Club or Chess Club.

Perhaps coincidently, about the time we began becoming more visible and active, we received notice to vacate our plush office on the top floor and move into the basement's SB-29. I checked out the new office first. I roamed throughout the basement offices but couldn't find office 29. I called the university's facility manager to inquire if a mistake had occurred. The woman said I'd taken a wrong turn. The *SB* referred to the subbasement. I had no idea a subbasement existed below the basement level. Besides informing me that the university had demoted us to the subbasement, she also mentioned that we had to share the office with the Muslim Student Association. The Climbing Club had never shared an office before. Apparently, this was the new world order. Some people claimed the university was punishing us for not knowing our proper place in the university's pecking order. No offense against the Muslim Student Association, but this organization had no connection to the Climbing Club. Besides, this office reassignment happened during the height of the Iranian hostage crisis. Most fellow students didn't look upon Muslims too kindly.

My next search found the cavernous entrance to the subbasement. In other places, we would call this a pipe chase, a place where architects place all the building's pipes, fittings, ductwork, conduits, sewer mainlines, rats, and misty vapors that permeate through black-mold-infused cinder-block walls. I wondered if a nuclear submarine, like the one my brother served on during the Vietnam War, would have looked like SB-29.

We decorated one half of the office with climbing posters and photos. Next to a poster of a winter climb of the Yocum Ridge on

Oregon's Mount Hood hung a poster of the Ayatollah Khomeini staring at us sternly, with the quote: "Death to America—we will fight you to the end!"

Before the move, I'd never met a Muslim before, so I had a vague interest in striking up a conversation. The Muslim students were always coming and going in and out of the office, but they seemed less inclined to speak with any of us. Besides, what's the right icebreaker with a group that espoused militant violence? "How's the hostage-taking going? Overthrow any governments or kill any infidels lately?"

They appeared to use the office for two reasons: as an undisturbed place to lay mats, face east, and silently pray to Allah, and to escape angry mobs. Many members of the Muslim Student Association picketed and demonstrated on campus, complaining about America and Americans. This didn't go over well with the student body. Angry mobs frequently beat and bloodied the Muslims, but the Muslims were adept at slipping by the mobs. Muslims at the University of Washington back then were fast. They should have tried out for the track team. After angry mobs began gathering after only a couple of minutes of the Muslims vocally denouncing America and everything it stands for, the fleet-footed Muslims ran for the security of the lockable office.

While in the office to plan climbing trips, we often heard elephant stomping followed by a frantic unlocking of the door as one or two heavily panting Muslims locked the door behind them in the nick of time before heavy pounding and shouting reverberated all the way from Mount Hood to the Ayatollah. Whenever I left the office in such situations, before unlocking the door, I shouted, "I'm Climbing Club—just the Climbing Club." I had to quickly shut and lock the door behind me before the mob burst through to attack the Muslims praying for our destruction.

Each group seemed to have less-than-pure thoughts and intentions. Where had the Virgin Mary, Our Lady of Fátima, and the calming force of Willi's apparition gone off to when we collectively needed them the most? These were heady times in the University of Washington's Climbing Club.

When All the Hurly-Burly's Been Said and Done

I've walked, walked, and walked. Sometimes I wonder if I've walked beyond the limits of any human-comprehensible metric. If I stretched all my walkings from end to end, how many earths would I have circumferenced? Despite all planetary circlings, nearly all have had a destination and been wholly immersed in wild, open spaces. This makes it incongruent that I would wind up living, working, and walking in San Juan's highly urbanized old-town red-light district.

The urbanized San Juan I speak of is not San Juan County in Colorado, Washington, or Utah. Nor is it the New Mexico hamlet or even the Mission San Juan Capistrano, even though swallows perform their own global circumferencing. If it had been, the swallows would have made good traveling companions. Unfortunately for me and my swallow-less walking pleasures, the San Juan I speak of is the Caribbean's ciudad de Puerto Rico.

I moved to San Juan wholly with a career in mind. If it had been for pleasure, I would have been in the San Juan Mountains, along the

San Juan River, or amongst tired birds in the Swallows Day Parade. But no, after that fateful career decision, I found myself stranded on an alien island with no car or no clear destination. I'm a mountain creature or a desert rat, not an inner-city cockroach. So, after too much confined urbanism, I longed for another type of walk—if even for the day.

Despite being both intrigued and repulsed by alien urban scenes, I wanted to experience other parts of the island. I longed for adventure.

I'm no urban junkie, craver of cholera, or denizen of the dystopian, I thought. *Dammit, I'm a mountaineer.*

The island's interior mountains called, "Come walk amongst my tropical hills and climb thy first summit." Granted, that was a metaphysical calling, and granted, the mountains of Puerto Rico aren't technically demanding like Yosemite's vertical walls. Nor are they draped in snow and ice like Mount Rainier, Denali, or even my spring break Yosemite. But they *are* mountains, and I heard their distant call.

I had only vague ideas about where I could find the island's mountains. In the pre-Internet days, we consumed electrons in wholly different ways. I had no guidebook. I had no map except for a free Puerto Rico road map produced by the Department of Transportation. The map depicted roads, cities, and towns, but no summits.

I asked several of the Puerto Rican rangers I worked with what the highest mountain in Puerto Rico was. Clearly, they never expended any of their electrons on such thoughts, but the best I could obtain was that Cerro de Punta was the highest and El Negro a close second. I didn't wholly trust this data, since I sensed the rangers gave me any answer that would end my incessant questioning and purge their electrons of the odd image of someone walking in the mountains—on purpose.

My Puerto Rican friends had no idea where Cerro de Punta and El Negro were located, but, presumably, they were somewhere in the island's interior. The consensus held that mountains weren't located anywhere in San Juan the city. My road map listed a forest reserve named Bosque Estatal de Toro Negro. *Surely*, I thought, *this must relate to El Negro, the mountain.* In hindsight, I deployed dubious logic, since *negro* simply means "black." It's not like there aren't other things named for this rarest of colors. This would be like an Argentinian swallow navigating home by flying to the first San Juan they see on a map. Regardless, blank regions around this El Negro became my new quest—my new destination. I foresaw I would be walking again soon.

Since I had no car on the island, I invited Dan to drive. Using my road map, I navigated him and his Ford Pinto to what appeared to be the closest road to Bosque Estatal de Toro Negro's north side. Dan parked the Pinto in the pouring rain. Getting wet mattered little in Puerto Rico, where it's always warm and wet, no matter the weather or time of day or night. So Dan and I shouldered packs and headed off into the dense tropical forest. Uphill served as our only guide.

It rained the whole way up the slope, but we eventually reached a summit. Shortly after arriving on top, a slight breeze parted the lower-lying gray tropical clouds enough for a view. Through the cloud parting we saw a significantly higher summit far to the south—much too far to reach by foot. We weren't on El Negro. Instead, we stood on a lesser summit. Dejected, I snapped a couple of photos before we walked back down through the rain and swirling clouds to Dan's Pinto.

Over twenty years later, I discovered El Negro isn't even Puerto Rico's second-highest summit, and we were nowhere near the true El Negro. The higher peak that we mistook for El Negro turned out to be Cerro de Punta—the island's highest peak. The mountain Dan and I stumbled upon was Piedra Blanca, the island's fourth-highest mountain.

Few things about this walk turned out as planned. Therefore, Dan and I sought other tropical mountains a few months later. This time, his Pinto took us to the El Yunque National Forest, the tropical rainforest on the island's far eastern end. From the main parking lot, we again shouldered packs and headed uphill with no idea where the slope would take us other than up. After a couple of miles of trailless rainforest and a gazillion tropical trees, the lessening slope indicated we were close to the top of something. From this high point, we saw another summit nearby, so we ascended both. As soon as we crested the second broad summit, we noticed on the far side an extremely high chain-link fence festooned with rolled razor wire. It looked like a hidden high-security concentration camp located in the middle of the jungle—the kind Rambo liberates.

As soon as we approached the fence, a jeep loaded with automatic-weapon-carrying Rambo-type soldiers in military fatigues rolled up out of nowhere. The soldiers filed out and blurted incomprehensible Spanish orders. Despite the jungle heat, a chill swept over me. They weren't there to give us an interpretive tour. Although they didn't escort us anywhere, clearly, we were being detained.

Oh crap. What did we stumble upon? I silently fumed as I looked from rifle to rifle.

After a brief questioning, the soldiers must have considered us non-terrorists and a non-threat. They released us with the instruction, "Leave immediately."

Before departing, I asked, "Where are we? What are the names of these peaks?"

The youngest soldier looked around to be sure no one listened or watched before he grudgingly answered, "Pico del Este." They stayed long enough for us to disappear back into the jungle for our quick departure.

Many years later, I learned Pico del Este is one of several sites within the US Army's Atlantic Fleet Weapons Facility, designed to be a control center and communications hub for guided-missile operations. This site specialized in electronic warfare training, radar surveillance, and communication protocols.

If only they specialized in mapmaking, I would have been on a different mountain.

⊛

Walking seems to belong to the same evolutionary branch as climbing, a branch far distant from caving. This is especially true for TAG caving. However, even TAG cavers will get out and walk a bit if it leads to a classic rappel or the discovery of a new pit. Cavers call walking while searching for new cave entrances "ridge-walking." It takes special eyes, ears, and noses to sniff out new entrances. In TAG country, it sometimes requires a gum-flapping, jawing, and chugging skill with holler-inhabiting landowners—one I remain especially inept at performing.

Private individuals own most land and caves within TAG. In these parts, privacy is often posted—and enforced. This is alien to my typical wandering background and inconsistent with my ability to negotiate with landowners. Consequently, most of my freedom ramblings and ridge-walkings have been on western public lands. I've ridge-walked in mountains and valleys ranging from Vancouver Island to the Grapevine Mountains, the Tongass to the Valley and Ridge, and from Hells Canyon to the Pennyroyal Plateau. I've also logged thousands of ridge-walking miles in the Guadalupe Mountains of

New Mexico and Texas. Despite hundreds, if not thousands, of miles, I proved adept at finding chiggers, poison ivy, ticks, cactus spines, blood-dripping lechuguilla spines, rattlesnake dens, an endless sea of more ridges, and thousands of charred sotol balls.

Among the abundant creosote bush, lechuguilla, claret cup cactus, ocotillo, and tarbush, the Guadalupe Mountains contain billions of succulent green sotol plants. Sotol's dagger-shaped lily leaves profusely radiate from the ball-shaped heart perched on a frail middle stem. This ungainly affair creates a round, top-heavy, bottle-brush profile. The sotol's hourglass shape only intensifies with age; as lower leaves die, the brown stubs remain attached to the plant's base, while the green leaves continue their radiating growth from the upper ball-shaped configuration.

One of the first parts of the sotol to burn when the many lightning fires sweep Chihuahuan Desert slopes is the plant's narrow mid-stem. This detaches the upper and lower sections, which causes the green ball-shaped upper part to begin rolling downslope. If the sotol ball is still on fire, then the flaming sotol ignites unburned lower slopes. In the Chihuahuan wildland fires I fought, fires commonly spread uphill by upwelling canyon winds, *and* downhill by rolling sotol flame balls. This is why firefighters, while conducting mop-up activities, partially bury smoking sotol balls so they don't burst into flames and begin rolling downhill, spreading the fire far and wide.

Whether rolling or not, the Guadalupe Mountains have millions, if not billions, of charred sotol balls spewed across near and distant ridges. Like mescal beans that sound like rattlesnakes, and rattlesnakes that sound like mescal beans, it's one of nature's many cruel jokes that, through binoculars from a distance, black sotol balls look remarkably like small and darkened cave entrances.

Spuds emit the most colorful language after the hour or more it takes them to descend from a far ridgetop, get rattled at by rattlesnakes, even more rattled at by dried mescal bean pods, pierced by hundreds of fishhook cactus spines, speared and shin-bled by lechuguilla daggers, and bedraggled by summer heat and thirst, only to find their exciting new cave turns out to be only a blackened sotol ball. After verbally offending the nearby creosote bushes and not bled-upon lechuguilla barbs, the spuds then pull themselves back up the slope, past more rattlesnakes, while collecting more fishhook spines and bleeding on more agaves, to return to the ridgetop to begin the search anew.

I, as ridge-walking spud, fought internal demons each time I spotted a distant black hole. I told myself, *It looks markedly like a black sotol ball. But if I wimp out and assume, I'll never find new caves.* So, down the long ridge slope I'd go, finding new rattlesnakes, spines, barbs, and blood-burnishing blemishes in the process—only to perform futile, energy-draining descent and eventual reascent. If I'd kept detailed notes, I could have mapped and inventoried every sotol plant in the Guadalupe Mountains.

Only one sotol ball turned out to have potential. And even *that* discovery remains, to this day, a mystery.

From my perch high on the plateaued ridge far above Yucca Canyon's farthest margin, I peered into the deepest of the park's remote canyons—West Slaughter Canyon. Through binoculars, I spotted a round black hole that, from my great distance, appeared much too large to be a mere black sotol ball, although such illusions had failed me many times before. As the park's cave specialist, I knew the location of all known caves. Unfortunately, this position didn't afford me the privilege of knowing the locations of all unknown caves.

Suddenly, I found myself talking to a pair of little cave specialists, one sitting on each shoulder.

Cave Specialist One pleaded with me, "But Dave, this is a new cave waiting for your discovery."

Cave Specialist Two kept interrupting as a nattering nabob of negativity, saying, "It's a waste of time, energy, and blood, since you know deep down it's only a sotol ball or a rock shadow. Not again! Don't do it, you fool!"

I chose the fool's path because I'd never find new caves if I avoided the expenditure of effort. Early explorers would have found all obvious cave entrances. So, down the slope I went. I knew distant destination views were fleeting and that I would soon lose all sight of the mysterious black smudge. So I took detailed notes of intermediate points and compass bearings to ensure I remained in line with my mystery hole.

After a tortuous descent, even by Guadalupe standards—not necessarily in rattlesnake counts, but by meeting every lechuguilla barb on West Slaughter Canyon's long and bloody descent—I fell and tripped multiple times, spewing more blood and more unspiritual words. I finally arrived on West Slaughter Canyon's shadowy bottom, right below the spot supposedly hiding my wondrous new cave discovery.

As soon as I ascended a few feet from the canyon's depth, a ten-foot-wide cave entrance appeared—not a sotol ball or illusionary shadow. As plain as my painfully throbbing legs and heaving chest, and as plain as the many lechuguilla spines still stuck in my shin and working their way deeper into bleeding flesh, I'd found a cave. I'd finally found one. I only had to go directly upslope—only two hundred more feet to go.

Blood surged through veins and out my open lacerations as I pushed my legs and lungs harder. I went as fast as I could, with no consideration for my remoteness or how far I was from help. I'd left no one a note about my intended location. Rescuers likely would never find my body if I hurt myself. Nonetheless, I let surging adrenaline get the best of me. Momentarily, I looked down to avoid a lechuguilla spine forest. After safely passing the spines, I looked up again to ensure my course remained true. As soon as I did, I caught a glimpse of a tawny mountain lion's rear end as it leapt into the cave—*my* cave.

I stood waiting, as still and with as narrow a profile as the nearby ocotillo. I waited and waited. The mountain lion didn't come out. I stayed put—intending to out-stubborn the beast. Inner demons once again took over, but instead of cave specialist versus cave specialist, the conflict became irrational caver versus a normal human being with a reasonable regard for safety. The fact that a mountain lion had disappeared in the hole probably meant cave passage existed beyond the entrance.

Finding a new cave is good. Let's check it out, the caver voice said to me.

The safety-conscious voice admonished, *Don't be an idiot. There's a mountain lion in the cave. Don't stick your fool head inside.*

I had no idea what to do. The lion must not have known I'd claimed ownership of *my* cave.

From the same rooted-ocotillo spot, I studied the entrance and my options. The buff-colored round entrance appeared to go back ten feet and then turn sharply right. The mountain lion must be somewhere to the right. I called to her. (No, I did not say, "Here, kitty kitty.") Regardless, she didn't answer back—not even to dare me. I calmly informed her of what I wanted to do in *my* cave, so please leave. She still did not answer or offer me a quarter—but neither did I. Knowing the stand-off couldn't go on indefinitely, I took one step forward. Then another, then another. As soon as I got fifty feet from the entrance, she let me know it was *her* cave.

I tried to turn my first and only time hearing a mountain lion in the wild into a conversation, but I could tell she wanted communication to remain one way. She hissed at me in a way that got her message across without the need for a universal translator. I didn't move, and her guttural hiss remained at an equal volume and intensity.

The safety me spoke loud enough for the dimwitted me to hear above the hiss. *It won't turn out well if you move forward. If you remain in place, she's trapped and has no place to escape. That's not good. If you want to go in the cave, back off and give her space. Maybe she'll come out.*

That sounded like good advice—too good for me to heed. I stepped back two feet, and her hissing stopped. But no tawny beast came out.

Maybe she went out a back entrance, I wondered.

I stepped forward two feet, and her conversation took up where she'd left off. There was no back entrance. I tried this experiment multiple times. There seemed to be a magical line unseen by any mere spud, but it meant something to her. When I crossed the line, she hissed. When I stepped back, her warnings subsided. Still, she never showed herself.

I'd come such a long distance and bled on so many cactus and agave spines. I wasn't so easily daunted. Not even a cornered mountain lion would prevent me from checking out *my* cave. This looked like a *real* cave, not just a shallow, disappointing rock shelter. A real cave. If it was big enough to hold a cougar, unseen around the corner, it was big enough to be a cave.

I had more than a fleeting thought to persevere despite the hissing. The caver in me said, *Just stick your head in enough to find out how large your cave is.* I wanted so badly to listen to the caver me and peer inside. If it went a long way, great. It was a real cave. If it didn't, I would be poking my head in face-to-face with an angry and very hoarse she-cougar.

What shall I do? I wondered.

In hindsight, my decision shouldn't have been so torturous. No matter if the cave continued, my claiming a new cave discovery wasn't worth the real possibility of the cougar maiming me, or worse. Both the mountain lion and the safety me finally won. After testing the cougar's patience for over half an hour, dejectedly, I made the long ascent back up to the ridgetop and the long walk home.

Career goals soon took me to Oregon. I never returned to the cave—*my* cave. I'm not fooling myself or doubting the veracity of it being a real cave. However, only naïvety and wishful thinking would assign the cave's ownership to anyone other than the feline. I've long since lost notes from this trip, as well as any clear memory of its precise location. Somewhere deep in West Slaughter Canyon's midsection remains a mysterious line that no one has yet crossed. It's the divide across which all wild places and beating hearts eventually reside.

⚶

From an early age, my heart beat fast over the unknown. Several years before the lion took up residence in *my* cave, I roamed the wildlands and crossed mysteries of a wholly different kind.

After I started my first federal position at Mount St. Helens, monument managers sent me and the other newbies to seasonal training. Recruits within both Mount Rainier National Park and the nearby, newly created Mount St. Helens National Volcanic Monument gathered together at the Cispus Job Corps Center located along the Cispus River in southwestern Washington. There must have been forty to fifty of us, all young, eager, and full of energy.

On the first day, after stepping off the bus and selecting a bunk for the remainder of the week, the majority of the campers began a friendly game of volleyball. I breathed deeply the hot, pine-scented air. Volleyball can never compare with exploring. I much preferred a walk along the nearby Yellowjacket Creek and a search for animal tracks. However, even the Yellowjacket Creek would have to wait. Instead, I turned toward nearby Tower Rock, a 3,337-foot basaltic plug that, according to Fred Beckey's brown book, might yield new climbing routes. I wanted to see for myself.

Based on my map, I figured I could get a sight of Tower Rock by strolling three-quarters of a mile down the main road that ran along the Cispus River floodplain and, at the 1,250-foot elevation level, veering onto a Forest Service logging road, heading directly south toward Tower Rock's precipitous north face. Walking alone along the Cispus River, I daydreamed of mountains, climbing, and new possibilities—just around the next corner.

In quiet solitude, I arrived at the junction with the Forest Service road leading toward my quest and caught my first glance of Tower Rock. I longed to feel its basaltic edges through rock shoes, or even boots. Standing alone in the middle of the intersection, I scanned the face, looking for natural climbing lines and new route potential. I must have lingered at that intersection for ten minutes before I turned up the dirt road leading directly to Tower Rock.

Suddenly, without warning, I had an intense feeling of being watched. I'd never had this feeling before, or since. Moments later, in the thick, overly dense young conifer stand located on my left, I heard a small branch snap as if someone had stepped on a dried and brittle branch lying on the thickly set forest floor.

Who could it be? I wondered. All other newly hired colleagues were still playing volleyball. I squinted into the densely packed pines, trying to discover who or what animal broke the branch. *Was it a deer? A bear? A cougar not wanting me to find her cave?* Whatever the cause, I couldn't shake my gut feeling—something was wrong. Someone, or something, still watched. However, the forest was too dense and the shadows too deep for my eyes to penetrate.

Deciding it must have been nothing, I turned back toward Tower Rock. I walked only forty more feet before I heard another twig snap approximately one hundred feet to my left. This was farther uphill from the last twig snap. The watcher had become a stalker. Despite having to abandon my closer inspection of Tower Rock, I heeded my gut and turned around.

Immediately, from the direction of the last twig snap, came a bloodcurdling roar, scream, and guttural laugh, all mixed into one hideous sound that reverberated off surrounding hills at the same instant that the twig snapping closed in fast. I saw nothing in the shadows, but I thought I heard something exhale.

I spent my entire young life in the Pacific Northwest woods, camping, fishing, hiking, and learning the flora and fauna. There's nothing—no known forest animal—that could even remotely come close to making the intense and hideous roar I heard in the Cispus woods. Even though I was normally a calm and rational person, the hair on the back of my neck stood on end as an intense wave roiled through me like a microburst from an ARkStorm. No hissing and cornered cougar from a Cueva de León made that sound, nor errant moose nor wounded bear. Whatever shook the valley and rattled my nerves, *it* didn't want me there, and it meant business. I needed no translation.

My too-short legs and too-shallow lungs couldn't move fast enough. Sounds of twigs breaking followed me down to the intersection with the main road. Once I was on pavement, my hair stood down, and my sense of being watched subsided. But I never looked back. On my way back to the Cispus Job Corps Center, I processed what had just happened. Nothing in my experience, training, or fanciful imagination could place a label on that sound.

The illustrious Sir Isaac Newton, in his game-changing book *Principia: The Mathematical Principles of Natural Philosophy*, said, "We are to admit no more causes of natural things than such as are both true and sufficient to explain their appearances." This would be true and applicable enough if, I repeat *if*, I'd experienced a natural sound within our known world. However, sometimes, the most fanciful explanations *are* the most simple and logical.

By the time I returned to the camp, my pace and breathing had returned to normal. The other recruits were still playing volleyball. I silently returned to my bunk. I told no one. As a new seasonal federal employee within a land management agency, having a reputation as an irrational crackpot wouldn't serve my career well. Besides, I had no proof of my chance encounter. I put such foolish thoughts aside and continued with the training and the beginning of my science career.

A year or so later, while other family members were watching TV, I—engrossed in thinking, reading climbing books, recalling old mountainous adventures, and planning new alpine feats of greatness—suddenly heard background sounds coming from the TV in the other room. The sounds yanked me from my mental nirvana and plopped me right back to my literally hair-raising Cispus woods encounter. Through plaster walls, white paint, and concert posters came the identical ominous and unmistakable bloodcurdling roar, scream, and guttural laugh. This time, instead of coming from the coniferous thickets of the Cispus River Valley, it came from my parents' living room TV set.

I rushed in and asked, "What are you watching?"

My father, in his typical non-emotive manner, calmly said, "It's a documentary on Sasquatch. Supposedly, some hunters recorded Bigfoot sounds ..."

My father couldn't make out why I became so animated. I'd told no one of the Cispus roar. My eyes and ears remained transfixed on the documentary's sounds. They exactly matched the roar I'd heard in the Cispus River Valley—exactly!

Growing up in the Pacific Northwest, I'd heard Bigfoot stories and rumors, but I'd placed as much stock in them as I had in the Loch Ness Monster, UFOs, and alien abductions. But an unsettling realization began sinking in. My walk to Tower Rock, while I was deeply immersed in my first-ascent obsession, caused me to step into an otherworldly unknown. I'd *had* a Bigfoot encounter. This became my truth from that point on; however, despite my conviction, I remained as silent on the experience as a fog hanging over a Skamania County alder thicket.

I argued with myself over a purely logical process, much like Occam's razor: if all simple, common, and logical explanations have been exhausted, the answer must lie somewhere within the next simplest explanation, however uncommon or illogical it at first appears (a loose paraphrase). The Cispus River is the heart of rumored Bigfoot territory. Therefore, despite all the Bigfoot hoaxes, all the laughs, and how unscientific it all sounded, I became convinced that some Bigfoot stories must be true.

After arriving at that conclusion, I felt no inclination to advertise my newfound belief or psychosis. I saw no chance that my unsubstantiated observation would contribute to the equation or convince society at large. Therefore, I remained silent. However, enough time has elapsed, and I've matured and developed perspective—or perhaps I'm simply lapsing into just plain curmudgeoness. Regardless, I no longer care.

I'm a science-oriented fellow. I have both bachelor of science and master of science degrees. In addition, I've worked in science and resource management for over thirty years. I've always placed a high value on logic and reason, and I've prided myself on suppressing emotional reactions so that I may concentrate on using logic to resolve life's puzzles. Therefore, this Sasquatch encounter posed a dilemma. Do I base my beliefs on known scientific principles, or do I succumb to unproven emotional speculation?

My confidence grew upon further thought, It is *not* speculative. I kept coming back to the notion that my conclusions were logically based. It's not logical for any known species to have made that distinctive marrow-depleting roar.

Another quandary I've wrestled with relates to what would happen after someone eventually provides credible proof of Bigfoot's existence. It's likely that timid believers who'd remained silent will pour out of the woods with their own Bigfoot experiences. I don't want to be *that* kind—too unseemly and too pathetic to own up to their conviction until it becomes socially safe to do so. How cheesy! If I claim to walk the talk, then I shall own up to my beliefs and observation and come out of the Cispus woods: I had a Bigfoot encounter.

Perhaps I'll reconsider if ridicule forces me into the life of a circus freak on the freak-show circuit or the state takes me and my psychosis away. Could my logic be flawed? Could my inputs be unsupported?

Could my basic premise be weak? I'll leave some ponderings to philosophers. That I am not. I'm merely a walker.

So with that, I'll simply walk on ...

Skooged Again

I spent hours, days, weeks, and years scanning, scrutinizing, and parceling old photographs, new photographs, reports, maps, comments, and anything short of Ouija boards, looking for clues to potential new climbs in the North Cascades. I longed to put up new routes, to go where no one had trod before, to carve my own path—preferably on new summits. But Hermann Ulrichs's times have passed, and there aren't many unclimbed mountains anymore in the Cascades. Therefore, out of necessity, my singular desire, from early on, focused upon new routes on previously climbed peaks.

I soon discovered that if previous generations left a ridge or face unclimbed, it might have been for good reason. Like that snake-infested quarry near Crow Butte State Park. Who wants to climb a pile of friable and disintegrating rock? While I wanted first ascents, I had limits. I wanted my first ascents to mean something. I sought to create a testament to my style and grace—a living legacy. One can't have that by chasing every crap pile out there.

Another barrier to putting up new routes is, sadly, that more people than just I want first ascents. Increasingly, my contemporaries were beating me to the range's better lines. "What's left for spuds?" I mused.

It certainly didn't help that at the time, I was pushing to start a career with the National Park Service, and, as such, I often lived out of state, except for the inhospitable winter months. Consequently, while I spent hours planning climbs in minutiae, others took the initiative, climbed the route, and *stole* my first ascent.

My planned first ascents fell off my list like clockwork—and sometimes at an alarming pace. I vividly remember reading that Gary Brill and Lowell Skoog had beat me to a first ascent from my cherished list. Although I no longer remember which route it was, the fact that I couldn't just sit around dawdling while I made up my mind had a profound impact on me. I realized that I had serious, non-spud, competition.

At that time, I'd never heard of either one of them. *Is Brill a songwriter from the famous Brill Building? And what kind of name is Skoog? How dare he steal my climb!*

Later, the team of Lowell and Gordy Skoog stole another one of my first ascents. I thought, *Did I read that correctly—Lowell and Gordy Skoog? What—there are more of them? There's two Skoogs? How can I compete with that? I don't even have one Skoog, but he's got two!*

I grew to hate Skoog. This is no easy task, since I've always prided myself on being a kind and decent person. Hate is ugly. I felt bad that I held such negative thoughts about any human, especially a fellow climber. Even a Skoog.

One by one, other climbers began stealing *my* first ascents. My well-studied but never-executed to-do list grew shorter every year. Other thieves and usurpers lurked out there too, not just a Skoog. But it no longer mattered. Skoog became an omnipresent symbol for anyone and everyone who stole my cherished first ascents. It also no longer mattered that sometimes, out of my ignorance, the usurper's first ascent predated my adding it to my list. How dare someone climb a route before I had the opportunity to discover it and place it on *my* climb list! I imagined scrunching my face and shaking an outstretched fist like Captain Kirk had in *Star Trek II: The Wrath of Khan*. But instead of defiantly screaming, "K-H-A-N!" I would scream, "S-K-O-O-G!"

Well, that never happened. But when I sat idly at home, not making first ascents, I had lots of time to imagine.

It's true that some people are lowlifes and despicable. This includes climbers. To ascend to the top of any endeavor requires a singular focus and drive. These traits sometimes conflict with human kindness, decency, and social graces. I imagined Lowell Skoog to be a miserable excuse for a human being. It made my ill feelings toward him less unsettling.

Kirk couldn't escape his Khan forever. Nor could I mine. It didn't take long for Skoog's and my paths to converge. The first encounter took place in Seattle's Wallingford District at the end-of-the-climbing-season bash. The bash was a long-held tradition among the Seattle area's climbing who's who, as well as the occasional spud Don Goodman had kindly invited.

Before hearing their names, I could see the respect other climbers held for them merely by the reaction that erupted when they walked through the door. Carla Firey received the largest eruption. The instant the crowd saw that she'd walked in, a wave of warm affection and greetings swept through the room, as if they'd all shared countless bivouacs, weathered countless storms, and endured trying times together. If there ever had been such a thing as 1960s and 1970s Pacific Northwest royalty, Carla Firey would have been a crown princess.

The crowd gave an equally warm greeting, although not quite as reverent, to a tall, friendly, and unassuming person carrying a warm smile. He looked like a thinner and lankier version of Clark Kent. As he walked by, someone rushed past me and gave this lanky fellow a big hug and said, "I'm so pleased you could come, Lowell."

I stared at him for the longest time because didn't Sun Tzu in *The Art of War* say something about knowing thy enemy? I didn't have to scrutinize for very long to discover a potentially unsettling truth.

Perhaps Skoog wasn't evil incarnate.

What? Had Skoog turned my whole world topsy-turvy? He seemed to be the nicest, kindest, most humble, and most decent human being possible. I stood in shock and disbelief. *How could Lowell Skoog be a decent human being?* I wondered. *How dare he reduce my rational indignation to nothing more than ugly spite and petty jealousy!* Dang, that Skoog. He took *that* from me too!

For the next five minutes, I jockeyed in and out among the crowd to be within earshot of the Skoog while trying to appear to be doing anything other than what I precisely had been doing. What I overheard in those five minutes gave me pause. He seemed nice, normal, pleasant, unassuming, even a little shy and bashful. He *was* Clark Kent.

Instead of being mad at him, or envious of him, for stealing *my* first ascents, I felt like I should just go up and willingly hand him the entirety of my now dwindling list: "Here have them. You're much more deserving of first ascents than I've been or could ever hope to be." From that point on, I accepted my spudness, and I never felt Skooged again.

The Skoog factor seemed to have brought out the dark side in me that I'd never known existed. That is *not* who I am. However, I long ago purged my dark forces. I realized that I had no true ill will toward anyone, not even Skoog. I accepted that I'd had my chances and opportunities. I could have gotten off my butt and taken the bold step to forge my own routes. If I hadn't and others had, it would only be a reflection on me. To climb at high levels and put up classic new lines requires a burning commitment and drive.

Everett Darr, famed pioneer North Cascade climber and Hermann Ulrichs's contemporary, once offered his belief that technical skill isn't the most important element for success on a hard mountain in remote wilderness because most Cascade climbs aren't *that* technically difficult. He felt nerves and commitment were far more important for success. Referring to modern-day climbers, he once offered his comparison of modern-day climbers to the pioneer climbers of the 1930s. He said modern-day climbers weren't any better than climbers in the 1930s. They were only better educated. As for his and Joe Leuthold's unsuccessful 1935 attempt on Bonanza Peak, he felt they failed on that enigmatic and classic mountain due solely to his, not Joe Leuthold's, lack of courage.

In my case, while I had the burning desire and passion for new routes, my commitment to the cause hadn't risen to the level of a Joe Leuthold—or a Lowell Skoog. This may explain why Skoog *is* Clark Kent, Tom Hanks, Joe Leuthold, and Mozart all rolled into one, while I'm standing alone, blended into the crowd, while eavesdropping on other climbers' conversations.

I long ago recovered from my Skoog affliction, much the way Antonio Salieri in the movie *Amadeus* recovered from his affliction. In the movie, fate struck Salieri with the blow of sharing the same time and place as Mozart. Antonio believed God's cruelty gave him the ambition of a Mozart but the talent of a Salieri.

In his old age, as hospital aides wheeled Salieri off through the insane asylum halls and he passed the decrepit, pathetic, and wretchedly insane, he touched each one, claiming to be the patron saint of the mediocrities. As he passed, he absolved each of the sin of being born mediocre—in his mind, and mine, the worst affliction for anyone with ambition.

However, unlike Salieri, I stayed free from the mental institute. Antonio Salieri derived solace by absolving others of their shared state of mediocracy. I find little solace in absolving myself, or anyone, of this wretchedness, because, like alcoholism, one never fully recovers from mediocracy—or a case of the Skoog. I carry this darkness with me for the rest of my life as a constant reminder that destiny has a place reserved for all the countless and nameless non-Skoogs out there.

Secrets to Hide, Freaks Inside

Some communities can't soar. It's as if society and fate had preordained them for failure, sometimes through no fault of their own. Many of the world's richest cave regions are also the most desperately poor economically. Soil nutrients, vital for prosperous agriculture, leach through sinkholes into underlying caves and flush downstream. Consequently, agricultural communities in cave regions are often hard hit and have high unemployment. With no steady income, the unemployed often find creative ways to put food on the table. Kentucky's Mammoth Cave region is no exception.

Rural Kentucky didn't share the successes brought to others during the Gilded Age, the Progressive Age, and ages beyond. In increasing numbers, in the years between the two world wars, affluent tourists flocked to the celebrated Mammoth Cave. Poor area residents began to realize that cave roadside attractions bring in outside money. Therefore, they began seeking their own caves to lure in tourist dollars. Instead of following the wind, they followed the money. However, for a newly discovered cave to outcompete Mammoth Cave's attraction, it had to be bigger or better—or at least visitors had to think it was. Entrepreneurial residents searched far and wide for new cave discoveries. If they found a promising new commercial cave, they kept it secret until they could secure the rights to the cave entrance.

Since property rights laws work best on a two-dimensional surface, cave promoters found it easy to take advantage of subsurface anomalies such as caves. Cave holes became loopholes. If a person owned a cave entrance and wanted to develop the underlying cave, no laws could stop a neighbor from digging into the cave from adjoining property, be the first to develop the cave, and invite ticket-buying visitors. Such an unscrupulous scenario, with people desperate for money in a poor time, became ripe for competition and exploitation—even the use of vicious, underhanded, and unethical business practices. So began the Kentucky Cave Wars.

During the 1920s, the height of the Kentucky Cave Wars, cave owners commonly attempted to lead tourists to mistake their unremarkable cave for the world-famous Mammoth Cave. This led unknowing visitors to off-route destinations. Cave owners also commonly marketed their cave as being distinctive from Mammoth Cave, no matter how deceitful the claim or how outlandishly garish the theme—anything to lead the curious-minded tourist into thinking one cave more freakishly curious than another. If this meant constructing fake waterfalls; claiming water drips were the Virgin Mary's tears; turning fragile cave formations into commercial product look-alikes; constructing fake stalactites that looked like the baby Jesus; offering boat rides on fake, artificially colored lakes; or claiming underground rivers were made of blood, so be it. Capitalism ran amok. Bounded by no ethical standards, the skies were the limit when it came to hustling tourist dollars. Some promoters' ideas succeeded, others didn't. It didn't matter if visitors felt conned or not, because promoters didn't depend on return visitors, and there were no ticket refunds.

The Kentucky Cave Wars went on for years and led to the death of poor Floyd Collins and the birth of the media's sensational interest in cave rescues and cave deaths. By his thirty-seventh year, Floyd Collins had become adept at discovering Kentucky caves, just not ones close enough to the road to be of interest as a tourist show cave. This pursuit led him in January 1925, alone, to push deeper into the diminutive Sand Cave. While he was crawling through a tight crawlway, a rock shifted and pinned his leg. He couldn't move forward or back, or reach the offending rock. Days later, hopeful rescuers also couldn't reach the rock that held Floyd in its vice-like grip. The gathering crowd of radio and newspaper reporters began presenting blow-by-blow descriptions to their national audience and the tens of thousands of interested bystanders who hung on the ensuing drama. Their coverage included direct interviews with Floyd, since he was within earshot. The fate and spectacle of the trapped Kentucky farm boy resonated with the American public as they witnessed his slow demise until Floyd succumbed to hunger, thirst, and exposure.

The media attention to Floyd's death did little to quell the Kentucky Cave Wars or the insatiable drive of other poor Kentucky farm boys to search for the next Mammoth Cave. However, there's a time and place for everything. Just as George Harrison once prophetically stated that "all things must pass," the onset of the Depression meant there were fewer tourists coming into Kentucky's cave country and less disposable cash. Also, visitors began to wise up to bald-faced deceptions and obvious cons. Equally so, the true owners of the more popular caves were becoming more adept at spoiling deceptions and devious practices. Therefore, the Kentucky Cave Wars eventually came to an end.

Nonetheless, there remain remnants of that era that continue to influence the public's perception of caves. Continuing for many years, cave promotions touted caves as fanciful or freakish curiosities of nature. Cave visitors didn't see caves as fragile and unique ecosystems containing sensitive and interdependent species and natural processes. People wanted entertainment. Instead of experiencing a fascinating interplay between biological, chemical, environmental, and hydrologic processes, they saw baby Jesus's look-alikes, George Washington's silhouette, a Native American papoose, baby elephants, flying monkeys, the Shroud of Turin, kissing angels, or hunks of cauliflower. Mental associations stretched already stretched common sense, the more outlandish and freakish, the better; however, easily common and understood look-alikes proliferated. Cave features named after food became immensely popular and equally relatable. Promoters were quick to remind exiting tourists that refrigerated magnets of the same food item were for sale at the gift shop conveniently located at the end of the tour—and with the day's special, they could get a hundred dollars off, and the promoter would even throw in a genuine Indian arrowhead for an additional fifty dollars.

⚭

Commercial exploitation or not, big caves are getting harder and harder to find. There are still many important discoveries, just not by me. It takes a lot of work, a lot of time and toil, a lot of patience to outwait mountain lions, and a lot of energy spent. Although not as appealing as finding an entirely new cave, cavers continually make exciting discoveries by simply connecting two already known nearby caves. If there are two caves located only a few thousand feet apart, cavers would surely attempt to find a passage that connects them. A few hundred feet of new cave passage may connect two five-mile-long caves, thus instantaneously creating a respectable ten-mile-long cave. This is how the world's longest cave came to be (from a human perspective). Kentucky's Mammoth Cave is now well over four hundred miles long.

Much of Mammoth Cave's phenomenal growth came about from connections with other nearby caves. Linkages, or the hope of such, continue to the present day. However, the biggest and most notorious connection occurred in 1972, when now famous explorers discovered a cave passage that linked Mammoth Cave with the nearby expanding Flint Ridge Cave System. This legendary connection of two great cave systems actively provides ongoing motivations for the possibility that additional linkages between other great cave systems, and even lesser ones, will expand our known cave universe and hopefully, just maybe, add another entry into the hallowed cave connection hall of fame.

Prior to the landmark 1972 connection, cavers assigned an individual personality to each separate cave. As such, distinct caving scenes and cultural constructs developed side by side, despite the proximity of area caves or their eventual connection.

Caves within each cultural cluster twisted under limestone ridges capped with protective-surface sandstone layers. Without the more water-resistant sandstone caprock, surface streams and erosion would quickly cut down into caverns, turning long caves into a series of truncated shorter segments. Where surface erosion found its way past the protective sandstone layer is where we find today's surface valleys. Therefore, connections between cave systems usually mean finding if there are any remaining cave passages under surface valleys that would enable intrepid cavers to crawl from one ridge cave into an adjoining ridge cave system.

Before the *big* connection, there were caves under Mammoth Cave Ridge and caves under Flint Ridge. Many cavers developed a loyalty to and affection for the caves within one ridge and competed with the cavers devoted to the adjoining ridges. It was a less exploitive and less unscrupulous version of the Kentucky Cave Wars. Most of the time, it consisted of friendly, competitive rivalry, although at its worst, it could deviate into snobby condescension. Not unlike the supposed superiority of the FM radio format in the 1970s compared with the pedestrian AM format, many cavers espoused the Flint Ridge caves as having an aura and distinctiveness that the Mammoth Ridge caves lacked, even though Mammoth continued to hold an appeal for the masses. Notwithstanding these rivalries, these two nearby cave systems were ripe for the search for a physical connection.

Connectionitis began in earnest on the Flint Ridge side in 1955, when cavers found a link between Floyd Collins's Crystal Cave and Unknown Cave. Explorers then linked Colossal and Salt Caves. Soon after, this, too, merged into the expanding Crystal-Unknown Cave pairing.

Sometimes connecting popular caves can lead to friction when deciding what to name the newly expanded cave. To be fair to specific cave devotees and their sensitivities, what should we call any new integrated cave system? Is one or more of the historic names lost or absorbed by another cave's name, or do we simply hyphenate to infinity? Does the name *Floyd Collins's Crystal-Unknown-Colossal-Salt Integrated Cave System* roll off the tongue? Renaming a cave is a big deal to many devoted and loyal cavers. Fortunately, for the sake of brevity, in this example, the cave groups settled on the *Flint Ridge Cave System*.

This naming controversy became even more acute after six cavers in 1972 found a tight cave passage under Houchins Valley that connected the Mammoth Cave System with the Flint Ridge System.

If the connection passage isn't torturous enough, the controversy over naming convention became even more challenging. Through connections, we already lost the names of Roppel Cave, Morrison Cave, Bedquilt Cave, Proctor Cave, Floyd Collins's Crystal Cave, Unknown Cave, Salt Cave, and Colossal Cave, so Flint Ridge cavers didn't want to lose the name of their cherished ridge. In addition, any name may need revision upon future connection with other nearby caves. Caves are located nearby in Joppa Ridge and Toohey Ridge, but other adjoining ridges contain the biggies—the Whigpistle-Martin-Ridge-Jackpot Cave System and the Fisher Ridge Cave System. Currently, the Fisher Ridge Cave System is one of the longest caves in the world. This would be a cherished, or despised, connection. It all depends on personal perspective and to what lengths we go to preserve a cave's historic legacy.

For a number of years, rumors have floated around that cavers had already found a connection between the Mammoth and Flint Cave Systems, but they kept it a secret. Many explorers didn't want the Mammoth-Flint-Ridge Cave System juggernaut to absorb their favorite local cave.

Even if cavers find a universally liked name for an integrated cave system, must the cave community revisit it with each new subsequent connection? Perhaps all caves will eventually connect, ranging from the Mammoth-Flint-Ridge Cave System, Carlsbad Caverns, Underground Seattle, Underground Atlanta, Area 51, North Dakota nuclear missile silos, and New York City sewer system to the White House's underground labyrinth for President Kennedy's secret rendezvous. If Mammoth Cave keeps growing and connecting, it may eventually take over the world. If so, how does this differ from a parasite taking over and absorbing any host it comes across?

Well, perhaps these last few speculations are a little extreme and overkill. Nonetheless, the cave community has hotly debated cave connections and the loss of unique cave cultures and identities since bruised egos come about with each new connection. With each new discovery, cave maps may not be the only thing needing adjustment.

☙❧

Unlike climbers with their climbs, cavers often can't enter caves impromptu. Many are privately owned, and landowner permission is required. Even if the cave is on public land, many entrances are gated and locked, so cavers need permission *and* a key. Climbers usually don't have to contend with this since most mountains are on public land, and mountains are much harder to gate, fence, or restrict access to—even if someone wanted to do such a bizarre thing.

Climbers may have to register for their climb, but this may only involve signing out at a trailhead booklet or, at the most, making a quick stop at a contact station. While overnight backcountry camping may be more involved, registering for day climbing is often no more than a simple annoyance.

Some caves are accessible only if a person joins an established project organized by a cave group. Project caving requires group membership, registration, and admission. Once on a project trip, cavers must follow rigid project rules and schedules. The National Speleological Society (NSS) and the Cave Research Foundation (CRF) manage most cave projects, but there's likely a plethora of site-specific and localized projects as well.

Both the NSS and CRF support officially designated projects throughout the country. For instance, I've participated with the NSS in California's Marble Mountain Wilderness, the CRF in Kentucky's Flint Ridge, Arkansas's Ozark region, and New Mexico's caves in the

Guadalupe Mountains. Most project caving involves cave survey or cave cleanup activities. Although project caving tends to be more scripted than my preference, large groups require structure and standards. The group is responsible for the safety of a wide array of strangers with varying skill levels. In addition, the organization and the managing owner, agency, or landowner sign an official agreement, so if any member misbehaves or doesn't accomplish tasks assigned by the agreement, the cave owner may terminate the agreement and deny all subsequent access.

There are many cave projects in the United States that I would love to have participated in, especially within the alpine caves of Montana's remote Bob Marshall Wilderness Complex. Caves within The Bob require a combination of alpine climbing and alpine caving that's the epitome of a perfect cave trip. I'm now too out of shape to enjoy such miseries, but in my heyday, that would have been fine caving indeed.

Projects I participated in were much more accessible, such as Mammoth Cave, right off the tourist trail near the lower Echo River section. This type of caving is even suitable for spuds. Project managers assigned our team to check out a few small, mostly water-filled passages, and if any of them go, to perform mop-up surveys as needed. Even though the leads were literally fifty feet off the show-cave trail, many weren't on the map. Maybe earlier explorers thought, *If there are still miles of unexplored walking passages to explore that push the cave's outer perimeters and into totally new areas, why would anyone want to wallow in tight water-filled holes in the center of already known cave passages?*

Although not glamorous, bold, or adventurous, mop-up surveys suited me fine. I liked the thought of finding new cave passages in the middle of the beaten path. Besides, I'd been caving in dry and desert caves for a long time, so a little muddy wet-suit caving provided a welcome diversion—and the Mammoth Cave region is famous for its river caves. If someone wanted to stay dry and clean, then why cave in Kentucky? I wanted to savor local muddy tight-ceiling sucking airholes.

Surprisingly, we found a going passage after only a few minutes of searching. This side passage required a wet dunk-under. While swimming in the main cave stream, River Styx, we noticed a small, unmapped side stream. This River Styx tributary had only an inch or two of air space. At first glance, this low air space extended only for a few feet before opening up again on the far side.

Not wanting to kick up any waves that would reduce the limited air space, I silently floated into the restriction on my back—headfirst. I pressed my nose and lips against the ceiling and breathed from the one-inch air space, but this only elicited images of water torture and drowning. Entering the passage sideways was out of the question, as was the floating-face-down-into-the-water option, so this only left entering head up, feetfirst. With my head still in the main passage, I probed the inner passage with the full extent of my gangly legs. I felt for free air space or additional constrictions.

I was pleasantly surprised when my boots flopped in open air. Invigorated and confident from the successful test, I plunged headfirst after sucking in as much air as my lungs could hold. Well before panic set in, I popped into a standing-room passage with a beautiful little rivulet gurgling against my slickened wet suit. The other two cavers soon joined me and marveled at the new cave passage so close to the tourist trail. We named this new River Styx tributary Hades.

Fortunately for me, the park's cave biologist had joined our group. Within this newly found stream, Rick pointed to a little white critter swimming merrily in short, jerking motions. The biologist identified the merry creature as the extremely rare and endangered Kentucky cave shrimp. Rick expressed *his* merriment too, for he said he'd been working as the park's cave biologist for nearly twenty years and it was only the second Kentucky cave shrimp he'd ever seen. Much to everyone else's merriment, we soon saw another, then another, and then another. Within a span of only a few feet, we found eight. Rick shared his observation that Hades appeared to hold the highest concentration of the endangered shrimp within the entire Mammoth-Flint Cave System.

I thought to myself, *Cool.* I also wondered if the Mammoth-Flint Cave System extended across the state line into Tennessee, would biologists embroil themselves in the same kinds of naming consternations the cavers in the Mammoth-Flint Cave System connection controversy had by calling it the Kentucky-Tennessee cave shrimp? Likely not. Regardless of any range extension, the diminutive shrimp will likely remain as currently named.

The end of our mop-up survey ended my fanciful mind wanderings. We soon returned through the shallow restriction and popped up next to the chrome handrail along the visitor path. There were no cave tours then, so we savored the moment alone. I savored it again a few days later when I returned with hydrological monitoring equipment.

At the time, I was living in the park for three months to finish the coursework needed for my master of science degree from Western Kentucky University. To compensate the government for letting me live in park housing, I helped them by surveying and mapping sinkholes vulnerable to potential contamination threats. I traced water pathways from each sinkhole in the project area to discover where it entered known cave passages and waterways. There were several known potential water-quality threats to the cave and the cave's aquifer, including oil wells and oil storage tanks, but we didn't know where these sinkholes connected with the cave.

Using fluorescent dyes, for three months, I traced sinkholes' flow paths in and around the developed areas of Mammoth Cave National Park. I placed in the water special charcoal packets that absorbed any fluorescent dyes that happened to flow by. After placing many charcoal packets throughout the cave, I then injected dye into one sinkhole at a time. By routinely testing each receiving packet throughout my testing network, I could determine what path the dye must have taken through the cave. On a whim, I placed a packet in the Hades stream next to where we'd seen the endangered shrimp.

Of all my testing locations, the only dye that entered the Hades stream came from those I injected in a sinkhole downhill of the park's only gas station. This test indicated that any gas spill at this service station would likely quickly spread its contamination to the world's highest concentration of the endangered Kentucky cave shrimp. Clearly, cave managers had to do something to mitigate this threat.

Fortunately, the gas station owner cooperated. He built a secondary containment berm so any spill would pool on pavement safely within the berm and not flow into the cave and kill any endangered shrimp or other aquatic species. Classic resource management in action. This wouldn't have been possible if it weren't for cooperative agreements between the National Park Service, Western Kentucky University, and cave project leaders within the Cave Research Foundation.

Caves are much more than a playground for the human species or freakish curiosities. There are wide varieties of organisms that call caves home. We humans are but intruders into their domain. Kentucky's cave regions contain an especially rich biodiversity. This is but one reason the Mammoth-Flint Ridge Cave System is one of the few ecological habitats designated as both a World Heritage Site *and* an International Biosphere Reserve.

Cave critters can go down cave passages that humans could never fit inside, so from their perspective, Mammoth Cave is much bigger than mere humans can comprehend, and there are infinitely more connections than we've ever imagined. While many of these passages may be too small for humans to fit into, water pollution would have no problem following. Increasingly, rare cave organisms are becoming even more rare—often threatened by our surface actions and inactions. From that perspective, while hydrological connections aren't as glorious as the 1972 epic joining of Mammoth Cave with the Flint Ridge Cave System, from the perspective of the cave's ecosystem, sometimes it's the little connections that are even more significant.

Cucamonga Sunrise

*A*s golden and sweet as Cucamonga honey under the blue warmth of a midafternoon. It rarely gets better than this. Such is the image conjured when my mind drifts between the fine line between rock climbing and spirituality. A person can get to know a climber's soul through their climbs—but not all ascents take place on rock, snow, or ice. Some climbs lead toward higher planes with a deeper meaning and a deeper verve—at the cusp of being art. Of the souls I've known, the one who has gotten the closest to such stately realms is Dan—soft-spoken and patient Dan.

In another time and place, I imagine Dan as a hippie. Not the shifty, flighty, or druggie type, but the optimistic, kindhearted soul searching for the Age of Aquarius within the Age of Reagan. Who wouldn't want to climb out of such places?

Before I met Dan, I don't believe I had a favorite type of rock climb. All were appealing, although not all were spud accessible. I lived for cracks, chimneys, slabs, faces, arêtes, walls, and whatnot. They all inspired magic, thrills, and a means to understand thyself. Before I met Dan, I climbed a lot of faces, not necessarily because I had an affinity for face climbing. It had to do with cracks were too painful and walls intimidating.

No matter how much finesse and style one has, vertical and overhanging climbs require upper-body strength and a bold spirit. Some spuds have neither. Strength isn't a benefit for low-angle friction climbing. Of much more importance on slabs are determination, concentration, and the slow, methodical movement of an artist in search of their soul. Brute force can sometimes hurl a person over a steep and physical cliff, but such antics on slabs would only burn rubber and stretch rope. Friction climbing is better suited to my body style and limitations. However, once I met Dan, I appreciated that friction climbing is noble and filled with style and grace.

I met Dan through the University of Washington Climbing Club. He'd just moved to the gray, mist-smeared Northwest from golden-hued Southern California. Shortly before moving, Dan put up a classic first ascent in the higher-domed land above Yosemite, home of the placid waters and enchanted green subalpine meadows of Tuolumne.

Dan formed relationships with rocks and summits. If the personalities didn't sync, he kindly looked elsewhere. A climb meant nothing unless done with style. How could a climb ever become classic unless climbed with style? The epitome of Tuolumne and Yosemite Valley's class and style is the aptly named Crest Jewel on North Dome.

Dan eyed Crest Jewel's line for some time before laying any paint on canvas. When he finished, his art deserved to be in the Louvre, the Guggenheim, and The Metropolitan Museum of Art, all rolled into one. Before the paint had dried, Crest Jewel had become an instant classic. Upon completing that pièce de résistance, Dan moved to Seattle, enrolled in the University of Washington, popped into the Climbing Club's first meeting of the year, and struck up a conversation with a native spud.

Through his childlike eagerness and soft-spoken sensibilities, Dan's belief in the spirituality of climbs began to rub off. He cringed at reckless maniacs who sought brute physical challenges at the expense of the experience. I might not have had the strength and boldness for the vertical, but I sensed a subtlety and beauty in the minute. Nearly hidden subtle curvature deflections are just enough for a carefully placed soft rubber shoe. A sloping depression accepts an inverted palm. Rising in perfect balance, you learn how much friction a palm can generate—and sustain. Such magic moments give rise to the notion that through climbs, you can feel, if not see, the meaning of beauty, style, grace. Dan opened a new and alluring world. Typically, he led most pitches. The spud just looked, learned, and followed.

Over the years, Dan and I occasionally climbed together, but I've always regretted never climbing with him on his favorite Tuolumne domes. Without hesitation, I said yes when invited on the first attempt of a new route on his beloved North Dome—the stately dome floating over Yosemite Valley opposite the more famous bifurcated Half Dome and right next to Tuolumne. Dan nearly owns North Dome, with Crest Jewel in 1981, then Dakshina in 1983. He returned the following year for a first free ascent of Dakshina. In 2002, he returned for the Crest Jewel Direct. Always believing that North Dome still held secret classics, he called me in 2004 for what he said might be his last foray to North Dome. Although woefully out of climbing shape, I packed with gleeful abandon for a five-day exploration.

I'd never touched North Dome rock, breathed North Dome air, or heard North Dome's spirit or vivacity. Previously, every time I'd been to Yosemite, snow and clouds had draped the valley and washed its edges with gray cascades and rivulets. Gray-dabbed rocks are picturesque but aren't appealing to the technical climber. Gray-slimed rock doesn't exude the warmth expected of golden Cucamonga honey—Californian dome climbing at its best. We pushed on, nonetheless. Every part of our attempt was a new experience for me.

"Look!" I exclaimed. "Yosemite rock with no snow and ice or dripping clouds!"

After parking at Porcupine Flat, we took the easy trail on the backside that led to the top. The trail provided us an easy summit and a tremendous view of upper Yosemite Valley. For the rappel down the massive, slabby south face, we used bolts from Dan's earlier climbs. However, the rappels broke our sprightly verve. Getting to where we wanted to go required rappelling at a steep diagonal. On the entire rappel, we fought and defied Newton's third law of motion. Gravity and other physical forces pulling us in one direction seemed greater than any opposing force, keeping us in line with where we wanted to go. (Not exactly a direct paraphrase of Newton.) Carrying a sixty-five-pound pack against a forty-five-degree angled pull tested my shoes' friction limits on the glacier-polished surface. If friction failed, gravity would gladly have propelled me and my pack on a wild pendulum ride across Crest Jewel, Crest Jewel Direct, Dakshina, and hitherto yet unnamed Hindi-sounding Dan routes. I had a tenseness that no *Om mani padme hum* mantra could silence, while Dan remained calm and serene, as if he were at home. Perhaps he was.

To lower my sense of gravity and vulnerability to pendulums, I tethered the Grendel-like pack to my harness. Big mistake, but Dan didn't—wouldn't—laugh or mock my silly antics. Tethering the pack lowered my center of gravity as intended, but scraping the sixty-five-pound pack along the rock's steep diagonal exposed me to an even greater potential for a wild ride of the pendulum kind.

Om mani padme hum.

Technique, style, or mantras didn't keep me on the rock and on rappel. Newer sticky climbing shoe rubber did. I'm forever grateful for the miracles of modern climbing technologies. If I'd been still wearing my EB Super Grattons, my skinless carcass would have been sweeping North Dome's broad south face by then.

Feet, don't fail me now, I thought. I've always loved Little Feat's song "Sailin' Shoes," but I never wanted to put it into practice on North Dome.

After 16 billion rappels, we reached the monster slab's toe and the end of our mantra saga—and nearly the end of my once illustrious and glorious pack. Dragging it on eight hundred feet of rock hadn't been kind to my old friend. Both the pack and I were in shatters. Even Dan admitted being tired.

Dan found the loveliest camp location for tracking the golden light's tranquil descent across Half Dome's blank northwest face. Not quite Cucamonga honey, but the next best thing.

We hadn't been tracing the golden arc for long before a lone climber hailed. We motioned for him to join us. He stumbled closer, along with his Grendel-like pack—clearly leading and pushing limply from behind. He'd just finished a solo aid route on Washington Column.

"For three days now, I've not had any real food," he said as he tore into what we had to offer. While he enjoyed the food, most of all, he welcomed real conversation.

After my rappelling ordeal, I found talking took too much effort. I mostly sat idle as the Washington Column climber and Dan recounted climbing memories. Later, I transferred my remaining energy to watching the shimmering cosmic glow off Half Dome's northwest face.

The next day, Dan and I explored the first obstacle—getting past a dramatic overhanging arch blocking the beautifully long slab and face that ran to the summit. If successful, this would likely be another of Dan's North Dome classics.

I belayed as Dan began the slow *tink-tink* hand-drilling required for the first bolt hole. Hand-drilling bolts is slow and tedious, and my muscles were still shredded. But with the sun's soothing rays, I didn't mind.

Later, a stranger approached at what had to be ten miles an hour. He soon joined me on my sun-warmed perch. *Hiking* isn't even the proper word for it since he seemed to float uphill. This fit floater obviously didn't believe in the Don Whillans's conditioning theory.

With a broad smile, Dennis introduced himself. Dan remembered meeting him once before. Good climbers often know each other. Dennis had never heard of me—and likely never will. The Dennises of the world rarely have more than a passing acquaintance with spuds.

In time, Dan and Dennis took turns bolting and creeping ever slowly up to the overhanging arch. Important progress, but painfully slow. I belayed both. This turned out to consume the extent of our waning light and Dan's and Dennis's waning drilling muscles. I momentarily thought of offering to give it a spell at the bit. But my forearms were so out of shape, I didn't think I would have been much help, considering the effort of switching positions on the rope. Besides, the light faded almost as fast as Dan's and Dennis's will to continue. As it turned out, Dennis had other plans that didn't involve North Dome. He'd merely dropped by to say hello as he passed through the area. As soon as our feet touched horizontal rock, Dennis dashed back to the Valley for adventures unseen. Dan and I returned to camp.

The next day dawned with cloud-filled skies that threatened to rain or snow. It had the look of typical North Cascades weather—and my typical Yosemite outing. I knew the Cucamonga honey wouldn't last. We now faced the prospects of exposure on a high slab during unsettled weather. Instead, we began the first ascent of a short new route lower and off to the side. We got to the top of the first pitch when clouds grew even more threatening. Briskly, we dashed back to camp, gathered our stuff, and began the long hike along the Dome's big thick toe to eventually arrive at the Porcupine Flat Trail leading us back to the safety of our car.

The first ascent of this anticipated new North Dome classic was not to be—at least for me. Four years later, Dan returned with a couple of other people and completed the main new route. He bestowed it the name Nataraj as a nod and continuum of his Hindi theme. In Hindi, this means "lord of dance." While I didn't participate in its first ascent, this may be the closest I'll ever come to dancing with Yosemite's domed deities. The dance first entered my dreams and subconsciousness nearly a quarter century earlier when Dan demonstrated that spirituality can exist in climbing art. While Cucamonga honey may lead to golden, sweet climbs, it also forever grants spuds the warmest of Cucamonga sunsets to last a lifetime.

Cursed Be the Tie That Binds

One of the most frequent questions non-cavers have upon first meeting cavers is, Don't you ever get stuck? At first blush, this question is a non sequitur, since unless the person asking is also stuck in a cave, clearly the caver they're asking isn't stuck in a cave. Therefore, if they had been stuck, it didn't last. However, on my first caving trip to Alaska, far more than a fleeting moment caused me to question that non sequitur.

My packs, caving gear, wet suit, and I joyously soaked in the scenery on the long ferry ride to Prince William Island from Ketchikan, Alaska. This trip allowed me to fulfill personal interests *and* serve a greater public good at the same time. Can't get any better than that.

The ferry ride and soaking took place in the early 1990s, back when the Tongass National Forest found itself in the throes of its forests being overcut *and* its ecosystem being irreparably harmed. Despite the largess, forest managers on the nation's largest national forest had boxed themselves into a quandary. Large swaths of the forest held muskeg bog expanses, which stunted the vigorous growth needed for maximum timber and pulp production. Trees, like people, don't like waterlogged roots. Trees, under such waterlogged conditions, grow slowly or poorly. As for people, they move to Phoenix.

The best soil drainage on the Tongass is over limestone and marble bedrock containing abundant caves and karst. Karst soils don't get waterlogged because excess water drains through caves. This enables trees around caves to grow bigger and stronger. So, when the Forest Service received their unsustainable harvest mandates from Washington, D.C.—the demand to overcut the forest—the agency turned toward their caves. Increasingly, the agency began selling harvest permits in and around fragile cave systems. Therein lies the rub—the pesky environmental laws and regulations protecting fragile caves and karst. Who snuck those in without Congress noticing or giving them a chance to subvert?

The rub lies in cave protection laws, such as the Federal Cave Resources Protection Act, which requires forest managers to protect and properly manage significant caves and not just push timber volume. Cave protection laws slowed timber production on the Tongass because it took time for politicians to find ways to waive or circumvent environmental laws. In the meanwhile, forest managers attempted to serve both masters. To do this, they needed to know the location of undiscovered fragile caves in relation to recorded timber sales. To further that goal, forest managers signed a partnership agreement with a coalition of cavers. The cavers obtained access to caves to discover and explore, while the federal government obtained access to resource data they could manipulate, avoid, ignore, bury, or circumvent to their heart's content. In government vernacular—a win-win. No one asked the trees or the caves how they considered this arrangement.

During my Tongass surveying week, the Forest Service gave us a free helicopter ride to one remote subalpine meadow and limestone outcroppings to survey partially explored caves. Even though they were only a few miles from the road, the thick brush separating the two would have taken my pack and me days to negotiate. And when it comes to timber sales, time is money. As the helicopter easily sailed over horrendous brush fields, I laughed and mocked the devil's club and slide alder from the window.

I got the better of you this time! I mused over the whir of the blades.

On the next day, I rappelled into one of Alaska's deepest caves. The cave protects its deeper bowels with a tight horizontal crawl turned on its end, which serves as the cave's internal anal sphincter. The cave's vertical intestinal tube was a couple of hundred feet long, or should I say deep. To ease getting down the two-hundred-foot vertical intestinal tube, I tethered my pack by dangling it from my harness and hung it near my feet. While on rappel, I let gravity do its trick, for both the pack and me. To get through tight spots, I simply bounced on the rope long enough to de-wedge myself enough to pop out below any controlling sphincter muscles and wedge again at the next lower constriction. If my pack hung up, I just stomped on it, which created a series of tether-length tumbles. I, and my pack, continued down this long vertical slot by a series of controlled jumps, wedges, and plunges—moving deeper into Alaska's marbled lower intestines.

An immense snow cone greeted us at the bottom of the vertical slot. Snow falling through the shaft over the years had never melted in the cave's cold dampness, so the snow accumulated and grew bigger. If left undisturbed, both snow cones and trees grow big on the Tongass. Fortunately for us, the snow cone hadn't grown so much that it blocked or stopped up the rest of the colon.

After a long day of cave exploration, surveying, and mapping, a watch alerted us to turn around and head out. I soon discovered an issue. The same bouncing on the rope to pop through tight spots on the descent wouldn't work for the climb out. The limited space in which to lift my knees made matters worse. Climbing a cave rope, like climbing a ladder, requires the caver to lift the knees—to step up, one step at a time. If the slot is no wider than the climber's body, there's no room to lift and bend the knees during each attempted lifting motion. In this Alaskan cave, the slot was narrow in width despite being long in the other dimension. As such, I couldn't lift my knees in the direction needed. I could barely lift them at ninety degrees from the direction knees naturally articulate.

Forcing bones, joints, and cartilage to work against hundreds of thousands of years of human evolution, I could make an inch or two of progress at a time by keeping my body twisted—my hips and knees on one plane, and my shoulders and head contorted ninety degrees. This ungainly position allowed me to make slow but steady progress.

While I could contort my body to ooze up past cave restrictions, I had limited control over my tethered pack hanging sullenly from a sling tied to my harness. Murphy's law being what it is, my pack didn't miss a single opportunity to find, and wedge with, every constriction, protrusion, or crystal within the entire miserable slot.

No matter how hard I strained, I couldn't budge my pack once entombed. Eron likely waited far ahead, out of sight and unaware of my predicament. Kevin, directly below me, couldn't easily hide his growing impatience with my pack, and me, blocking his only way out of the cave. The stuck pack tethered to my harness prevented me from moving forward, but the narrowness of the slot prevented me from reaching down to free the pack. Both the pack and I were in a bind. Visions of being stuck and dying, and of being Alaska's Floyd Collins, flashed through my head and ever-reddening brow.

After more than a two-hour struggle, I had to resort to less safe methods. I unhooked from the rope. Although the slot fell away more than two hundred feet below me, my falling seemed highly unlikely, since even with all my energy, I couldn't move even an inch, let alone two hundred feet. Untying from the rope and pack allowed me to get into a slightly different position. Holding the pack's tether in my hand, I repeatedly kicked the pack to dislodge it from its vise-like grip. Another hour of me pulling, while Kevin pushed, gave me a new perspective of and meaning for *futility*. After another couple of hours, and at the limits of my endurance and Kevin's patience, the pack chose to free itself. It must have been satisfied that its cruel intent worked: to whip and frazzle me into submission. Embarrassment coursed through my body upon the realization that I'd inconvenienced Kevin immensely.

By this time, the night had already transitioned into a new day, albeit still in the wee hours of the morning. With the last of my dissipated energy, I dry heaved the pack onto the marble surface under a wondrously constriction-free starlit night. The Milky Way stood in bold contrast and appeared more expansive than I'd remembered. Kevin, stuck below me the whole time, seemed less than thrilled with me, the Milky Way, or anything else in the cosmos. So too was Eron, since he had no idea what had taken so long or if anything had gone wrong. For Eron, the wait, worry, and wonder had grown hard to endure.

Human bodies, and even minds, eventually recover from such abuse. Fortunately for the caves and karst, our mapping and inventory produced enough information to confirm that federal cave protection laws apply—even on the Tongass.

☙❧

Over the years, I found myself testing that non sequitur more often than I would like to admit; however, each time, as luck would have it, I found a means to ensure that my stuckness remained only a temporary condition.

Many years ago, I ended up in central Oregon for a series of meetings—for what, I no longer have any recollection. I did, however, feel the pull of central Oregon's lava fields. I knew then, as I do now, that volcanoes filled central Oregon with lava flows, and within those flows are some of the nation's most intriguing lava tube caves. So, after the conclusion of each day's meetings, I quickly changed into suitable clothing and mental state, piled into the rental car, and headed out to search for caves.

On one late-afternoon adventure, I sought a specific lava tube I'd read about years before in one of Bill's many write-ups and trip reports. I brought with me no location information beyond a vague and cryptic note I'd scribbled before leaving home earlier that week. But in case I found the tube, I packed one handheld flashlight.

For this intriguing ice cave, I had a little more to go on. By *ice cave*, I don't mean the cave formed in ice. There are caves in real ice and in real glaciers, but most ice caves are in lava. The ice is only *in* them—like the snow cone in that deep Tongass cave. Many lava ice caves are located in high desert regions, where it may get warm in the summer. But it also gets darn cold in the winter. During winter's coldness, air does what it does everywhere else—it flows into low spaces, not unlike how it pulls in hapless and unprepared cavers while on business trips.

Cold winter air sinks into the depths of caves and, upon contact with damp groundwater seeping out of the caves, forms ice deposits.

The summer's warmth doesn't penetrate the cave's bowels because warm air doesn't sink. Only the cold sinks. Therefore, in properly shaped lava caves, cold air that descends in the winter remains trapped until an influx of new cold air and new moisture arrives the following winter. Over years, such caves develop near-permanent layers of ice. Hence the name "ice cave."

It had been a long time since I'd been in an ice cave. I wanted to at least find its entrance. Through luck and determination, I found it about one hour before darkness. After all the time and distance to get there, I couldn't remain content with just finding the cave. I needed to probe its depth—and its ice. So, casting safety, common sense, and good judgment aside, and armed only with one handheld flashlight, I entered the darkness, hoping the cold air would lead to ice.

I left no note with anyone about where I planned to explore, other than that I was presumably in central Oregon, where I'd planned to attend a weeklong meeting. No one knew I'd parked my car up a lonely and rarely visited Forest Service road. No one knew where I'd headed out in the trailless forests. If I had a problem, all anyone would know was that I would miss the next day's meeting. I knew I shouldn't enter caves alone and without telling anyone. I knew I shouldn't go into caves without the proper helmet and safety gear. I should have known obsessions are often too strong to overcome with rational thoughts and knowledge. I should have listened to my knowledge and gut.

My cautious descent to the lower regions turned out uneventful. I reached the top of the last short drop leading to the cave's end. I shone the light to the actual bottom—a small pool of water rimmed with an ice shelf. The drop was only fifteen feet—an easy haunch slide. I couldn't tell myself I'd gone through the entire cave if I hadn't. Common sense and rationality should have prevailed.

171

I reached the lower pool by holding tight to a firm handhold, putting my full weight upon it, and lowering away. Since I would need this handhold to climb back up, I made sure my feet touched the ice shelf bottom before I let go of the hold. The very tips of my feet could barely reach the near-level floor on the shore of the lake. I thought, *No problem*. So I let go. My lying prone in the middle of the ice-coated pond happened so fast. Isn't gravity grand? I found myself suddenly cold, suddenly cursing, and suddenly wondering what happened.

Fortunately, my wet and bluing fingers were tightly wrapped around the one miniature flashlight, and it still worked—the flashlight, less so my fingers. I scampered out of the water onto the level ice shelf encircling the pond. With a thud and splash, I ended up lying face down in the slushy pond. Trying not to panic, I forced my logical problem-solving self to take control. Mind you, this is the same logical problem-solving self that almost shared a cave with a cougar.

It appeared the level ice shelf encircling the pond wasn't exactly level—almost, but not exactly. The smooth-as-glass ice had no imperfection, bump, crystal, or embedded dust necessary for a boot's grip. Each futile attempt landed me back in the water. If I couldn't stand on the shelf, I couldn't reach the one and only handhold needed to climb out. "Well, Dave," I reflected out loud, "if you were inclined to an emotional response, now would be a good time to panic."

If I dropped and broke the flashlight, I would be in trouble. If I didn't get out before it ran out of battery life, I would be in big trouble. If I didn't get out before the cold seeped any further into my body's core, I would be in the exact situation I found myself in—in real trouble.

Since struggles and thrashes proved futile in extracting me from the water, I resigned to the inevitable. Standing in knee-deep water, I scanned my options. It wasn't like I had a pack holding an assortment of emergency equipment, climbing gear, or safety gadgets. I had only my one flashlight, skill, determination, and willpower.

In other words, I was all alone and helpless.

There had to be another handhold. Even a minute one would do. If so, I could summon all my strength and climbing skill to make it work. It had to work. I'm a firm believer that when a person's life depends on it, they can accomplish great feats.

All potentially usable holds on all walls were at the maximum extent of my outstretched hand and arm. I could barely touch one meager hold with the tip of my middle finger. To use the hold, I needed to pull with sideways pressure. However, the slightest sideward pull on the one fingerhold caused the finger to slip off the icy depression, and I would end up back to the all-too-familiar ice puddle. It didn't help that I only had a handheld flashlight. Holding the light required a hand. Climbing out required both hands.

Dilemma.

I held the flashlight in my teeth, but reaching for a hold at my skeletal limits necessitated I hold my head, and teeth, in ways that shed no light on the hold. Therefore, I needed to memorize hold locations and hold the flashlight in clenched teeth while reaching with all the elasticity and stretch I could muster for the now unseen hold, all without causing any motion or vibration that would plunge me off my fragile ice footing. The probability of this maneuver going well faded upon each futile attempt.

I revisited the lake bottom for the next unknown elapsed minutes. Or hours? Eventually, another try provided me with an extra quarter inch of body elasticity. My fingertip felt a slight dimple that could serve as a hold. I pressed sideways on it to lever my body up slightly higher on the ice shelf. The increased height allowed me to place a finger of my other hand on a minute nubbin. The rest of my body stretched across the pond to an ice-coated nubbin that miraculously held my boot tread. One more nubbin got me up out of the pit and back to the security of ice-free level rock flooring. A couple of minutes later, I taunted fate and escaped the cave.

The evening's light had long since passed below the horizon. The stiff breeze quickly reminded me of my wetness. What I didn't need reminding of was how stupid I'd been to descend that last drop. Why did I go in alone? What did it serve, other than my own selfish impulses?

No cave is worth dying for, and especially for no greater benefit to humankind, cave-kind, or mountain-kind. This trip had been pointless. Rescuers wouldn't have found my body for years. With these thoughts surging through my slightly warming veins, I limped back to my car.

The next day, I told no one of my previous evening's adventure. It would've been too embarrassing. I never told my wife. I hope she doesn't read this chapter. Perhaps not all non-caver questions are non sequiturs.

Darkness Cometh

From a young spud's age, I've felt the pull of Wyoming's Teton Range and its alluring summits. But I never succumbed until well into my declining middle-age spud years, when Andrew rang me up and invited me to join him and two of his New Jersey friends on a Teton adventure. Although my internal fires still burned intensely, a mirror would have plainly exposed the fact that my external parts had softened after years of slovenly non-exercise and non-climbing. In total disregard of the obvious, I accepted Andrew's offer and proposed that we climb the challenging Grand Teton North Face. However, recognizing that the most ambitious climb I'd attempted in years was a climb off the sofa, I hatched a plan for us to climb, in quick succession, two other Teton classics—first a moderate route, then a harder route, and finally the North Face. In hindsight, the illogical notion that climbing two mountains in as many days would prepare my woefully out-of-shape body to tackle the dangerous and foreboding North Face was merely a morphed and rebooted Don Whillans training philosophy that had consistently failed me in the past. However, some spuds need to learn the hard way.

For the easiest of the three, we chose Mount Moran's moderate in difficulty but long CMC route.

Mount Moran is the bulky giant that towers over Jackson Lake. The CMC route climbs to the summit from along the impressive black dike that's clearly visible from the valley.

Long routes on tall and bulky mountains often equate to taking a long time to climb. This is especially true when at least one climber is far from his physical prime. Our plans involved ascending to a notch called Drizzlepuss the first day. On the second day, we planned to ascend the peak and return to the valley bottom in time to pack for the more challenging summit on the following day.

On the valley bottom, blown-down trees covering what seemed like multiple square miles caused us to laboriously step and climb over each windfall. Negotiating the downed trees was like spending a full day on a stair-step exercise machine with a heavy pack. Nature's stair-step machine grew weary on the spud's mind and muscles. We arrived so late at Drizzlepuss that I was too exhausted to enjoy, or notice, its alpine charm.

The next day, the climb above Drizzlepuss reminded us of the definition of *long*. Each rope length higher appeared not to get us any closer to the summit, which was still brooding and laughing at us from high above. I lost all count of the number of rope-length pitches we climbed on that massive face, but apparently, we made progress, since we arrived on the broad 12,605-foot summit as the sun's rays faded on the far western horizon.

Andrew called for a vote on whether to continue down in the dark or settle in for an unplanned bivouac at the 12,000-foot level on Moran's exposed, cold, and windswept alpine shoulder. Since I'd spent unplanned bivouacs in cold places before, I voted to continue down in the dark, at least to a balmier elevation. The New Jersey contingent wanted to wait for the comforts of light. The New Jersey voters dominated, so we prepared to spend the night in an alcove at the gates of heaven. We pooled and divided equally our combined sum of a small tin of sardines and three small caramel cubes. Pretty meager pickings for four cold and tired adults to last ten hours—or more.

We were already as cold as the darkness when shivering commenced. To get out of the wind as best we could, we packed into a tiny dish-shaped depression. We tied ourselves into the wall to keep from falling. We made sure knots were tight.

After swallowing the last of my water, three-quarters of a caramel piece, and two sardines, I turned to thoughts other than the cold night's slow procession. I tried a multitude of mind games to keep my head occupied and force time to pass quickly. Nothing worked. I kept staring to the east, looking for the first glimmer of the rising sun.

My position afforded an unobstructed view of the dark night sky. I spent hours gazing at the wondrous Milky Way, but sleeplessness, cold, and discomfort prevented me from enjoying it more than in passing. Time seemed to have slowed. The stars and heavens rotated, but the sky remained just as dark, just as glorious, and just as miserable.

No matter how much I appreciated the dark, at that moment, I longed for light's warm embrace. Finally, after having mocked me long enough by slowing the passage of time, the mountain gods eventually lifted the golden globe upon the horizon. Out from the darkened ashes, the phoenix once again took flight. While basking in the first warming rays, we untangled ropes and rearticulated cold, stiff, and weary bodies so we could prepare for the long descent.

How much more frightful and daunting would it have been on that frigid night if we hadn't had faith and the prior knowledge of the dark and cold? That after a calculable amount of time, light would return? The sun's predictability gives hope and comfort to those enduring the cold and dark. No matter how miserable it gets, there will always be a degree of hope that comes from the conviction that the sun *will* rise. We can then endure that known commodity. Imagine if someone didn't know when the sun would return—if ever. If the night's coldness persisted for weeks or more, then there would have been no question if we'd stay on the mountain or attempt the dangerous descent in the dark. There's strength and warmth in both knowledge and faith.

After we reached the bottom of the mountain, the long and tortuous trip through the blown-down trees and around Leigh Lake took just as much time in this direction as it had in the other. We reached our cars as nightfall came upon us.

Mount Moran's CMC route was to be our warm-up climb before jumping to increasingly harder climbs and culminating our week with the challenging North Face of Grand Teton. Humbled by having this warm-up climb kick our butts, none of us felt motivated for any more climbing, hiking, or physical exertion. The New Jersey folks drove to the airport, hoping to catch an early flight back. I moose-watched in the morning, followed by basking in the sun's warm embrace for the remainder of the day.

Our chase of the light and dark is nothing new. Going back millennia, countless peoples and philosophers have pondered the nature of light and dark. How would you describe a star to someone who'd never seen one—or a million? How would you describe light to someone who'd seen only darkness? What is the relatable experience?

The poet Mary Oliver once said, "Someone I loved once gave me a box full of darkness. It took me years to understand that this too, was a gift." For me, few experiences have been as relatable to Mary Oliver's box of darkness as that Mount Moran night under the infinite stars, constellations, meteors, comets, planets, asteroids, nebulas, galaxies, and the immensity of Milky Way's broad arc.

One of the fundamental concepts of the real world is that as time progresses, our universe is incrementally progressing from structured order to homogeneous disorder; unique and special clusters progress to a homogeneous mix of the average—the mundane. This progression is occurring at the cosmic level down to the subatomic, as well as driving the aging forces that befall all corporeal beings. In our universe of chaotic disorder, caving and climbing offer a richness that lies only within the extreme margins at either end.

Nothing Succeeds Like Excess

Some people envision a mountain landscape as peaceful and pastoral. This may be the case for some foothills or for low, rounded old mountains victimized by weathering, such as the Appalachians. Because time has weathered steeper features, some climbers consider them tame. Therefore, climbers often seek out unusual conditions, such as frozen waterfalls or ice-choked ice runnels in the winter, to increase the technical challenge.

For actively forming mountains, it's a clash of the titans, a war of the worlds. Younger mountains host competitions between mighty Earth forces pushing mountains higher and erosion tearing them down. Actively forming mountains usually provide the greatest interest to traditional mountaineers. Steep faces, sharp ridges, imposing buttresses, and somber bastions stand as grand fortresses against the ever-present erosional onslaught. Earth forces haven't finished tearing down these technical challenges.

Within this harsh environment, climbers pit their soft tissues and friable bones against calving glaciers, icy torrents, collapsing snow bridges, rockfalls, avalanches, pounding wind and ice storms, lightning, severe cold or tortuous heat, and the ever-constant danger of gravity. The wise climber proceeds through the front lines, attempting to avoid frontal assaults, since humans are woefully outmatched. A strong body remains a necessity, but climbers challenge difficult mountains with their heads. The best defense is stealth and avoidance, especially within the most violent and harshest mountain region—the alpine zone.

Oscar Wilde's famous quote, "Nothing succeeds like excess," seems a perfect match for the idiosyncrasy common to many master alpinists. To climb in peak performance, many masters sacrificed moderation for the potential successes of excess. If nature aligns the forces in the human body, mind, and spirit just right, then climbers may attain wondrous successes; however, if misaligned, results and failure are consequential. Either way, human history is fascinating at either extreme.

❧

With such a compelling name, prominent horn shape, and rich climbing history, Mount Triumph long attracted my interest. Similarly, it didn't take long to talk Derek, the same Derek from the Mount Bad adventure, into a climb of Mount Triumph's classic and hauntingly lovely northeast arête route.

As in many routes in the North Cascades, the trailhead starts from an old logging road. We measured distance not in miles but in stumps and logging slash. We parked for free, since our climb took place long before the implementation of the myriad user fees federal agencies now charge. At the trailhead, we donned heavy packs burdened with ropes, slings, chocks, carabiners, crampons, ice ax, ice screws, and snow flukes, as well as normal backpacking equipment.

As we slogged toward Mount Triumph, we passed through typical lowland and mid-slope Pacific Northwest forests. Green dominates. I've always marveled at how many shades and hues of green there actually are. The light-green new-growth Pacific silver fir tips contrasted with the darker blue-green older needles of mountain hemlock. Salmonberry and red huckleberry leaves provided a showing of light greens, while club and true mosses, salal, and the occasional sedge or trillium formed the darker greens. Red alder, western redcedar, maidenhair fern, and a plethora of other lush species provided various transitional greens.

For me, Northwest coastal forests mark home: The verdant greens framed by gray skies and the dank, pungent odors of the green-carpeted forest floor. The various forms of the ever-frequent rain and glimpses of pileated woodpeckers through the trees, winter wrens in the shrubs, dippers bobbing along streams, and banana slugs underfoot. Home is vibrant, comforting, and somber.

I'm reminded of a comment my mother made years ago. As an artist, her standard rule for painting Pacific Northwest forests was "paint it dark."

"Forests are always dark," she frequently said while engrossed in creating one of her oil paintings. She thought if the sun's obscured behind a water-laden gray sky, then forests are dark. If the sun's out in all its vibrant glory, then the lush forest casts deep and impenetrable shadows. The forests are dark, at least in the understory.

While on the way to Mount Triumph, we plodded through the dark understory, one step at a time, creeping ever closer to our single-minded goal—Mount Triumph's northeast arête.

As we ascended, tall, lush green trees and shrubs of the lowlands slowly gave way to isolated clumps of fir separated by heather patches and dabbles of multicolored lichen. The woodpeckers and dippers disappeared, and ptarmigans and mountain goats took their place within the starkly austere land of white and gray.

The dullness of the glacier's and snow's whiteness made the multicolored splotches from airborne residues and pink or green algae and microorganisms growing on the surface stand out in vivid display. The Northwest's high country is truly a land of gray. The sky is gray. The confining colossal mountain walls are gray granite, granodiorite, gabbro, gneiss, schist, or other transitional varieties of igneous or metamorphic rocks typical of the North Cascades.

On the hike into Mount Triumph, my gray ponderings gave way to mindless and time-consuming mental exercises. *Exercise* is much too alive and invigorating of a term for what went through my gray matter. To while away time without having to think of aching and tired muscles, any random thought shielded me from the pain and repetition—the more time-consuming and mindlessly easy, the better. I often counted steps and racked my brain to remember the words to hopefully forgotten mindless pop songs, such as "Mellow Yellow" or anything by Tony Orlando and Dawn.

Mental tricks must have worked, for suddenly, the magical, serrated, awe-inspiring southern Picket Range jarred me from my gray daze. A chill ran down my spine. The climbs, the legends, the lore, the mighty Picket Range—the most remote, challenging, and ass-kicking alpine-breathing entity in the United States outside Alaska.

Famous hard-core climbers made history in the Pickets—climbers such as Beckey, Bertulis, Cooper, Degenhardt, Strandberg, and Firey. Intrepid explorers penetrated its depths and added color to the remote range's lore and mystique. Even Hermann Ulrichs didn't make it into the Pickets' heart. It sustained me and provided sustenance that made a bland dinner seem even more austere and tasteless. How can any dinner compete with the Pickets?

We bivouacked near a tarn adjacent to gray glacier-polished granodiorite slabs. Glaciers reign supreme in this land—if not now, then back in the glorious Pleistocene. Glaciers created or modified everything in sight. The Pleistocene's mighty ice rivers carved the deep Goodell Creek Valley that falls off beyond the tarn. As moving ice scours and plucks away softer rocks while carving valley into mountain flanks, it occasionally hits harder obstructions, such as granite. Being more resistant to erosion, granite, gneiss, schist, and other hard rocks remain firm against the glacier's onslaught. Instead of tearing them down or plucking them out, like a boulder in a mountain stream, ice simply flows around and polishes more resistant rocks. Eventually, glaciers leave in place glistening granitic towers and smooth, polished slabs.

The same glacier that polished the slabs next to my sleeping bag likely carved Mount Triumph's steep glacial headwalls, like the looming northeast face, nearby sharpened ridges, and northeast arête slicing into sky-blue perfection. From a distance, Mount Triumph had a near-perfect bell shape. It looked exactly like the mountain in the Paramount Pictures logo.

Thoughts of a fitful collision of rock and ice under the most brilliant starry skies imaginable kept me awake most of the night. Eventually, a weary body overcame my active mind, and I drifted off to sleep, although from my dreams, I never left.

As I learned on Mount Bad, the alpine climber races against time. Not only are climbs and approaches usually long, but time affects what climbers refer to as objective hazards. Objective hazards are those dangers the climber has little control over, such as avalanches, rockfalls, and storms. However, objective hazards don't lurk randomly around every corner, waiting to hurl themselves at unsuspecting climbers. There's some degree of predictiveness to these hazards that an experienced climber can use to their advantage by reading subtle signs and adjusting behavior accordingly. The smart climber then reduces risks and develops a higher degree of control over fate. This is a powerful tool that climbers hone only by experience.

A mistake many novice climbers make is being overconfident, wherein they put too much faith in their perceived control. No alpine climber is in control. Experience only increases your odds; it doesn't eliminate them. Life within this realm is still a toss of the laughing bones. Wise climbers are acutely aware of nature's humbling powers.

In our case, we knew time wasn't on our side. So we woke and broke camp in the predawn hours. An alpine start often begins at two or three o'clock in the morning. It was going to be a long day, so we wanted an extra cushion of time to deal with the unexpected. In addition, storms pelt mountains in the afternoon, so it's good to be well on the way back by then. We also planned to be high above the glacier before the morning sun melted any ice that was holding loose rocks in place. I didn't want a repeat of the Mount Bad epic.

Frozen firm, freeze-thaw, then rock avalanche volley—the endless erosional cycle carves into mountains. It's the alpine zone's daily ritual, with the resulting forces tearing the mountains apart, filling up the oceans, bending ice ax shafts, and sending climbers scurrying for cover. The alpine zone constantly reminds climbers that this is the mountain's domain—not a human's.

Ah, couloirs!

Ice-filled couloirs are the epitome of class, style, grace, and beauty. If heaven were a climb, it would be a snow- and ice-filled runnel slicing deep into an alpine mountain's northern flank, with surrounding, foreboding rock bastions keeping the climb in a perpetual twilight. In the stillness of dawn, crampons squeak with sound firmness.

I palmed my ice ax. It felt good. The ice ax's swing is in both mathematical and artistic cold precision and purity as it arcs across azure skies and ends with a thud aided by an outstretched arm and inward, warm beating heart. The ice ax and I fell into a poetic rhythm, in sync with pulsating beats and breath. Swing, swing, crampon, crampon, swing, swing, crampon, crampon—I effortlessly flowed upward as smooth as water and air flowed down. I sustained the yin and yang of nature's ebb and flow, taking unspoken clues raining down from the mountain's inner voices.

Granted, the mountain gods created couloirs as rivers of detritus in order to expunge and vomit unwanted material. Couloirs are also the home of rockfalls and avalanches. I guess you can't have one without the other. Small price to pay for a slice of heaven.

Glaciers are flowing rivers of ice. As flowing ice encounters the many twists, bends, and obstructions typically found in mountain valleys, instead of creating turbulence, as in a stream, the rigid glacier cracks and heaves. *Crevasse* is a fancy term for a large ice crack. Crevasses may be up to two hundred feet deep. Falling into a crevasse isn't advisable, should you ever have an inclination. Even if you survived the fall, you would likely encounter one of three scenarios: trapped, with no way to climb out until the cold saps your energy and you die; firmly wedged in a constriction until you die; or lastly, plunging into the icy meltwater of the glacier's innards, where the internal plumbing whisks you into the glacier's lower intestines—until you die. The common element in all scenarios is death. An experienced and prepared climber uses their rope and ice ax to increase their chances, but falling into a glacier unroped is not wise, welcomed, or encouraged. "Do not attempt this at home."

Unmelted winter snow often buries and hides crevasses in the spring and early summer. On the surface, snow may bridge the gap of a crevasse, making it appear as if it's solid below, despite the bridge being only a few inches thin. A person walking on a fragile snow bridge could easily plunge into the icy depths below.

To lessen the chances of falling into a crevasse, climbers cross glaciers in the early-morning hours, when the snow is colder, firm, and consolidated. Warmth from the sun weakens snow bridges and makes them less safe for both novice and uber climber alike. Wise mountaineers cross glaciers as early as possible.

In the crisp predawn hours on this snowy, wintry day, Derek and I were on the edge of the small glacier on the western margin of the North Cascades. We strapped crampons onto boots in anticipation of crossing the glacier. Crampons are rigid frames containing sharp spikes. Once the crampon is strapped on the boot, the majority of its spikes point straight down, with two or so pointing forward. The sharp spikes enable spuds to climb steep and even overhanging ice, make glacier crossings a breeze, and allow inattentive spuds to aerate their calves and decorate the ice with red Jackson Pollock splatters.

At the glacier's edge, we also re-bonded with sacred ice axes. On lower-angled snow, climbers don't use the ax for ascent. They use it as a backup safety device in case the climber falls or slips. As a spud begins to slide, the other climbers jam their axes into the snow, with the addition of a rope, to bring the spud to a full stop. Climbers call this a self-arrest. They must learn various methods of self-arrest in case the fall is headfirst, feetfirst, back first, or stomach first.

Besides arresting their own slips, experienced climbers use an ice ax to stop their partner's fall. Climbers protect themselves while crossing glaciers, in climber's parlance, by roping up. Without the ability to belay and self-arrest, roping up is highly dangerous because if someone were to fall into a crevasse, then everyone tied into the same rope would also fall in. This is what caused the Edward Whymper party's epic 1865 Matterhorn tragedy. However, if properly trained and equipped, a climber's self-arrest stops the fall of anyone else tied into the same rope. Therefore, if any climber were to break through a snow bridge, any other member of the rope party can safely stop the fall and not share the same fate as Edward Whymper.

With our crampons on our feet and ice axes firmly planted in hands, Derek and I roped up and gingerly began the traverse across the glacier that precariously hung on Mount Triumph's glacier-polished slabs. Mount Triumph's bluish shadow fell upon the southern Picket Range's jagged silhouette, which loomed across the intervening valley's dark nothingness. As we continued across the icy moon canvas, Mount Triumph's looming and horrendously steep east face suddenly appeared crowding and oppressive. The somber recess below the overhanging face was far too chasmy for even moonlight to penetrate.

While contemplating big-scale marvels and colossal mountains, I began noticing tiny wonders of nature. Mysterious worlds exist in a plethora of scales—most beyond our typical notice. Within the range of our headlamps, there were thousands of ice worms crawling on the glacier's surface. Ice worms live in glaciers and permanent snowfields in Washington and British Columbia. They're nondescript one-inch-long worms that spend their entire lives within ice. Not the tequila variety, but actual native worms that evolved to occupy this highly specific niche. With the right atmospheric conditions, ice worms rise to the surface en masse. This day was apparently a good time for both ice worms and climbers, since the specific alpine conditions brought us both together in this same place and time.

Despite the summit being a long way off, it still beckoned. We left the ice worm world behind. Apparently, the worms didn't feel the same pull. Wormless, we gingerly crossed a delicate snow bridge over the bergschrund leading to the jutting rampart that marked the beginning of the northeast ridge.

From this point forward, we expected a typical alpine rock climb, so we'd brought typical rock-climbing gear: rope, harness, slings, carabiners, and climbing protection known as chocks. Instead, we found snow, ice, and iced-up rock—places where typical rock-climbing hardware is useless.

Hermann Ulrichs preferred climbing unroped over dealing with ropes, belaying equipment, and other weighty impediments. This purity-of-motion ethic stopped him from attaining some summits. Derek and I didn't want to squander our opportunity to reach the summit, so we used the rope. One of the most rewarding and beautiful aspects of alpine climbs is when the roped team develops a smooth, fast, graceful, and rhythmic leapfrogging of rope lengths, or pitches. When each pitch progresses smoothly in an elegant fashion, it demonstrates that a team can be more than the sum of its individual parts. A good climbing team develops a strong bond and rapport. In addition, they can often sense what the other is thinking without the need for spoken words. Sadly, Hermann Ulrichs never had the privilege of being part of such a climbing team. On our Mount Triumph climb, Derek and I came close.

Once we crossed the glacier, we expected to stow our crampons and ice axes away and don rock-climbing gear. However, it was still too early in the year, and the snow and ice on the northeast ridge hadn't melted yet. Instead of climbing enjoyable sun-warmed rock up the sharp rock ridge slicing glacial ice on either side, we met one of the hardest climbing conditions alpine climbers encounter.

Iced-up rock is especially difficult, since you don't have solid holds common on rock. Also, the ice isn't deep enough to sink an ice ax into. Therefore, nothing works well, and climbers have to resort to dangerous climbing on glazed-over rock. In these situations, the metal spikes on the crampons generate sparks as they slip and slide off glacier-polished ice-free slabs.

Under such hideous conditions, where there isn't iced-up rock, there are deep, loose, powdery snowdrifts. When snow gets too dry and fluffy, it provides no solid purchase for the ice ax or footing for a boot. To climb higher, we trenched and wallowed through two-to-three-foot layers of loose snow to locate any secure ice or rock below. It was a blind search for meager rewards. Derek and I both knew, without saying a word, that neither of us could afford to fall. If either one of us were to fall, we would share the same fate as Edward Whymper's party on the Matterhorn. I had to force away thoughts that Mount Triumph looks remarkably like a small Matterhorn.

I love ridge and arête climbs. Ridges are safer from objective hazards. There are few things as nerve-wracking as the whir of unseen rock projectiles traveling at maximum speed over and around your head when you're in a confining couloir. But more than safety, a mountain's spine has natural elegance. Sharp ridges offer commanding and airy scenery. On ridges, air and views drop off on either side, leaving you alone at heaven's throne. On the rare day of sunshine, the rope between in-sync partners leads further into nirvana. On either side lie white, glistening rivers of ice that freeze the moment in time and space. It's in these moments that climbing, art, ballet, poetry, and spirituality morph into one.

The strong, biting wind indicated we were nearing the summit. From the summit's small rock jumble, we saw the earth's curvature and dozens of peaks, spreading from British Columbia to Washington. I sat on the summit with sublime contentment, staring toward Mount Slesse, Mount Despair, the Picket Range, and the blanket of dark-gray fog engulfing and confining the lowland valleys. The thick lowland fog made the peaks appear to float in space.

Far to the west, somewhere deep within the featureless fog plain, lay the Puget Sound metropolis. I tried to imagine people holed up in their Seattle cocoons, looking out windows at, from their perspective, miserable weather. How different perspective alters one's viewpoint—literarily and figuratively.

I've never been one to whoop and holler upon reaching a summit. To me, this is brash and disrespectful. If I did, I would expect the mountain to strike me down for being rude and insolent. The more important or meaningful the climb, the quieter and more reflective I become. I've never felt as peaceful or filled with a sense of purpose as I do while standing on alpine summits.

I've always wondered if the magic can last. Will there be a day when I gaze from lofty heights only to feel lonely and view the adventure as mere work? Will I wonder, *Why bother?* I hope not, but in case this does happen, I want to savor every summit moment. Sublime alpine moments highlight the deep connections and shared moments offered by alpine grandeur.

Our typical descent meant we had only a few mishaps and miniature epics. We descended the ridge, crossed the glacier, and, as the sun began to set, quickly shot past the site of our previous night's bivouac. We spent an unplanned night on slabs so we could hike out safely the next day.

Alpenglow lit the mountain slope in various shades of yellow and orange that truly looked like a phosphorescent glow. Tired but content, I quickly fell asleep, encased in my bivouac sack and memories yet to be.

I awoke to the typical Pacific Northwest gray and overcast morning, but it didn't matter. We'd summited, and we were on the way out. What a glorious way to spend a birthday! I'd turned twenty-one. However, I had no time to dawdle or celebrate. We loaded our gear and headed downhill. We made good time, especially after we hooked up with the trail. Our fast descent lasted until we lost the trail and our route was slowed by thick, tangly brush. We didn't experience the typically horrendous North Cascades brush, but it became thick and penetrating, nonetheless.

The North Cascades and the coast ranges of British Columbia and southeast Alaska are notorious for their nearly impenetrable brush. The tangle of bushes, vines, and small tree shoots forms a barrier that a climber often must climb over, under, or through. Going through means you must push the brush aside to part the individual entangled strands enough to squeeze through. The main problem is your pack, ice axes, crampons, and other climbing paraphernalia constantly get hung up in the brush. In these situations, trying to free tangles on the blind side of your backpack is infuriating and nearly futile. Sometimes, it works best to hurl yourself pack first against the wall of brush, hoping that, when you crash, your total mass and inertia will be enough to make forward progress against the defending brush wall. A refined technique it isn't.

Climbing over brush is extremely tiring, for every other step, a foot plunges through a gap or weak spot in the brush, and you usually end up upside down with your head in a pool of mud. Trying to get up takes all your remaining energy, since, with a heavy pack strapped on your back, you're like a turtle turned on its shell and struggling to right itself.

In heavy brush, I resort to crawling on hands and knees under it only when I'm too weary to care about dignity. However, brush is usually too thick to let you see anyone else, even when inches away.

Derek and I stayed together through the brush by following each other's cries, curses, grunts, groans, and whimpers. The worst part of brush in the North Cascades is the notorious devil's club. The Latin name, *horridus*, says it all. It's quite a lovely plant, but its distinctiveness comes from its half-inch-long needle-sharp spines that profusely decorate the stems. I break my vow not to holler and scream in the mountains when accidently grabbing a devil's club.

Fortunately, we grabbed no devil's club, and we managed to find the trail with only a couple of lost hours. No sooner than finding the trail we came upon a backcountry ranger hiking up. I recognized him.

I'd met Saul the previous year. He had a dream job as a backcountry ranger in North Cascades National Park. I asked him what he was doing there.

Saul replied, "Coming to rescue you."

Typically, park rangers don't send out search parties for people who are only a day late. But apparently, my father became worried and called the park. Being a service agency, the park dispatched a search party of one after receiving the call from a concerned family member. I apologized to Saul because we didn't need rescuing.

He said, "That's alright. It's training week for the new rangers." He was glad to get out of the office.

On the way back to the trailhead, Saul strode along with us, talking of climbs and the North Cascades. He mentioned that climbers had recently completed the first ascent of Mount Triumph's overhanging east face—the ominous and shadowed wall we'd traversed under on the way to the northeast ridge.

I felt outclassed. Who would have thought climbers could have enough training, skill, talent, equipment, and boldness to ascend something as terrorizingly overhanging as the east face? Well, I knew it was a common practice on sun-warmed rock in Yosemite. But there, on a cold, wet, and icy alpine wall?

Climbing has become much more technically advanced since Hermann Ulrichs's day. Since my day also, for that matter. Apparently, these climbers had to resort to aid-climbing and sleeping in Yosemite Valley-style portaledges, which is much like sleeping in a hammock strung to a few pieces of protection or small metal pieces wedged in the rock. To each their own. Everyone has their own preferred style and type of climbing.

After returning to Seattle, I had no time to plan my next adventure because I needed to head off to the desert Southwest to start my new summer job. Career aspirations impeded my climbing ambitions. For much of my life, this quandary tugged me in all directions—other than up. I was too career-minded to become a climbing bum, but my climbing addiction was far too advanced to let a career take me over completely.

This pull is the downfall of many climbers. With the need to settle down, have a degree of financial security, be socially acceptable, and ease into middle age—and the eventual resulting fitness decay—most climbers either retire from harder climbs or fade into mediocrity. As a backcountry ranger, Saul attempted to have it both ways—a life in the mountains *and* a career.

Career thoughts continued to weigh on me well beyond our stroll down from Mount Triumph. Three years after Saul's rescue, he helped establish the North Cascades Institute, a nonprofit organization dedicated to environmental education and the North Cascades ecosystem. A few climbers are persistent enough to continue with first ascents and climbing at high levels, while others, such as Saul, use their energies to benefit the wider society.

What about me? I mused. *I have good ideas too! Couldn't I use my abundant and restless energy for something as lasting and meaningful as an environmental institute? I haven't made many first ascents or climbed at a high level. Apparently, I'm no Lowell Skoog or Saul Weisberg. Shouldn't I use my energy, motivation, and enthusiasm for something useful? Am I perpetually confined to following the footsteps of others and wallowing in the deep snows of mediocrity? Have I fallen into a couloir that leads in only two dimensions and affords limited views and perspectives?*

It takes a special breed to step into the unknown, whether summit, career, or life's many choices. I may never have fully resolved all life, caving, and climbing internal conflicts, but no one gets to the summit in one leap. It takes a continual series of steps, complete with missteps and mini-Triumphs along the way.

Toward the Sun
and Beyond

A warm, fuchsia-filled, sunny day will surely guarantee climbers will be out in droves on Devils Tower, the strikingly bold monstrosity that juts over twelve hundred feet above the winding Belle Fourche River. It was even more crowded after Mateo Pee Pee and Barney invited me on one of their challenging climbs on the Tower's west face—the side that dominates the view from the park's visitor center and the telescopes specifically mounted to provide gawking visitors a close-up view of climbers' antics. Whether in Eldorado Canyon or Devils Tower, I've never liked being under the microscope, but this didn't deter me from accepting the chance to climb such a classic-looking side of the Tower.

Mateo Pee Pee, the strongest of the three of us, naturally took the lead. The first pitch ran up to a series of expansion bolts and a hanging belay. A hanging belay means there's no ledge to stand on. I intended to belay Mateo Pee Pee on the second pitch by hanging my entire weight from the bolts drilled into the rock. My useless feet hung limp below. Somewhere farther below, Barney drifted between bouts of listlessness and napping. Despite it being a short pitch, it served to better set up a proper belay at the hardest part of the climb—the long and much harder second pitch.

While the visitor center's telescopes got a good view of our climbing party, I, from the confines of the hanging belay bolts directly below Mateo Pee Pee, received a close-up view of his brand-new floral-patterned lavender-and-fuchsia Lycra tights, which he, for some reason, proudly displayed for all to see.

The floral-pattered lavender-and-fuchsia spectacle made easy work of the first fifty feet from the hanging belay despite it being vertical and having very few substantive holds. However, something at fifty feet out caused the Lycra-tighted climbing master to hesitate. It must have gotten much harder. Dan's hesitation in the Henrys didn't turn out well. I hoped the same dynamic wasn't at play on Devils Tower's west face. With multiple attempts to overcome whatever obstacle it was, Mateo Pee Pee retreated each time to the same minute holds.

How has he kept hanging on? I wondered. *Does he not tire?* However, I'd learned not to doubt the Master Pee Pee.

While still clinging to who-knows-what, he called out, "Dave, will you—"

Without warning, he became airborne, but my attentive belay kept his fall to the minimum. As soon as he impacted the rock, he shouted an excited utterance that I shall not repeat here. Fearing serious injuries, while still holding him by the rope in my firm grip, I shouted, "Are you okay?"

"No, goddamn it."

Again, I repeated, "Are you hurt? What's the matter?"

"I ripped my goddamn new Lycra tights."

My unsympathetic response didn't endear me to Mateo Pee Pee, since it betrayed the fact that I didn't cherish his hideous lavender-and-fuchsia floral Lycra tights spectacle as much as he apparently had. But unbeknownst to both of us, his devotion to his hideous tights would soon save his life.

Mateo Pee Pee's anger over his ripped tights had put him in a mental state not conducive to any more leading that day. I hadn't known Mateo to retreat before—or since. He asked me to lower him to the hanging belay. He'd had it for the day.

As soon as we were back on solid ground, next to the now wide-awake Barney, I looked up to where we'd been just moments before. At that instance, a bolt of lightning came out of nowhere and blasted the Tower at exactly the spot where Mateo Pee Pee had struggled and fallen just moments before. The lightning blasted a shallow hole in the rock, sending sharp rock fragments to the three of us. I ducked from the worst of the volley but got clipped on the chin and hand. Barney and Mateo also escaped with only minor cuts and mere flesh wounds. If Mateo hadn't ripped his tights and asked to retreat, 300 million volts and thirty thousand amps would have passed from his strike point and out his fingertips to the negatively charged rock surface. I, being tied to the rock directly below the strike zone, would not have fared much better.

Shaken, but with only minor cuts and scrapes, we retreated to Barney and Mateo Pee Pee's shared apartment next to the visitor center. We had a beer and relaxed our taught nerves. A few minutes later, I drove the one mile to the Devils Tower Junction store, located right outside the monument's boundary.

While I was enjoying my quickly melting ice cream, Sarah, an off-duty ranger friend, ran up to me, frantically yelling, "You're alive!"

Calmly, I replied, "Am I not supposed to be?"

Less calmly, she responded, "Who died? Barney?"

"What are you talking about?" I asked. "What's the matter with you?"

"Through the telescope, a park visitor saw lightning strike us and thought they saw at least one body fall. We looked at the sign-out register and saw your names. The witness's description fit Barney. Is he alright?"

Apparently, while scanning the Tower from one of the telescopes, a park visitor spotted the lighting strike and saw the whole thing. According to the witness, this bizarre incident originated from one cloud, the only cloud. This small, puffy white cloud high above the Tower off the eastern side wouldn't have been visible to any west-face climber. The visitor saw a lightning bolt leave the cloud. But instead of making a direct hit, it circled around the Tower to eventually strike on the opposite side. In hindsight, it seems improbable that the lightning bolt would, by chance, circle halfway around the Tower only to land right where Mateo Pee Pee had ripped his Lycra tights. Could Mateo Pee Pee's wrath have conjured the lightning to punish the offending rock for ripping his tights? Or were the Tower spirits so offended by his culturally insensitive lavender-and-fuchsia Lycra tights that they tried to smite poor Pee Pee? If so, that's some serious juju. Regardless, unless purely coincidental, it seems logical that this one-in-a-million strike would have been purposefully seeking the offending floral tights.

Sarah, Barney, Mateo Pee Pee, and I were grateful that no one fell and no one died—at least not this day. The falling body must have been a rock or an illusion. Sarah used the radio to call off the rescue and body recovery. Some of the visitors looked disappointed that no entertaining body recovery had followed.

୧ৡৡ

It may have been an epiphany that brought me to Wyoming's Black Hills. Epiphanies have a way of recharting and resetting a person's trajectory, whether they know it or not.

The film *Close Encounters of the Third Kind* and I shared the same trajectory, at least in timing. Filming began the same year I began climbing. Dramatic Devils Tower images flickered across the silver screen and splattered boldly into my visual sphere at precisely the perfect time to imprint on a young tater tot's impressionable mind.

However, it might have been that once I became a climber, the Tower's striking profile drew me in to climb the beautiful, scale the superlative, and check off a classic. Regardless of the source, like a fire that takes to a grass expanse, something drew me to Devils Tower. I salivated over climbing its steep columns and looking out upon the prairie from its lofty gray-hummocked promontory.

Poor Seattle climbers living on a seasonal salary and with college expenses can't afford to travel to far-off Devils Tower. It might as well have been in a different galaxy. That left only dreaming, studying photographs, and reading the expanding exploits of others. However, that didn't stop me from applying for a seasonal job in the nation's first national monument.

In 1986, I packed my wee Ford Fiesta and pointed her toward first contact. I had but two thoughts: it would be a good career move, and I could climb every day in the Tower's summer playground. Beyond those data inputs and what I learned through the movie, I knew little of the Tower, despite it having captivated souls ranging from the Lakota, Theodore Roosevelt, park visitors, and technical climbing master Todd Skinner—and if we can believe Hollywood, an occasional wayward alien.

The other two climbing rangers that summer, Mateo Pee Pee and Barney, also came to climb. Yes, it was a good job, but we were there to climb—not only on weekends but after work, before work, during lunch breaks, whenever. We climbed as often as we wanted, as we had a premier climbing playground literally right out our front doors.

When Mateo Pee Pee and Barney were off climbing things beyond my abilities, I sought out other partners for less ambitious ascents. The campground provided a reliable place for climbers to congregate, swap stories, and brag. However, my climbing colleagues in the campground didn't share my sense of community. As the park's lead law enforcement ranger, this meant that instead of climbing hardware, such as chocks and ropes, I carried a revolver, handcuffs, mace, and a police baton. I enforced laws. This created, or at least implied, a cultural barrier and noncompatible perceptions and worldviews. Climbing bums attempting to scam free camping don't often emit warm, friendly feelings toward law enforcement rangers.

When I approached climbers lawfully just hanging out in their campsite, they commonly replied, "We'll be leaving soon."

In which case, I would usually say, "Why would you? This is your site, isn't it?"

"Sure, but I thought you were coming to chase us off."

"I hate to break it to you, but I don't get up in the morning wondering whose rights and privileges I'll assault today, which heads I'll crack, or whom I'll torment." I often capped off my pontifications with, "Perhaps I was just coming by to say hello and see how your climb went earlier in the day. Was that you I saw climbing the overhanging Billie Bear Cranks the Rad?"

"Oh wow. No way, man," the climber would often say before pausing as if trying to wrap their head around the incongruent logical nuances inherent in multidimensional quantum theory. "I never met a ranger who wasn't here just to run us off. Wow, I'm not sure how to respond."

"You could start by saying hello."

֍

One key takeaway I learned from years of working on contentious public resource issues is that communication across the aisle has less to do with facts, figures, and data than it has with perspective and worldview. If it would be in the best economic interest for a coal miner to shut down a coal mine and transition into a non-mining livelihood, there would be both resistance and trust issues. Until the root of their resistance and distrust is resolved, from their perspective and their reality, pushing facts and figures will likely elicit only strong emotional responses and their digging even deeper into their entrenched opinion. I bring this up in relation to Devils Tower because the sheer striking presence of Devils Tower brings together people with wildly different perspectives and worldviews—some quite alien. This, in turn, develops wide-ranging trust issues and can serve as a good example of what not to do.

It's little wonder that the aliens in Steven Spielberg's movie *Close Encounters of the Third Kind* chose Devils Tower for first contact, since, for a long time, the Tower had been a point of cultural convergence. Vortexes have a way of drawing in people from all quarters, complete with diverse purposes and final destinations. Devils Tower is no exception.

Before arriving at Devils Tower, I hadn't given much thought to other Devils Tower viewpoints and perspectives. Clearly, it's a visually striking volcanic remnant that Theodore Roosevelt believed worthy of protection (based on his emotional connection with the Tower from his ranching days in North Dakota's Badlands). And clearly, the

Tower contains outstanding rock-climbing opportunities. That was the depth of my knowledge and awareness of the Tower's significance at the time.

When I was a child, weekly television series and Hollywood movies provided my primary exposure to Native American cultures. We called them Indians in those days. I'd seen *Jeremiah Johnson, F Troop, A Man Called Horse, Little Big Man*, and every John Wayne and Clint Eastwood western. I was a devoted follower of the Cartwright clan on their Ponderosa ranch. TV shows, even *F Troop*, weren't exactly an accurate depiction of Native Americans to help me form a proper frame of reference and worldview. But, nonetheless, that was my neighborhood.

While I was working on the Navajo Reservation at Canyon de Chelly National Monument and then on the sacred lands of the Lakota at Devils Tower, it slowly began to sink in that there can be multiple forms of relationships with the same piece of real estate—and not all compatible with each other. Our universe isn't black and white. It's an expanding and ever-changing universal arc of gray—especially on the piece of real estate that many people now call Devils Tower.

In the spring of my Devils Tower season, at the convergence of the Great Plains and the foothills of the Black Hills in Wyoming's isolated northeast corner, the Lakota were openly talking about their sacred sun dance ceremony. This was a chance and fleeting encounter, since our trails intersected only at that very moment. I ended up being a minor observing party to the Lakota's first sun dance ceremony held in several generations on their sacred Devils Tower real estate.

Upon first sight, it's hard for observers not to feel awe at the dramatic thumb sticking out from the flat Dakota prairies. The Tower's steep columns and gashes boldly contrast with the surroundings. Geologically, it's the central core of an ancient volcanic vent. The surrounding rolling mixed prairies and forests are the Black Hills' western outlier. The Tower has an immense physical presence on the skyline throughout this corner of the prairie. I can easily imagine why this imposing landmark would be so significant to so many cultural traditions.

As many as twenty tribes, not just the Lakota, hold Devils Tower sacred. They include the Arapahoe, Northern Cheyenne, Crow, Kiowa, and Eastern Shoshone. With such diverse cultural interests and histories, there's likely a wide variety of perceived Tower personalities. Native cultures know Devils Tower by many names, including Grey Buffalo Horn and Bear Lodge. None of these names conjure images of the Devil. This inaccurate association with the Devil is insulting to Native Plains peoples, since they hold Bear Lodge, not the Devil, sacred. One of the Native cultures' most sacred forms of worship, far removed from Devil imagery, is their traditional sun dance ceremony.

The Lakota held sun dances at the sacred Bear Lodge for countless generations. After the US government moved the Lakota to the Pine Ridge Reservation, the government enacted strict laws intended to break traditional tribal customs, including the sun dance. After the Tower became a national monument, the government forbade sun dances at Devils Tower. The Lakota's last legal traditional sun dance was held in 1881. It had been even longer since they last held it in the shadow of the Tower.

The government's ban and suppression of native cultural practices continued for generations and had many long-lasting consequences—including worsening many of the tribe's biggest challenges. The federal government had taken a nomadic hunting tribe, forced them onto parched land, and demanded that they farm. If the government had found the lands suitable for farming, they wouldn't have designated it an Indian reservation. The government also forbade the tribe to use their own social structure. Instead, it set up a controlling system in which the tribe became dependent on the federal government for everything. As a part of this forced assimilation, the government forbade traditional cultural practices. Considering the many bans and restrictions, elder tribal members had a challenging time keeping their cultural heritage alive and exposing younger generations to their history and way of life. Without this continuity, elders feared for the future of their rich culture.

Over the years, the US government and the National Park Service, which manages Devils Tower National Monument, slowly softened their ban on traditional cultural practices. Consequently, the Lakota officially petitioned the government to use Devils Tower for a sun dance. The National Park Service agreed.

I worked at Devils Tower National Monument in 1986. Summer-hired rangers had no say or involvement in any of the major decisions. I only assisted with logistics and served as an interested observer. The only instruction we spuds received from park managers was that the Lakota were granted permission to hold their sun dance, and the National Park Service wanted the event to proceed without incident—zero. I took this instruction to mean not only wanting no incident from the Lakota but also wanting no problem or complication from the National Park Service. This spud picked up the message, and this spud understood. I also understood the agency wanted the ceremony to go smoothly as a small gesture to past mistreatment. But perhaps, most of all, the agency didn't want bad public relations.

The park manager's tenseness became even more acute when rumors swirled that Russell Means, Dennis Banks, and other members of the American Indian Movement (AIM) planned to stage a demonstration.

The agency feared AIM might use the event to protest or even perform an armed takeover not unlike the Wounded Knee incident that occurred only thirteen years previously.

In 1973, AIM members, including the Lakota Russell Means and the Minnesota-born Ojibwe Dennis Banks, took over the town of Wounded Knee, South Dakota, in protest. Demonstrators intended to shed light on the tribal chairman's nepotism and corruption, as well as the hiring of a private militia as muscle to enact a brutal crackdown on the chairman's detractors and opponents. AIM's siege lasted seventy-one days and resulted in at least two deaths and several injuries. The National Park Service feared another such tense, dangerous, and bad publicity event occurring at their quiet and peaceful Devils Tower. Nothing ever happened at Devils Tower National Monument, and the National Park Service was fully determined to keep it that way.

The prairie dogs were at full attention and chirping excitedly as approximately twenty Lakota arrived at Devils Tower to begin their preparations for the sun dance. I was one of a handful of park staff who met them and discussed logistics. My eyes naturally gravitated to Russell Means, whom my supervisor had pointed out to me beforehand. With a sigh of relief, my supervisor whispered that Dennis Banks never showed up.

Perhaps this sun dance will be an actual dance and ceremony after all, I thought, *and not a tense political act of defiance. Maybe Devils Tower won't be a replay of Wounded Knee.* Nonetheless, I remained as silent and nonintrusive as I could. I listened intently so I might not unintentionally spud things up. Being silent and not burdened with the responsibilities of management afforded me the freedom just to watch the personal dynamics of conversations, behaviors, and antics—whichever way they might play out.

By actively listening, I could see that the Lakota were clearly waiting for someone who'd not yet arrived. There were several smaller groups engaged in nervous small talk. The most nervous appeared to be the National Park Service contingent. While we waited, the larger group had no real center. Russell Means led one conversation. I believed people in his group were members of AIM, since park managers looked worried. The AIM members were full of nervous energy, as if they were poised for something to happen. But overall, few seemed to be waiting well.

Eventually, the invited speaker arrived. She walked slowly up to the group. As soon as people saw who was approaching, an immediate reverent silence fell upon the crowd. She floated through the center of the group, not by maneuvering around the randomly placed people but as if the hands of God had parted the group like the Red Sea. Half the crowd flowed in one direction, and the other half sliced off in an almost scripted, synchronized fashion. All eyes were on her, and they were alert and attentive. I understood, without doubt—in an unspoken truth—that she held power, influence, and a respect that starkly contrasted with her youth and diminutive physical stature.

Despite the wind, her lack of projection, and her nearly inaudible volume, the crowd heard every word she spoke. No other sound came to our ears, not even casual rustling of clothing. No other person talked, whispered, coughed, or moved. Even the wind seemed to silence itself.

She didn't speak long. Softly, she said the only purpose for gathering was to hold their sacred sun dance at their sacred tower. With slightly piercing eyes, she gazed at the AIMS contingent. She said she didn't want their sacred sun dance co-opted as a vehicle for political or social demonstration. She didn't want to jeopardize the tribe's use of the

Tower for future sun dances. In addition, she clearly stated this was a particularly politically sensitive time with their Black Hills land-claim lawsuit. The Lakota had waited far too long for a legal victory, and she didn't want it jeopardized by rash or restless hotheads. She again glanced at the AIMS contingent. I saw Russell Means silently nod. When she left, the crowd parted once more, providing her a free and respectful corridor, only to fill in behind her and reconverge upon her silent passing.

When I first began recalling these events, I couldn't remember the name of the mesmerizing Lakota speaker or her official title. I recalled her being soft-spoken and a frail wisp of a woman. I can't recall her age, for my memory fails me on this detail. I believe my image of her as frail and wispy wasn't based on her advanced age but instead on her slight frame and almost inaudibly soft voice. I assumed she must have been the tribal leader, but modern-day googling indicated that the first woman tribal leader wasn't until years later. Her influence must have been cultural or spiritual rather than from holding any formal office.

An Internet search eventually jogged my memory, surfacing the identity of this larger-than-life presence: Charlotte Black Elk, the great-granddaughter of the famous Lakota medicine and holy man Black Elk, who was cousin to Crazy Horse. At the time, Charlotte Black Elk served as the tribal council secretary. But even more than that, she was the driving force behind the modern Lakota's efforts to resolve their monumental legal land dispute with the US government.

Even now, the Black Hills lawsuit and land dispute remain unresolved. The Fort Laramie Treaty of 1868 granted the entire Black Hills region to the Lakota people, with a guarantee that white settlers wouldn't build or reside on Lakota land. However, six years later, General George Custer (yes, *that* General Custer) announced the discovery of gold in the Black Hills and changed things forever. Gold seekers, politicians, and government leaders weren't going to let something like a legally binding treaty stand in the way of riches and greed. The non-Lakota violated the treaty—and dramatically so.

Generations later, the Lakota took the US government to court. The 1980 court decision held that the government had violated the treaty; however, the court believed evacuating all the non-Lakota towns, communities, and individuals would be impractical. Instead, the court ordered the US government to compensate the tribe financially.

The tribe tried to have the feds take the money back, since they wanted the Black Hills, not hush or appeasement money. The Lakota refused to access the funds sitting in the escrow account. At the time of the sun dance, Congress was considering the tribe's petition to resolve their Black Hills claim. Charlotte Black Elk didn't want to lose the political headway the tribe had been making to get the Black Hills back. She clearly made her point.

Since both the Lakota and the National Park Service wanted the event to go smoothly, what could go wrong? Enter my supervisor—likable and well-intentioned, but even by 1986 standards, not culturally sensitive. His instructions to me were to avoid going anywhere near the Lakota encampment during the duration of their stay. His reasoning: "Injuns are always up to no good. So if you go close to them Injuns, you'll end up seeing what they're doing, and we'll have to respond. So, it's best if we don't know what the no-good things that them Injuns are doing."

I cringed at things he later said directly to the Lakota—things I'm sure offended. The tribal representative appeared to take his unintended slights in stride. I suspect they were used to it. However, they increasingly presented more of their daily logistical requests directly to me. Perhaps this is why one of the organizers invited me, as the only non-Lakota, to their sacred sun dance ceremony.

I felt deeply honored. Perhaps my naïve childhood fantasy of acceptance into the Native American fold, just like in the movies, would finally come true. I knew enough to know that the Lakota's invitation was just a casual invite. I also knew enough to know my park duties would conflict with watching the entire ceremony, even if that was what that kind person offered. Nonetheless, I took him up on the invitation. I would have been crazy not to.

On duty and in full uniform, I traveled to the sun dance, complete with my freshly oiled Model 66 stainless steel .357 Magnum revolver, PR24 side-handle police baton, chrome handcuffs, extra rounds of ammunition in two quick-drop leather pouches, pepper spray canisters, wide-brimmed Stetson uniform hat, shiny badge, and two-way Motorola radio holstered in a leather pouch firmly attached to my polished cordovan duty belt. I parked the police cruiser—equipped with its law enforcement light bar, sirens, external speakers, and spotlight—well out of sight of the ceremony, which was already in progress. And to remain unnoticed, I quietly approached from the rear.

As I approached the ceremony, the entire crowd was kneeling in a silent circle with all heads bowed. I stood approximately one hundred feet away—a respectable distance for an invited interloper. They appeared to be praying. The silence broke as one person began softly saying something. I couldn't tell if it was speech, song, chant, or prayer, but the mood was clearly serious and reverent. Except for the soft mumblings of the one, the entire scene was tranquil and serene.

Suddenly, at the height of silence, my previously quiet radio blurted a megaphone-level reveille. Through the cackling Motorola, my anxious and exasperated supervisor shouted, "You are *not* with them Injuns, are you? They're always up to no good! I told you ..."

My frantic lurching for the off button took an eternity. I imagined that the sharp soundwaves were reverberating off Mount Rushmore and Crazy Horse monuments on the other side of the Black Hills at that very moment. From the corners of my flushed eyes, I saw that the entire sun dance had stopped and every head was turned toward me to see what the ceremony-killing ruckus was that had so offended their long-awaited sacredness.

I held my head down to avoid seeing their contempt as I silently slunk off in shame.

The following day, before the ceremony's next phase, I located the person who'd invited me. I mustered the courage for a heartfelt, though mumbled, apology. He'd heard the interruption, but until I apologized, he hadn't known what or who had caused the commotion. He was polite enough about it, but I sensed I would receive no further invitations to the remaining ceremony. Even if he'd extended an offer, I knew better than to show my face or radio again.

That was the extent of my exposure to the Lakota sun dance ceremony.

Only later did I begin to grasp the deeper meaning and significance of the sun dance and the role that Bear Lodge plays. More than a mere climber's playland, the Tower is part of a spiritual journey for the Lakota, beginning at Hinhan Kaga Paha (the Black Hill's Harney Peak) at the spring equinox. From what this ignorant non-Lakota can tell, this spiritual journey continues in procession through the center of the Black Hills, to end at the summer solstice under their sacred Bear Lodge. Only if the individual's spiritual journey is complete does Bear Lodge transition into Grey Buffalo Horn and that person pass into the next higher plane of spiritual existence. Without successfully going through this entire process, a person's journey remains incomplete.

I didn't know anything about this during my seasonal Devils Tower experience in 1986. However, I had a basic sense that they viewed the Tower in deeply spiritual ways that I couldn't comprehend. This piqued my curiosity. I'd never met a people who held such a strong and deeply spiritual connection with the land. The Lakota's land ethic and worldview were at odds with our notion that land is strictly an asset and commodity we can simply buy, sell, dispose of, transfer, or, in the case of the Black Hills, take. However, the Lakota's traditional land ethic and spiritual relationship with the land conflicts with climbers' needs and desires to trod on land that others hold as sacred. From that perspective, I can see that non-Lakota people drilling bolt holes in the Tower, excavating dirt and flowers that may be in the way of climbing protection, and trespassing across its sacred surface with glaringly bold lavender-and-fuchsia floral Lycra tights is an affront to their sacred Tower. While I can't imagine we should outright ban any further climbing and recreational use of the Tower, in the complex world of land management, we can no longer afford to hold such a singular vision of parklands—and its people.

After the sun dance ended and the Lakota went to their modern homes, I strolled across the ceremonial grounds and throughout the Devils Tower landscape, looking for a means to connect and understand. I found only softly crushed prairie grasses in the fields off the Joyner Ridge Trail, with the Tower still silently looming above and casting its greenish-gray shadow onto the undulating lonely expanse of prairie. I felt there had to be some tangible connection, since the tribe and I had momentarily shared the same space and time. I'd always felt I had a deep connection with land, and certain places can prompt my mind to conjure its own spiritual wanderings, however poorly formed. But these prior experiences were insufficient to prepare me for my present journey. I grew to understand there may be some trails that simply can't be taken by others, and there's no way around harsh realities.

Still remaining at the foot of Devils Tower at the site of the recent sun dance, I gazed across the prairie expanse. I knew something historic and profound had transpired, something more than the mere expanding of the worldview of a naïve suburban trail wanderer. I also felt things would likely never be the same on this patch of sacred prairie, as if the stark gray thumb jutting into the sky, which I'd never failed to notice before, suddenly appeared to me in a different light.

Years later, as I write this, I'm uneasy with the awareness of how much time has passed since this sun dance and my reflective ponderings. With a critical eye that only time can clarify, I wonder if there has been much progress in any journey. For the individual Lakota, only the practitioners and their spiritual advisors can know. However, for their broader societal journeys, my backward assessment doesn't provide me encouragement. It's true, the federal government gave the Lakota permission to hold additional sun dances, but many tribal members would likely claim they can't have progress as a supposedly sovereign nation if they must seek permission to hold or observe traditional ceremonies.

The Lakota have other struggles and challenges as well. Lakota and their Dakota relatives on another nearby reservation had not long ago spent a considerable amount of time fighting the construction of a long-distance regional transmission natural gas pipeline immediately adjacent to their reservation. They felt the pipeline would impact the tribe's only water supply. The developers claimed it wouldn't harm reservation water. But others have taken advantage of Native Americans for a long time with false promises, and exploiters have dumped their wastes on tribal lands, giving the tribe little to no voice in decisions. The tribes often remain understandably skeptical and untrusting. They also took it as a negative sign that government officials made several efforts to shorten the pipeline environmental review and public input period. Regardless of the degree of impact, such approaches don't help heal old wounds.

Despite decades of effort, the Black Hills lawsuit is still unsettled, and the tribe is still not touching the escrow account. During my last count, it has grown to the tidy sum of over $1.3 billion. This money could go a long way, since there are pervasive social and health issues throughout the reservation. Unemployment is at over 80 percent. Poverty, tuberculosis, and diabetes are rampant, and reservation residents have some of the shortest life expectancies in the Western world. Sitting on this amount of cash places the Lakota and the entire Sioux Nation in a no-win scenario: either take the much-needed money to deal with the many internal challenges facing their people or, once again, capitulate and reinforce the centuries-old norm that it's acceptable for the federal government to take advantage of and ignore Native Americans while seizing their lawfully held land and resources when and where they (we) want. This situation doesn't seem to represent much progress.

To address tribal concerns that climbing their sacred tower desecrates their religious and spiritual experience, park managers closed all climbing in June—the tribe's more sacred time of the year for their Grey Buffalo Horn and Black Hills journey. The National Park Service likely saw this as a reasonable accommodation and gesture of respect. However, many in the climbing community saw it differently, and they objected.

To them, the federal government implemented a law banning climbing based on a singular religious purpose, making it thereby unconstitutional. To address these concerns, the National Park Service changed the June closure from a legal requirement to a recommended voluntary restriction. Despite the voluntary ban being in place for more than a generation, judging from news stories and restless vibes, neither side of the issue has been satisfied. News reports show that many climbers refuse to abide by the voluntary ban, and it appears the tribes may be developing further legal strategies to better fulfill this quest and journey in the realm where spiritual and legal trails converge.

As for me, many things have changed since I basked in the glow of Devils Tower's gray ramparts and gazed at the dark shadow cutting arcs in the clear prairie night. I've placed my fingers against the Tower's sun-warmed rock, and from an upper perch, I've gazed across the wondrous prairie expanse. But I like to think I've made progress in my journey. I now see the Tower as much more. The paths and trail intersections helped me see beyond the notion that landscapes are merely ecological habitats, sporting gym, or pleasure grounds for personal entertainment. I also grew to understand that we all can form deep spiritual meaning and connections with the land if we expand our worldview beyond our self-imposed bubbles and open our minds to accept diverse relationships with the land. However, how these various land ethics would mesh with current land laws and restrictions remains unclear. For instance, could there ever be a way that spiritual ownership and rights could transfer with a sale and be recorded in the deed filed at the county courthouse? Without a formal way for society to recognize the intangible and spiritual value of land, our trails may never truly intersect. With no intersection, how could there be true understanding, respect, and progress?

I now see that these Devils Tower experiences helped guide me down my own path. Where it leads, I can't say. But I instinctively know something changed after I passed under the Tower's soft gray glow and witnessed the Lakota's relationship with their Bear Lodge.

Perhaps what's more important is to have and partake in journeys in the first place. I respect the sun dance and that this may be the Lakota's chosen path for reaching their Grey Buffalo Horn. I know now that I must follow my own journey toward this same destination, not as some white man's co-opted version of Native American spirituality reminiscent of naïve childhood fantasies or B-rated Hollywood movies, but as something unique and meaningful for me.

The Tower has also seen other returns, including that of impacted wildlife—but with caveats. Bouncing back from their once perilous journey, peregrine falcons are returning to Devils Tower only to find they must share nest sites with climbers. The intersection of several simultaneous journeys indicates that a new day has dawned at Devils Tower. Because, on any given day, doesn't the sun shine on us all equally? And isn't there a little Grey Buffalo Horn in every one of us?

On the Shoulders of Giants

$\mathcal{T}$he stiff wind coming across Windy Pass's barren crest caused me to lean in at a right angle to Mount St. Helens's gaping maw and steaming caldera rising to the left of my angulated stance. I'd never liked cold introductions, but I summoned the courage to meekly knock on the tiny, well-used, wind-buffeted trailer. Scientific curiosity, a desire for adventure, and youthful excitement led me here. Who's to say how much of anyone's actions are due to free will and how much higher forces orchestrate them all—even higher than those beating and swaying the trailer with each successive gust.

I'd recently begun working for the Forest Service as a seasonal interpretive naturalist within the newly created Mount St. Helens National Volcanic Monument. I'd just given a Windy Ridge talk. In wild animations uncharacteristic of my natural self, I'd recounted the events on the fateful day of the volcano's May 18, 1980, eruption and the instantaneous blast that tore all trees from this previously unnamed forested ridge and reshaped the entire landscape as far as the eye could see.

Curiosity led me to ask fellow Forest Service employees about the lone trailer parked on the ridge between the torn-apart mountain and the infamous Spirit Lake, shimmering in the sunlight and wind-driven wavelets. My better-informed friends told me the trailer belonged to a rarely seen volcanologist studying the mountain's eruption. Perhaps sensing my curiosity, they also shared with me rumors that he consistently searched for nontechnical research assistance. Only later did I learn that these were code words for miserable and tiresome grunt work that no one else wants to do. I had no overt science knowledge or ambition at the time, but I always held a high regard for curiosity and unanswered questions. Simply put, the mysterious researcher in the wind-blown trailer intrigued me enough to overcome my natural shyness.

My meek knock produced a tremendous crashing sound from inside, followed by a hurried voice shouting, "Door's open!"

Firmly holding the rickety door so the wind didn't tear it from its hinges and hurl it to Spirit Lake's log-strewn waters, I opened the door and stepped into the beginning of the commitment, passion, and search for scientific understanding that dominated the rest of my life.

Once safely inside, I began introducing myself to Harry Glicken, a United States Geological Survey volcanologist. I continued with the introduction, but he seemed more interested in and distracted by his attempt to fry eggs in a frying pan over the tiny lit stove. He seemed friendly and talkative despite his fixation and intense concentration on frying eggs. His frying antics became aggressive despite frying being an otherwise common chore. His antics and movements were anything but smooth; instead, he lurched from task to task. With each jerking movement, he bumped against a perilous stack of dirty dishes, books, towels, and an assortment of clothes, both clean and dirty, eventually sending all the contents crashing into smaller piles that littered the floor. He didn't seem to notice the confusion and disarray—or care.

While he was attempting to crack another egg, it slipped from his hands and landed on the edge of the stove. By this time, the animated story of his volcano research had built to such a crescendo that he didn't notice the egg dribbling down the countertop on its way to the piles of papers and strewn kitchen implements accumulating on the floor. I interrupted his animated monologue to point out the egg still slowly running down the stove and kitchen wall. I sensed he heard but, just like he approached the rest of his surroundings, didn't care.

I sat in wonder, listening to his frantic storytelling, which was complete with arm waving that led to the crashing of the last remaining upright stacks of dishevelment. I focused my mind on his volcano knowledge and storytelling, but my eyes still tracked the dribbling egg and his total lack of awareness or concern. As my gaze drilled down to the oozing rivulet, I noted a succession of older dried egg layers under this younger deposit—all having oozed roughly the same path down the counter's cheap, fabricated facing. It became a lesson in sedimentology, for I noticed that other walls had dried flow deposits of unknown substances as well.

How can someone live like this? I wondered. With apologies to Lady Macbeth, I thought, *Go get some water, and wash this filthy witness from the land, or at least the walls and floor!* However, despite the squalor, I could have stayed put for hours. Time indeed passeth like a shadow, but I had little understanding then that when I passed through his sedimentary layers, I had little chance of returning unaltered.

Harry, and his passion, came to study Mount St. Helens's pyroclastic flow deposits, one of the many complex remnant features from the May 18, 1980, eruption. When the mountain blew on that fateful day, it behaved wildly differently than typical eruptions seen in the news or from volcanoes portrayed by Hollywood. News stories of

Hawaiian eruptions usually show lava rivers flowing downhill, slowly cooling until they finally turn into stone.

Cascade volcanoes usually don't spew slowly flowing rivers of lava. Mount St. Helens's May 18, 1980, eruption surely had none. The only rivers from this eruption were fast-flowing mud avalanches and instantaneous air blasts. Cascade volcanoes often contain pent-up gas and pent-up energy waiting for the right trigger. Like an exploding pressure cooker or rupturing pressurized tire, once released, pent-up energy blasting miles into the air clears away any plug or material standing in its way. Accompanying violent explosions are often a mixture of swirling superheated gases and hot and partially molten material that flows down the mountain. However, this hot gas is mostly heavier than air. So, instead of flowing slowly down the mountain as sticky molten lava does, this superheated river of gas flows down the mountain at hundreds of miles an hour, picking up rocks and ash along the way, while instantaneously vaporizing any burnable object in its path.

Volcanologists call these superheated gases and ash flows pyroclastic flows. *Pyro* means "born of fire," while *clastic* refers to "consisting of rock." Although technical sounding, the name is highly apt, since pyroclastic flows contain a mixture of gases, ash particles, and molten lava fragments—heated to well over a thousand degrees Fahrenheit. Pyroclastic flows swirl downhill at near supersonic speeds. No one can outrun a pyroclastic flow—or even see it coming.

As Harry Glicken continued his morning ritual in the Windy Ridge trailer—complete with gyrations, spouted superlatives, and more kitchen crashing—he filled me with volcanic blast and pyroclastic flow power and awe. I imagined that Harry Glicken's excited whirlwind calamity could captivate any audience.

Well beyond his egg-soaked kitchen piles and debris, Harry believed studying pyroclastic flow remnant piles and deposits would offer important insights into these fascinating and destructive phenomena. However, deposits aren't in convenient lab settings. Collecting data required long hours of dangerous grunt work in less-than-ideal field conditions. Harry had no grad students to perform such tasks and often few willing volunteers.

I blurted out, without hesitation, "Sign me up."

Perhaps due to my climbing experience, or maybe because I kept willingly accepting an escalating series of the most unappealing grunge tasks imaginable, by the end of the day, my remedial job consisted of chopping steps in the steep, crumbling, loosely held walls of ash particles and trying not to fall while balancing on near-vertical ash walls by standing on crumbling ash nubbins. Handholds were useless; besides, I needed hands to carefully chip friable ash samples from wherever Harry pointed. I then dutifully chipped the sample out of the wall and placed it in a numbered plastic bag. I yelled out the bag number to Harry as I tossed the sample to his anticipating hands. He caught each tossed bag without dropping one, despite our never being close together. He made sure he'd be standing clear if—when—I fell.

Serious injuries would likely have resulted if I'd come off any of my ashen stances. As many aspiring climbers soon learn, I'd disciplined my mind not to fall. With laser focus, my world held only ash samples, plastic bags, Harry's pointing fingers, and my crumbling stances. Every time I looked down at Harry, I sensed his pleasure in not being the one collecting samples.

I also noticed that the pyroclastic flow deposits transformed Harry. He was no longer the disheveled, awkward person constantly crashing into chaotic surroundings. When conducting science, he became focused and disciplined, and he presented an air of confidence, knowledge, and wisdom. He, like other volcanic rivers, had a natural flow. Volcanic blast zones and pyroclastic wastelands are typically ill-fitting garments. But for Harry, they cleaved well to his mold. The worse conditions became, the more they seemed to fit. I could see why his colleagues respected him.

I never caught Harry short of words or inhibited from using them to fill empty spaces. Everything he did seemed to have multiple layers. Some were obvious, while others were subtle, but all swirled, as do all pyroclastic flows. However, Harry's flowed at normal body temperature and human speed. Buried within his cacophonic deluge, I began picking up fragments of Harry the person that flowed beyond Harry the researcher. I gleaned that elements of both haunted him.

Harry had become fast friends with David Johnson, a fellow United States Geologic Survey volcanologist. In 1980, they were sharing volcano-watching duties on an unnamed ridge and high point north of Mount St. Helens. The United States Geologic Survey scheduled Harry to observe the mountain from this unnamed ridge on May 18, 1980. However, Harry wanted to make a supply run into town, so he asked David to cover his volcano-watching shift. Unexpectedly, later that morning, the mountain woke from its long slumber when the north side suddenly bulged and convulsed. David knew a big eruption was imminent. He had just enough time to warn the radio dispatchers. Seconds after the warning, the mountain exploded. Instead of the blast shooting skyward, this eruption blew out the mountain's north side, directly at David.

No one saw David Johnson again. To honor him, the federal government officially named the observation post Johnson Ridge. The fact that a friend died while taking his scheduled post still clearly haunted Harry. I sensed he constantly wrestled with these and other thoughts. Only when speaking of his dear friend did Harry pause, stumble, and appear at a loss for words. There were some unknowns that Harry's research project was ill-equipped to answer.

After a full day of data collection, we stumbled, bedraggled, into Harry's trailer just after sunset. Harry thanked me for my help, and he offered to fry some eggs. Apparently, he was quite the egg man. I declined his gracious offer. Slurping eggs took more energy than my tired and sore muscles felt up to.

As we parted, the crashing sounds emanating from his tiny trailer followed me the entire distance to my car. As I opened the door, a wind gust from across the barren ridge ripped the door from my grip. I must have been tired. I scrambled in, closed the door, and returned home for a long night's sleep.

I helped Harry out a few more times. Each trip was like the first. His talking remained a constant during all our additional sampling adventures. Forever talkative, Harry went on about volcanoes, life, science, geology, and more volcanoes. His passion seemed timeless, but unfortunately, his clock wasn't.

After the last of the summer field season, I never saw Harry Glicken again. Eight years later, while he was studying pyroclastic flows in Japan, Mount Unzen suddenly erupted on June 3, 1991. The volcano's blast claimed Harry's life, as well as the lives of forty-two other unsuspecting bystanders.

Harry died before the publication of his dissertation. However, scientists had widely circulated his maps, research, and insights on pyroclastic flows. One noted researcher called Harry's research "profound." Despite his short life, Harry's work influenced other volcanologists and led to a much deeper understanding of these powerful Earth forces. Harry Glicken also triggered in other people, including spuds, pent-up forces and a fascination with earth science that leads to a better understanding of the wonders and beauty inherent in the world around us.

❦

In 1675, when talking about his scientific accomplishments, Sir Isaac Newton famously said, "If I have seen further, it is by standing on the shoulders of giants." This metaphor perfectly encapsulates the scientific method and process, whereas each researcher's discovery builds upon earlier scientists' findings. While deeply immersed in the world of caves, I had the fortunate opportunity to cross paths with more than one giant.

Bring forth elixirs to slay my evil thirst. This thirst is not the kind that Good Samaritans can quench with water. Universal truth and understanding can be the grandest elixir of all. To fulfill my newfound ravaging, I attempted to engage every researcher who came through Carlsbad Caverns National Park in search of a research permit. As I filled out permits, I quizzed and prodded researchers and invited myself on their field studies. Some politely, others less so, told me to bug off, stating that they were only interested in getting their permit and heading out—alone. Others let me tag along and tolerated me incessantly asking probing questions. I found excitement in all their projects and topics.

Dr. Gill Harwood not only tolerated my attempts to learn, but she seemed to welcome them. She'd recently transferred to the University of East Anglia from the University of Newcastle upon Tyne. Although New Mexico is a long way from England, Gill passed through the area once or twice a year to continue her long-standing research on the park's Permian reef.

Gill specialized in evaporites and sedimentology within carbonate settings. Sedimentology, as the name implies, is the study of sedimentary rocks. They form by the accumulation of sand, silt, or other particles deposited by water, wind, or oozing egg yolk. Over time, particles coalesce to form sandstone, siltstone, and other sedimentary rocks. The deposition of limey and other carbonate minerals forms limestone. This is why we collectively call limestone and other related rocks carbonates.

Evaporates are still another sedimentary rock type. Evaporites form when water or another liquid evaporates away, leaving the remaining minerals that had been in the solution to coalesce into a distinctive new rock layer. Since Carlsbad Caverns lies in a massive limestone reef and the cave's dry air enabled a wide variety of evaporates to form, it's an alluring place for the few researchers specializing in evaporites and sedimentology within carbonate settings.

Gill Harwood didn't mind having me tag along and ask questions. She went out of her way to explain her research and point out tidbits. She showed me that it's often small, nuanced, and detailed observations that hint at a much grander meaning and significance. For instance, she had me look for fine details within each fossilized shell protruding from the cave's walls, which used to be an oceanic reef full of clams and other shelled critters. Usually, the fossil's shell contained small traces of coalesced sand. Gill pointed out that the top of the sand layer in many shells lay horizontal, as you would expect sand to accumulate. However, in other places on the cave walls, an unexplained force had tilted the sand layer in each shell—all in the same direction.

Gill's story to the spud said that all sand layers in all ancient shells were originally horizontal. But after fossilization, something acted on the reef/rock, tilting it in some locations and at certain times. Younger deposits formed later, after the reef's tilting, were the still horizontal shell sand. Armed with this and other knowledge, experts, such as Gill, read the rocks and fossils as you or I would read a book. Like a biography, the pages of this story chronicle what happened to this reef within the last few million years. Gill's research breathed life back into critters and a world long gone that had, up to recently, passed unnoticed by many previous researchers.

What I once thought was just a series of rocks now opened to me its continuous story of life and death spanning millions of years. Gill taught me how to read rocks, then piece these stories together to make sense of the world around us. Isn't this a wondrous gift to give to another human being?

Before Gill, I'd only met one person from Great Britain. Therefore, during slow fossil-gazing times, I barraged her with naïve and ignorant questions, like, "What's the difference between Great Britain, England, and the United Kingdom?" I asked her many Beatles questions because the only thing I knew about England came from the Beatles, Monty Python, and grade-school lessons on the American Revolutionary War. Gill crushed my disillusionment. She informed me that not everyone from Great Britain grew up in Liverpool or had private, inside Beatles anecdotes.

I didn't confine my barrage of questions to the Beatles. As a mountaineer and connoisseur of mountaineering literature, I knew the Cairngorms' role in ice-climbing history. I just didn't know how to pronounce it or where exactly the Cairngorms were. Since Gill represented everything British to me, I asked her *that* too. She explained it in a way a sedimentologist professor would explain evaporite mineralization to a three-year-old. She also explained that

Scotland isn't the same as England and patiently answered each of my pestering questions. She saw no end to my questions, but I saw no end to her patience.

A few weeks later, I received a package in the post from England (or United Kingdom/Great Britain—I still get things confused). It came from Gill. Opening it brought a smile to my customary non-emotive face. She'd sent me a book, *Mountaineering in Scotland*, by the famous Scottish climber William H. Murray. It's a well-known and respected book on Scottish winter mountaineering circles (yes, it's a small circle). I've treasured this book ever since.

Apparently, Gill remembered my curiosity about the Cairngorms. So, when she got back to England, she searched several bookstores for anything about winter mountaineering in Scotland. That was about the nicest thing anyone who barely knew me had ever done for me.

Gill remains forever a giant in scientific acumen, kind friendship, and inspiring leadership. She's also a role model for women in science. Her inspirational abilities extended far beyond the awards she received. Her openness, inclusion, and patience helped kindle my interest in science—especially earth science. Gill went out of her way as a true educator. She willingly molded all those passing by who demonstrated an interest and passion for learning. Gill didn't need to do any of this; she could easily have just grabbed her permit and told me to bugger off.

By the early 1990s, Gill stopped coming to Carlsbad Caverns. Over twenty-five years later, I had a spontaneous thought to call her up, reconnect, and say hello. Sadly, I learned that doctors had diagnosed her with cancer about the same time she stopped coming to Carlsbad Caverns. She had a long battle with this disease and finally succumbed on March 12, 1996.

In recognition of her contributions to evaporite and carbonate sedimentology, as well as her mentorship of young women interested in pursuing a science career, the British Sedimentological Research Group, with assistance from the International Association of Sedimentologists and the Geological Society of London, created a scholarship in honor of Gill. The Gill Harwood Memorial Fund offers support to women pursuing sedimentology studies. So far, there have been dozens of recipients—and still counting.

ॐ

One of the largest giants who passed through Carlsbad Caverns during my tenure was Diana Northup. I had the privilege and honor to also call her a friend. Her academic credentials and scientific interests developed over time. I met her during the final stages of her master of science degree thesis research project that focused on cave crickets. She lived and worked in Albuquerque but spent just as much time in Carlsbad. So much so that she and her husband, Ken, invested in a used miniature airplane they found at a cheap price. A plane enabled them to quickly fly back and forth as their busy schedule allowed.

After her cricket study and master of science degree, she pursued her PhD. But this time, not with such large critters as crickets. Instead, she focused on cave life she could see only under magnification, such as a microscope—or better yet, an optic or electron scanning microscope. The study of such organisms has opened the eyes of more than mere spuds. Her findings have the potential to influence critical research topics ranging from cures to debilitating diseases, such as cancer, to the potential discovery of life in outer space.

One of the biggest stumbling blocks in finding or imagining life in outer space is asking what it would eat, since doesn't all life on

230

earth eat carbon-based foodstuff? Isn't such carbon-based foodstuff limited to earth?

Well, not exactly. While most known organisms are carbon based and eat other carbon-based life, there are a few critters that gain sustenance from eating inorganic material, such as sulfur and manganese. Researchers have found mineral-eating critters in only a few extreme environments on earth, including deep oceanic volcanic vents and deep, undisturbed caves in southeastern New Mexico—such as Lechuguilla Cave.

Since her cricket-studying days, Diana Northup has left her mark as one of the world's premier experts in cave-oriented exobiology. Caves and deep-seated fissures on Mars, Titan, and other potential otherworldly bodies may one day hold secrets to life in outer space. If so, this would be one of humankind's greatest revelations. Even before that day comes, I present thanks to Diana Northup for her research efforts probing the boundaries of scientific understanding. Harry, Gill, and Diana clearly showed me that shoulders can do more than carry backpacks and haul ropes. Shoulders can also form the foundation that inspires others to reach even higher into an infinite universe.

Yes, Virginia, You DO Need a Stinking Permit

*I*n Shakespeare's ultimate tragedy, three witches tempt Macbeth to murder his king and seize the throne for himself. Blind ambition drove the dethroning of one king and the ascendency of another. Within the climbing world, pitons ruled supreme for nearly one hundred years, but they, too, eventually met a monarchy's end. During its reign, the piton had an unparalleled impact on the climber's world. Despite the negative impact, without pitons, climbing wouldn't be the same. Pitons provided the margin of safety climbers needed to push limits and raise the endeavor beyond merely a scramble amongst the Alps.

Pitons are metal spikes of various shapes and sizes that climbers hammer into rock crevices and use as anchors to provide a margin of safety. If a climber falls, the piton keeps the fallen from hitting the ground. Pitons served climbers in the way chocks do now; however, chocks are easy to remove and don't damage the rock. To remove a piton, the trailing climber hammers the piton from side to side, slowly loosening it until it pops out. Repeatedly hammering pitons in and out of the same crack eventually damages the rock and enlarges cracks.

Unsightly rock scars were the main reason climbers switched from pitons to clean chocks. Because of the ensuing clean-climbing revolution, pitons largely became obsolete by the late 1970s. When I began climbing, we could still readily purchase pitons. I have fond memories of perusing cardboard bins in Seattle's Swallows' Nest, eyeing pitons of all shapes and styles, angles, knife blades, bongs, Leepers, copperheads, and Realized Ultimate Reality Pitons (RURPs).

Clean climbing helped sustain the integrity of cracks from abuse; however, it brought with it other non-sustainable consequences. (Just to be clear, the term *abusing crack* may now create images different than intended.) Climbers drive pitons into cracks (the rock variety) despite the crack being full of dirt and plants. However, clean climbing requires the removal of offending dirt and vegetation. To the clean climber, dirt and plants in cracks are an evil hindrance, but to the environment and ecologists, they're habitat. Some rare plants grow only from cracks on cliffs.

Even more damaging to plants have been climbers' push to free-climb routes instead of simply aid-climb like in the days of old. Climbers' ethical rules state that climbing by stepping on or resting on pitons or other artificial items is aid-climbing, and aid-climbing isn't as pure as free-climbing, whereas the climber ascends using only natural features. Therefore, to free-climb a steep and hard vertical crack requires removing, or gardening, all the dirt, plants, and other slick things that get in the climber's way or collect moisture. Therefore, in the interest of better preserving cracks, we climbers have sacrificed plants and cliff habitat. This practice is just as non-sustainable as permanently scarring the cracks. It just depends on the observer's perspective.

Coloradoan Chip Salaun first brought up this concern in 1976 in the June issue of the now defunct climbing magazine *Off Belay*. He wrote an article lamenting climbers devegetating Longs Peak's alpine walls solely for the climbers' desire to avoid scarring the rock with pitons. After researching the topic in detail, including establishing monitoring plots throughout the vertical Diamond, he concluded that an occasional piton would be better ecologically. It grieved him to think that many alpine plants must die to provide climbers with a clean ascent.

This may be sacrilegious to many climbers, because without gardening, many world-famous climbing areas wouldn't be the meccas they are today. Paul Boving might never have been able to usher the 5.11 climbing level into Washington because he might not have been able to climb Thin Fingers with the thin crack filled with mud, soil, and plants. Therefore, climbers may ask, in a world of green, what's the harm of losing a few plants and soil? While Macbeth might have anguished over murdering the king, few climbers lose sleep over destroying microecological habitats if it means opening beautiful and challenging crack climbing areas like the Index Town Wall.

It would be all too easy to blame climbers and deem them abusive or insensitive, but this would be an either inaccurate or incomplete conclusion. Every type of activity produces impact, so few can claim the moral high ground in such a discussion.

Most climbers attempt to find an appropriate balance. The climber's dilemma becomes hard when their passion for climbing far exceeds their interest in botany or ecology. However, climbers *can* do it. Well-regarded climbers Todd Bibler and Greg Davis ended what would have been a first ascent because it would have crossed their personal ecological threshold.

Todd and Greg reached a ledge a short distance from the top of a new route on Longs Peak's The Diamond—the same peak whose lost alpine wildflowers pained Chip Salaun. Todd and Greg turned around on this new route because to continue would have required the desecration of a prolific green carpet of moss and ferns. They set that as their personal ethical limit.

It may be a different threshold for the next climbing party because there are few gardening ranger cops patrolling The Diamond. Therefore, some climbers may consider what's fair is foul, and what's foul is fair. In Todd Bibler and Greg Davis's case, although they never completed the route, they climbed it in good style.

We don't restrict such inner demons, quandaries, conflicts, inner turmoil, and owl-shrieking moralizations solely to climbing. Cavers have their share too—and then some. Perhaps the most notable ethical dilemma for cavers is digging.

The entrances to many of the world's most famous caves originally were too small for even the slightest person to fit through. For generations, cave explorers have been enlarging cave entrances. In deep and rich forests, this only requires digging through prodigious piles of pedology (or, in pedestrian speak, dirt). In other situations, cavers resort to chipping stone, flowstone, and bedrock—just enough to squeeze through. Explosives are a favorite fallback in cases where there's too much debris or bedrock for cavers to hand dig.

Bang—instant cave entrance.

A caver who used explosives to enlarge a cave entrance may be the same person who's repulsed when some "careless jerk" leaves a muddy boot print on flowstone or carves their initials in the rock. An enlarged entrance may cause significantly more harm to the cave environment than fingerprints, boot scuffs, or carved initials, but we all draw our own ethical lines and boundaries. I, too, have chipped at and enlarged cave passages to allow humans to squeeze past short restrictions. I can see the issue from all sides, so this is a conflicting issue that has few, if any, communal resolutions.

᎒᎓᎒

I'm torn and conflicted by the duality of the phrase "freedom of the hills." It's both a title and a wilderness ethic. The title: the Seattle-based publisher Mountaineers Books published *Mountaineering: The Freedom of the Hills*, an enduring classic book on mountaineering technique. The ethic: the book's title aptly touches upon a core sentiment that makes the mountain and wilderness experience unique. However, some claim that since we're loving nature to death, freedom sentiments in land management are as antiquated as alpenstocks and wood-framed Trapper Nelson backboards. Others claim that without freedom, we can have no wilderness.

I suspect I'm not the only one torn and conflicted.

I long for the freedom of the hills, where I may follow whatever path inspiration, fresh mind, and tired legs could take me. This is the way Hermann Ulrichs experienced *his* mountains. However, as a natural resource manager, I've seen firsthand the destruction that unregulated freedom-seeking herds have inflicted upon fragile environments. As I said, I'm conflicted.

I plainly see the need to regulate, restrict, and tightly manage wilderness use, but I also pine for the days before people of my ilk imposed such freedom-sucking restrictions. During such pining episodes, I often think back with fond memories of Washington's Enchantment Lakes region. These memories date back to long before the formalized, bureaucratized, stiflized, and enforcilized five permit zones era. Before permit requirements. Before nonrefundable permit fees. Before the annual permit lottery system that opens for only a two-week window in February. Before the annual March lottery drawing. Before the requirement to outline exact itineraries, with the name of every member of the climbing party—no exceptions. Before a separate parking permit was required to be obtained remotely and in advance, and certainly before the saying, "freedom of the hills" became oxymoronic.

What's next? A months-long waiting list to obtain my dry heaving permit and specify in advance each heaving location? I'm glad I went to the Enchantments before the regimented permit and lottery system. I've not been back since, and I likely will never return.

⚶

Once, well past my youthful "freedom of the hills" experiences, I happened, in a Yosemite National Park's ranger station, to obtain a five-day permit for an exploratory North Dome climb. With a deep sigh and pangs of regret, I resigned myself to proceed through all the required permits, processes, and procedures. By most modern standards, it didn't create excessive pain. It required no reservation a decade in advance. Unlike some rafting permits, it required no mega-jackpot statistical odds of drawing a winning lottery ticket. Other than requiring me to travel well out of my way for the application, the backcountry permit process wasn't *that* bad. However, after I obtained the permit, the ranger asked me how many bear canisters I needed.

Apparently, all backcountry permit holders must have and use bear-proof black cylinders for food storage. I fully understand the wildlife conservation need for them, but I'd never carried bear canisters before. He showed me a sample canister so I could judge how many I would need for my weeklong trip. Despite being not very large inside, each canister had huge exterior dimensions—approximately the size of two footballs. I figured I needed four but couldn't imagine having enough space for such monstrosities, so I paid my separate rental fee for three hardened bear-proof food canisters.

The ranger held the park information center's door open for me as I delicately balanced three over-bloated black cannisters in my hands and walked out into Yosemite Valley's heat. Then I staggered to the bus stop. At least it wasn't snowing *this* time. Getting out the door while balancing the three canisters proved not as hard as getting them on the bus. *The Freedom of the Hills* failed to cover this skill development. One canister brushed against the doorframe, rolled out of my hands, clanked on the ground, and then proceeded to roll under the bus. Setting the other two in the bus's entryway, which blocked anyone else from boarding, I crawled under the bus to retrieve the errant canister.

Once I was back out from under the bus, an irritated wannabe passenger helped me load all three canisters back in my arms so that I might take my seat and the bus could be on its way. I couldn't get all the canisters into the storage space at my feet, so I placed two on the empty seat next to me. I wished for seat belts to keep the canisters from rolling, which they were inclined to do upon the slightest bump in the shockless bus. I had things relatively under control until there were more passengers than there were available seats. Standing passengers began glowering at me and my selfish canisters. I relinquished the second seat after an elderly woman politely asked me to move. I stacked canisters on my former seat and stood over them, praying they wouldn't become animated. This worked well enough until it was time to exit. Getting off the bus required only three trips, two minutes, three rolling canisters, and countless irritated looks. Eventually, I succeeded in freeing myself and the cursed canisters from the bus ride from hell, but exhaustion sent me looking for a place to nap.

Despite my Lowe Nuptse being the largest commercially available backpack at the time (I'd purchased it years previously), its size still wouldn't hold all three canisters unless I discarded sleeping bag, tent, clothing, stove, water bottles, climbing rope, and climbing gear. It's not an option to go on a five-day climbing trip without climbing gear. I saw no other legal option. Since I was an environmentally conscious public servant, I couldn't see myself flaunting park and environmental regulations, but Newtonian physics allowed only so much space in a Nuptse. I couldn't serve *both* beasts.

In the end, under cloak of secrecy, I chose to carry one canister. If I passed through any canister-checking inspection, I could at least show the rangers that I indeed carried *a* canister. In camp, I otherwise would have hung my food from a tree, but I wasn't about to visibly post my flagrant canister violation to all passing rangers. So, I hid the bulk of my food in my sleeping bag, wrapped in the raincoat, and in other places as if they were contraband—all the while praying the canister police would never search.

My climbing obsession had turned me into a food smuggler. For the next few joyless days, I lived in constant fear of rangers catching me in my subversive act, fear of acquiring a nonenvironmentally friendly stigma, and fear of black-suited agents sending me to Guantánamo Bay's prison camp—all over bagels and Top Ramen not in a proper bear canister.

For the next few days, no matter how hungry I got or how nonsensical the item, I ate only food *not* stored in the single bear canister. I sought to eat my evidence as soon as possible. The stress continued for days and nights. But in the end, I suffered no inspection, no legal fine, and no imprisonment.

After an equally comical epic to return all three canisters, I finally rid myself of the encumbrances and guilt-provoking surreal monstrosities.

Somewhere along the line, we'd transformed "freedom of the hills" into "bureaucracy of the hills." However, I'm fully aware that there's a fine line between tragedy and comedy. I'm at least grateful that it now has been over twenty-five years, and no federal marshal agents have burst through my door and arrested me in front of my children or peering neighbors. I think I can safely say that I may finally be free from any tragic or legal repercussions of my ethical transgressions. But somehow, I think we'll never again have freedom in the hills as we originally envisioned and had grown accustomed to experiencing.

Wilderness and
the Mind of Man

The concept of wilderness is dependent upon personal interpretation and experience; therefore, noticeable conflicts can, and
do, arise when holders of wildly different perceptions collide. These
conflicts may be external or internal, while in some situations, they're
both. Such was the case with me many years ago within a dark and
austere mountain valley I've always treasured.

A quick glance at the map revealed the proximity of this mountain
valley to the lifeblood of the civilized world: roads, cities, televised
football highlights, strip malls, and smog-encrusted inversion layers.
But close inspection revealed a myriad of physical and psychological
barriers that separated the creature comforts of the lowlands from
the enticing real world beyond.

For reasons unknown, I hadn't yet visited this valley despite
spending years climbing and exploring alpine and subalpine regions
throughout the range. It brought me great pleasure just thinking that in
modern times, with everything tamed and conquered by humankind,
there remained a trailless, dark, dank, cold valley surrounded by dense,

nearly impenetrable vegetation intermixed with swift, braided glacial torrents and steep, foreboding ice cliffs clinging to encircling flanks. It was as if no one had told this magical realm that the Pleistocene epoch had temporarily retreated for more hospitable environs.

As dusk approached, my pulse quickened, for I approached the end of the road that marked the beginning of the route. I would soon, after all those years, experience this Ice Age relic firsthand—a valley that, for so long, had been a part of my collective consciousness and a symbol of wildness and all that's good.

I curled up in the open bed of my pickup, waiting for first light. Small bats, probably one of the *Myotis* species, darted about, catching moths in the star-filled night as I drifted into wondrous dreams.

As early dawn approached, I was on my way upon a well-maintained trail, which I expected to end soon. My well-thumbed description stated that the trail faded into thick brush, interspersed with cold and swift water crossings, before arriving at the valley proper. Obviously, this newer constructed trail postdated my information. The trail, which enabled me to breeze past slide alder, devil's club, and other biodefenses, ended at a gravel bar and a stream channel. To keep my boots and socks dry, I waded across the glacial water in bare feet.

Once I was beyond this ford, views straight toward the head of the valley opened, while at the same time, the encircling alpine walls loomed and closed in on my flanks. I would soon arrive in the heart of the fabled valley. The new trail directed and guided me into the inner realm of the valley of my dreams. The defenses were gone—the approach much too easy. I felt violated.

The beauty of the valley and the cold, dark, and dank positioning were as foreboding as expected. After being satisfied that the valley experience had placed my minuscule human existence in proper perspective, I turned to return to my artificial yet comfortable life that lay somewhere below. I began the descent along the little rivulet of water that connected the two worlds.

I covered some distance just following the meandering gravel bars, away from the annoying trail. While following the growing river through an incised gravel bar, I began noticing signs of the world below. I saw what appeared to be avocado peels plastered on glacier-smoothed boulders within the stream. Moments later, a white, globulous projectile barely missed me and landed in the milky torrents of the glacial stream. Being an inquisitive scientist, I investigated this unusual event. The flying white substance appeared to be mayonnaise.

Then it began to make sense: *I'm witnessing the birth of guacamole.* As this thought hit me, another glob of mayonnaise didn't, and landed in the stream.

Climbing up the twelve-foot-high gravel embankment to the higher floodplain above brought me face-to-face with a pair of humanoids and their bright-yellow tent. The two people were oblivious to the fact that I stood thirty feet from them or that scraps from their meal heaved into the river channel hadn't gone unnoticed. They also didn't seem to notice that they were desecrating my sacred valley and valley experience. They were lost in their own world and wilderness experience. I didn't want any further intrusions upon my perceptions, so I disappeared back to the river channel without detection.

Later, while on the well-maintained trail leading to the parking lot, I happened upon another pair of humans. I'd had two sightings in one day! Their attire appeared more appropriate for a formal Thanksgiving Day dinner than a primitive excursion. The male wore slacks and a nice buttoned-down shirt, no tie. The female wore a well-pressed dress and low-heeled shoes. In proper old-world English, with the appropriate diction and intonation, he queried, "What is the destination of this trail?"

Apparently, while out for a Sunday drive, they'd happened upon an unknown trailhead that they decided to investigate. After I briefed them on their whereabouts and the swift river ford awaiting them, we parted company. They continued their stroll toward the beginning of the glacial valley and their own wilderness adventure.

I didn't know it at the time, but a few years prior to my visit, the Forest Service extended the trail into the valley. The publishers of a popular hiking guide had also highlighted the trip. It listed the hike as an easy or moderate stroll. Therefore, in my process of converting my mental images and dreams of this wilderness valley into actual experience and reality, the wilderness qualities were, for me, forever diminished. Real wilderness qualities didn't live up to the imaginary, while at the same time, reality forever tainted my mental imagery.

While exploring alpine mountains, desert canyons, and cavernous mazes and passages, I've experienced much more remote and lonely places than this small cirque valley. However, since wilderness is a human construct, few places were as wild as the wildness that existed within the inner realm of my thoughts prior to my actual in-body visit.

I, of course, wasn't the first person to visit this wilderness. This valley, long before my existence, hosted countless hikers, climbers, sheepherders, miners, surveyors, trappers, prospectors, and Native Americans and their ancestors, continuing back into antiquity. Each person has probably enjoyed, in their own way, a wilderness experience and felt a similar loss as their experience diminished upon the advent of future generations—individuals who were developing their own perceptions.

How many people have pondered the wilderness characteristics of this valley? How long will people continue placing a value on wilderness? As the perception of wilderness shifts with time, reflecting ever-changing societal attitudes and moods, is the fundamental idea of wilderness even sustainable? If the differences between wilderness and non-wilderness become less and less distinct, will a time come when a distinction is even relevant?

At home, as I lie awake, comfortably encased within the sheets of my bed, I occasionally entertain thoughts of this valley, which exists far from my present location and frame of reference. Life, death, mountain building, and erosional processes within this cirque valley pass undetected, oblivious to our distant and silent thoughts and musings. Emotionless and detached, this glaciated alpine valley continues at its own pace and within its own reality despite momentary intrusions and ever-changing human perceptions.

The Long View

There are certain mountains that pull at a subconscious level, rewiring brains or stirring the spirits from deep within. From that point on, chemical stimuli and internal circuitry take over, and auto-electronic-neurotic responses overwhelm thoughtful or rational thought—or understanding.

Mount Rainier is one of those mountains and one of those forces.

When I was growing up in Seattle, the looming hulk of Mount Rainier cast its ominous shadow over the city. Its profile dominates the southern skyline so much that it encodes into our DNA in a manner not unlike how a fledgling instinctively knows which bird is its mother. There's an unspoken understanding between mother bird and her downy-clad chicklets, similar to the one that once existed between John Lennon and Paul McCartney, and between Mount Rainier and my psychosis.

Seattleites simply call it The Mountain. We need no further description. Because of this notoriety, the first question any non-climbing Seattleite excitedly asks after hearing that I'm a mountain climber is, "So, you've climbed Mount Rainier?"

"No, I've never made it to the top."

Clearly deflated and disappointed, they invariably say, "So, you're not a *real* climber, just a hiker?"

While I've had numerous attempts and got close once, despite Mount Rainier not being a green-book summit, I failed in each attempt. Consequently, to date, I'm one of the few Pacific Northwest mountaineers who have never climbed Mount Rainier. Therefore, I'm not a *real* climber. Such is the state of affairs when one mountain dominates a community's consciousness as much as Mount Rainier does for the Puget Sound metropolis.

This doesn't mean that my heart and soul don't reserve a special spot for this special mountain, despite it forever taunting me on every clear-day return visit to the Puget Sound Basin. It also doesn't mean that another skyline, absent my dear friend, doesn't appear achingly lonely, as if I've lost a protective and watchful close relative. Mount Rainier may no longer loom on my eye's horizon, but it has never left my side, synapses, or soul. Mount Rainier will always be with me.

◦❦◦

Mountains surrounding the resort town of Estes Park, Colorado, provide horizons all their own. There's little question about the identity of the dominant mountain in this resort town. Longs Peak is to Estes Park what Mount Rainier is to Seattle.

I became restless while between National Park summer seasonal positions. I needed adventure. I needed experiences. Michael Smithson, from Rocky Mountain National Park, offered me a dreamlike experience. He asked me to drop my temporary job taking phone orders for Recreational Equipment Incorporated (REI) so I could move to Rocky Mountain National Park and work as a winter volunteer for free.

I resigned the next day, packed my meager belongings, and moved to Colorado.

If I volunteered full-time, the park offered me free lodging in the outskirts of Estes Park. The government housing they offered exceeded my expectations. It wasn't a falling-down trailer. It didn't leak air, wind, or rain. It didn't smell of hantavirus, and it had no menagerie of snakes, scorpions, rodents, or mysterious pulsating growths. Most impressive of all, it had a commanding view of Longs Peak.

Not just the typical hulky, bulky, or obscured view. The mesmerizing view of Longs Peak dominated the skyline from the Estes Park side—the only side that knew witchery and sorcery. The side that hung in shadow. The side graced with The Diamond.

Longs Peak is tall, but by many measures, it's nondescript—all except for The Diamond. From many vantages, Longs Peak appears to be a high ridge with one protruding, minute nubbin. The nubbin reaches an elevation of 14,259 feet above sea level, which bestows it the distinction of being one of the seventy-eight mountains in the United States that rise above 14,000 feet. The nubbin's elevation grants Longs Peak the honor of being our nation's thirty-sixth tallest mountain. If it weren't for The Diamond, that would be the limit of Longs Peak's recognition.

Lying in the shadows of Longs Peak's east side are steep ramparts and cliffs. The ramparts culminate in a diamond-shaped vertical and overhanging cliff. This hallowed and storied cliff is one of the grandest and most intimidating alpine walls in the country. Knowing and fearing people speak of The Diamond in hushed and reverent tones—or simply remain silent and bow in tribute, respect, and deference.

Mountaineers long considered The Diamond unclimbable. Due to natural progression in climbing skill level, climbers would likely have succeeded by the late 1950s, but government timidity and bureaucracy reared its ugly head. Rocky Mountain National Park managers forbade climbing attempts on The Diamond until 1960. As soon as the park lifted the restrictions, ambitious climbers swarmed in, and The Diamond fell shortly later.

Thoughts of climbing The Diamond gave me the shakes. I shook out of fear and intimidation just as much as excitement and anticipation. I had no idea if I would ever be skilled or bold enough to tackle *the* wall. Or, more correctly, if The Diamond god would allow me the honor to pass unsmitten. One can't be too impertinent in the face of The Diamond god.

I gazed out the kitchen window to The Diamond's tantalizing shadows. While eating, washing dishes, or doing other household chores, I saw or thought about nothing else. It pulled, it beckoned, it called to me. We spoke. Well, The Diamond spoke. I listened and gave the appropriate thanks. Often, I rolled the window open to allow closer communication. I also frequently stepped outside in subzero temperatures to have fewer barriers between the face and me. I needed my face-to-face time. If I ever were to climb The Diamond, I must first demonstrate that I was worthy.

I certainly wasn't up to a winter ascent. My volunteer position in this magical park, with The Diamond window, ended before spring thaw—just in time to begin my new assignment at Devils Tower. I never returned in summer long enough to continue my communion with The Diamond. I, and The Diamond god, never learned if I was worthy—that unknown I carry with me into the present. Also remaining with me are the personal conversations I once had with Longs Peak. These internal conversations continue providing comfort, for I remain fully aware that not only did I speak to the mountain, but the mountain spoke back. The Diamond called out and granted me, for one winter, the exalted privilege of, while not walking with the gods, at least sharing a communion with one.

෧෮

Despite her not being a supreme being, I always found it easy to talk to Jean. We both worked for Michael as members of his interpretive team. I've rarely used the word *vivacious*. For that, I'm glad, since I saved it for someone like Jean, who could do the word justice. Jean enthusiastically talked to the extreme, but she could also listen. Once, while listening to Michael and me talk about climbing, she said, "If you're a climber, you should talk to Ken—he's also a climber." While Jean worked with people in the interpretive division, her significant other, Ken, worked alone with computers.

Within the next couple of days, I wandered into the IT department, where Ken worked as the park's computer specialist. I found it hard to imagine that Ken and Jean were a couple, since Jean's demeanor exuded joy and animation, while Ken's didn't. He spoke so softly that I had to lean in to check if his mouth moved air. While I invited him on a climb and attempted to engage him in climbing conversation, but terse answers were all I extracted from him—and quite painfully, at that. During this whole "conversation," he didn't look up once. He appeared totally disinterested.

The next day, Jean bounced over and asked if I'd introduced myself to Ken. I chose my words carefully, since I didn't want to be rude. "Yes, I did, but he seemed uninterested, so I let it be."

"Oh, that's silly. Ken is actually quite interested. That's just Ken. He's shy. Ask him again!"

My next visit and non-conversation went as the first. Jean's follow-up prodding also went as before: "Ken's shy, ask again!"

On my third attempt, Ken said to meet him at his place on Saturday morning. I had him repeat it several times so that one version hopefully would register at a volume audible to the human ear. As twice before, he never looked up to physically recognize my presence. Regardless, I now had a climbing plan, but with him being so reserved, I had no idea what to expect.

I met Ken at their place. Before we took off, Jean translated Ken's inaudible mumblings. According to her interpretation, if I got into Ken's car, he would drive us out to the nearby Lumpy Ridge, a well-regarded rock-climbing area overlooking Estes Park.

In deathly silence, Ken drove while I attempted futilely to strike up a conversation. It was going to be a long day.

As soon as we arrived at the Lumpy Ridge parking lot, Ken pulled out not only his climbing gear but his other personality. This other him burst forth like a Mount St. Helens pyroclastic flow. Perhaps he'd succumbed to a sorcerer's spell, either back at the office or there in the parking lot. But Ken became an entirely new person. He became more talkative and livelier than even Jean.

As we hiked to the first climb, Ken's wild hand and arm gyrations helped propel his boisterous words to form a four-dimensional storytelling style totally lacking commas, periods, or any indication of a pause. It was as if he attempted to make up for his time as a mute.

He turned out to be an absolute joy to climb with—one of my all-time favorite climbing partners. He had a fabulous talent for climbing, with a palpable and infectious excitement and enthusiasm for all things climbing related. My strength and climbing skill grew from merely being in his presence.

The next day, while at work, I stopped to say hello. He never looked up. He muttered something inaudible and devoid of emotion or sign of life. I wondered what I'd done wrong. I later sought Jean to translate.

She said, "That's just Ken."

The same scenario played out for the next couple of weeks. Around the office, home, and other alien places, I could tell from subtle perceptions and clues that Ken attempted to talk, but I received nothing audible that my brain registered as communication. It was not unlike when you intuitively know someone is watching you, but your eyes catch the sight of no one.

If all attempts to understand failed, I always turned to Jean for a translation. For her, it must have been humorous and painful to witness two extreme introverts attempting to communicate. Ken eventually grew comfortable enough with me that I didn't require Jean to translate, but still, his comfort zone remained on the sharp end of a rope.

Ken and I continued climbing together, and Jean's role transitioned from translator to facilitator. She could climb quite well, but she privately admitted to me that she never found much joy in rock climbing, certainly not at Ken's level. She never told Ken that she climbed only to share in his passion. If she'd had her druthers, Ken would reach out and climb with others so she wouldn't feel the pressure of being his main climbing partner.

Once, while beyond Ken's earshot, Jean whispered to me, "Ken's been pleading with me to climb harder routes." She didn't have the heart to tell him she had no interest. She handed me a list of routes he wanted to climb with her. She suggested that I recommend climbing them with Ken. She pleaded to me, "Please don't tell Ken about the list."

One by one, I suggested climbs from Jean's list. Each time, Ken perked up and expressed an interest, but each time, he hesitated before responding, "Jean's had her heart set on climbing this route with me. I'll have to ask her if it would be alright if we climb it without her."

Each time, Jean gave him her permission. "It's alright. Go on the climb with David. There will be other climbs."

Ken never caught on. Although once, while belaying, he exclaimed, "It's amazing that most of your climbing suggestions are ones I've always wanted badly to do that were high on my to-do list." Clearly astonished, he said, "It's as if, somehow, we're operating off the same list."

I said, "Amazing that it's working out this way." However, he expressed regret and guilt that we were leaving Jean out of *her* special list.

When I met Ken, he was a phenomenally better climber than I ever expected to be, but as time marched on, he grew even better, while I remained the same. With other partners, Ken graduated to steep free climbs on The Diamond and other hard test pieces. Before that ascendency, he once called me when I lived in New Mexico. He still lived in Colorado, and Colorado climbs still animated his very being, but it had been a long winter, and he wanted something warmer. He sought a partner to stretch cold and tired muscles in the warmth of southern California's Joshua Tree National Park—a rock-climbing paradise. I figured all the good climbers he knew were too busy, so he must have resorted to his B list. Without hesitance, I said, "Yes, of course."

A week later, Carlsbad Caverns National Park offered a special job opportunity that, from a career perspective, I couldn't pass up. If climbing had continued to rule my life as it had for so long, I would have dropped everything and anything for the chance to climb in JT with Ken. However, I'd been attempting to begin a real career. Little did I realize at the time, but that special detail assignment changed my life forever, helped kick-start my career, light my passion for cave science, and changed my life's trajectory.

I called Ken to cancel our JT climbing trip. Despondent, he said he'd already bought nonrefundable plane tickets. He also didn't understand why anyone would choose a job over climbing. He asked me to reconsider, especially at that late notice, since he wouldn't be able to find a replacement. I still declined. I mailed him a check to reimburse him for his unused plane ticket. I never climbed with Ken again. He continued with his climbing ascendency, and I continued along my path.

Warm memories of climbing with Ken continue to flood my thoughts more than twenty-five years after our trail divergence. My heart sank upon reading that he'd died from a sudden heart attack. I can't fathom how Colorado climbing, once filled with motion and emotion, can be so suddenly stilled. He remains one of my all-time favorite climbing partners and one of the most unique personalities I've ever met. Colorado climbing will never be the same. Longs may have caught my eye and lured me in, but Ken animated Colorado mountains and gave them their voice and soul.

Free Four

$\mathcal{A}$ quiet silence flowed out of Icicle Creek. The Snow Lakes trailhead sat as silent as an antique postcard. Most disturbing was the emptiness. At Eightmile Boulder, I waited alone. The time had passed.

Ghosts provided my only company. A chill brushed by, as if I'd caught a fleeting glimpse of a cougar before it bounced off to sights unseen. Suddenly, the valley grew both colder and older. I longed for the sparks, warmth, and smell of pine-pitch fires. Everything has its place and time, and I sensed Icicle Creek's time had passed.

I couldn't tell for sure what I'd expected, but not this. Perhaps I'd expected a Northwest version of Yosemite's Camp 4. Instead, I got a normal Forest Service campground. I got a Washington State's version of Sunnyside Campground.

Near the Merced River—under the shadow of Yosemite Falls, tucked to the side and out of sight of the exclusive Yosemite Lodge— once lived the enigmatic and once-fabled Camp 4. Camp 4 once held a vibrancy and warmth built and nurtured by countless wild fireside nights, boisterous storytelling, idol worshiping, and drunken comradery. The type of integrated resource that the cultural and historic resource management world calls a "cultural landscape"—the blending of people, time, and place that gives birth to something unique to experience.

During my Yosemite heyday, or should I say "what-the-hey" or "whatever the heyday," the National Park Service didn't appreciate this cultural landscape, so they had no desire to preserve the Camp 4 experience. They wanted to snub it out, quiet the stories, and bring forth their form of camping respectability. Mostly, they wanted the climbing bums out. They started with a renaming. Maps and signs no longer called it Camp 4. The purveyors of respectability rebirthed Camp 4 as Sunnyside Campground

To quiet climbers' gatherings, park managers placed log barriers throughout all campground open spaces. They turned an open-office business plan into a myriad of individual quiet cubicles. At first, climbers revolted by simply carrying, towing, or winching the logs away. Just as quickly, rangers put them back. A cat-and-mouse game became a local and nonpolitical version of the Cold War. Instead of the US and the Soviets fighting a proxy war in Vietnam, Korea, or Angola, the staid National Park Service and the remnant hippie culture fought a proxy log war within the boulder-strewn climbers' camp in Yosemite Valley. Newly arrived, naïve spuds hoping to experience a glimmer of the old Camp 4 experience became hapless victims of the power struggle.

Living and no-longer-living old-guard legends once graced Camp 4. Big Wall climbing pioneers, such as the stately Royal Robbins, the energetic Chuck Pratt, the spiritual Yvon Chouinard, and Warren Harding, with his wayward debauchery, made their mark on Camp 4. However, the next Yosemite generation turned the Camp 4 experience into a cultural phenomenon. It's they who haunt the hollowed spaces between strewn-about logs.

The Camp 4 generation included such noted climbing bums as Ron Kauk and Steve Roper. And lest I fail to include the greatest and most enigmatic Camp 4 climbing master—Jim "The Bird" Bridwell.

Eventually, many of the Camp 4 climbing bums moved on to far-flung walls in Asia, South America, and the Arctic, or they moved on to respectability and the safety of homes, jobs, and the tending of sore bodies. Sure, new climbers came and went, filtering through Camp 4 and then later, the rechristened Sunnyside Campground. But the vibe, dynamic, and culture had changed. Everything has a season, and for Camp 4, those days are gone.

Camp 4 sprung organically from purely practical needs. Young people spending their lives honing skills and techniques and putting up new challenging climbs couldn't afford to spend time and energy working jobs, acquiring money, or paying mortgages. So naturally, they had no money for a proper room at a refined vacation lodge. Besides, they sought comradery from a like-minded community, not an individual lodging experience. Therefore, in spring, they pitched tents in the nearby campground and stayed put until autumn's snows drove them to climbing areas farther south or park rangers hauled them to jail. They had no money for food, so scarfing from the nearby lodge's dumpsters provided sustenance at little to no cost. They also had no money or time for laundromats. But, like during my first Yosemite experience, the lodge's bathroom hand dryers provided a suitable alternative.

Back in the Camp 4 heyday, at the end of a long day of climbing, all legends, wannabe legends, and spuds sat together around a roaring campfire and listened in awe to tales from the mightier legends and climbing gods. The warm and carefree time made life more vivid and worth remembering.

Only recently has the National Park Service begun to appreciate the uniqueness of the Camp 4 cultural landscape during Yosemite's golden years. Perhaps it's easier for the National Park Service to exalt the hippie lifestyle when they no longer must manage a park around hippie unruliness. Now the park can look back fondly upon that era. Now they can go retro.

As a nod to the camp being a cultural landscape and park experience worthy of commemorating rather than stamping out and obliterating, the National Park Service returned Camp 4's original name. While appreciated, to some, this isn't unlike reading an exhibit in a museum. Park managers may have reestablished the old name, but they can't turn back the clock, can't breathe life back into the Camp 4 of new, and can't legislate a cultural phenomenon by administrative decree. You may drag the original members of Creedence back together, but somehow it won't be the same dynamic as Creedence of 1969.

The only remnants of the fabled patrons of the real Camp 4 are the silent ghosts that still ply Yosemite's walls during the day and fireside stories at night—at least in the minds of young climbers wishing to form a connection.

The closest I came to meeting a climbing legend at Camp 4 and striking up an organic conversation was one especially miserably cold and snowy spring evening. Mead Hargis, one of my Pacific Northwest climbing heroes, stopped by our Sunnyside campsite. Long before, he'd left the Northwest and moved to Yosemite, not as a climbing bum but as a National Park Service ranger—just like me. He saw few climbers on that snowy evening other than our group, which was huddled around the fire to keep warm. He stopped by to say hello and spread a little cheer to what looked to him like uncomfortable and despondent climbers. With his lively personality, he talked of Yosemite, climbing, and whatnot. His warm gesture to cold compatriots hinted at the comradery of Camp 4 of old.

My climbing partners later told me of Mead's visit and warm conversation, since I'd already crawled off to my sleeping bag and was fast asleep. I missed it all.

❧

Back at the lonely and silent Icicle Canyon, I still sought ghosts and remnant outlying Icicle Canyon experiences because the Icicle had once been the Northwest's Camp 4. Instead of Ron Kauk, Steve Roper, and Jim Bridwell, Icicle's Camp 4, during Creedence Clearwater Revival's heyday, had Mark, Jay, Jim, Julie, Pat, Steve, Carla, Don, and Mead (yes, *that* Mead).

With a lonely and forlorn sadness, while camped at the deserted Eightmile Campground below Eightmile Boulder, I kept an eye and ear out for any of the legends who'd forged the Pacific Northwest's version of Camp 4. Castle Rock, Snow Creek Wall, Peshastin Pinnacles, and Midnight Rock climbers once filtered in and out of multiple gatherings along Icicle Creek to tell stories, see old friends, and plan the next day's explorations. Many forces and factors led to the demise of the Icicle as a climbing scene and cultural phenomenon—different forces than at Camp 4, but gone, nonetheless. This breakup happened just a few short years before my first entry into Icicle Canyon, where I drifted from site to site, looking for something to happen—but left sitting silent among ghosts.

Icicle's time had passed.

Northwest Climbing in the Time of Creedence

*P*issing vinegar, sporting fresh ideas, and armed with unlimited possibilities, the late 1960s Pacific Northwest climbing generation set out to make their mark. Mark they did—and then some. Carefree friends in a less-than-carefree time. Solidarity and friendship bonded them, but competition, heady times, and surging youthful energy propelled the close-knit group to classic status.

Hermann Ulrich might have been Muddy Waters, and Fred Beckey might have been Elvis, but the Pacific Northwest leading climbers of the late 1960s were Creedence, Lynyrd Skynyrd, Steppenwolf, The Band, the Grateful Dead, and the British Invasion all rolled into one. Like Creedence, the climbers were around for only a few short years, but within this euphoric blink, they spawned enduring classics of unequaled style and grace.

Commitment, comradery, and contagious convergence marked this area, but the taint of death and disillusionment followed close behind. In the immortal words of Shakespeare's *Macbeth*, "What's done cannot be undone." Innocence lost can't be recaptured, but it can be treasured. I walked in their shadows and slunk upon their hollowed stage, but uttered not even a whispering cadence, no sound or fury—signifying nothing. Yet the shadows carried me on in exalted bliss and reverence for their deeds and sub-deeds. A generation like that comes around only every so often.

This story revealed itself with discomfort. Their story isn't fully my story, and I only met but a few. We played in different bands. With Hermann Ulrichs and climbers from the 1930s, I had the comfort of detached time and distance. However, I'm separated from the Creedence climbers by only twelve or so years. But much happened in the Pacific Northwest, the nation, and the world in those crowded few years. The era is too contemporary to be remote, yet too distant to be familiar. In addition, many Creedence climbers still walk the earth and climb its crests. However, as with Hermann Ulrichs and Fred Beckey, we all shared the same rocks and mountains. Even more so, we shared a bond with the climbing experience that transcends time, clique, and cohort. However, this story isn't as much their story. Instead, it's a story of the influence they had upon those forced by circumstances to follow their trailing rope and strive for the same distant summits—metaphorically or otherwise. It's in the fleeting moments after riding through a storm's wildest hurly-burly that our experiences merge and connect—the place where mountains, people, and experiences become indistinguishable from one another.

No matter how robustly they lived their lives, it's an inescapable fact that, like characters in many Shakespearean tales, the Creedence climbers knew tragedy. Discomfort over how to handle other people's deaths and despair gave pause to my earliest draft. Jim Madsen meant too much for me to exploit and reduce his story to a single fall. However, for Northwest climbers who followed, he and others within this narrow window became the classic climbing line-up, not unlike rock stars from the classic rock era. There could be no true discussion of classic rock without also telling of Jimi Hendrix's, Janis Joplin's, and Jim Morrison's falls. Their deaths marked not just an end to three remarkable individuals, but also to a critical inflection point in the overall sixties' youthful counterculture and the end of youthful innocence.

The baby boomers fractured and faced disillusionment after weathering combined calamities ranging from the Vietnam War, Watergate, and Altamont to disco. Therefore, to put classic rock in the context of history and place, one *must* discuss Jimi Hendrix, Janis Joplin, and Jim Morrison. Their deaths wouldn't have been such watershed events if they hadn't shone so brightly on our stage or shared their music, souls, and vibrancy. Their lives inspired; therefore, sharing their deaths becomes a collective celebration of their contributions. This turns caricatures and clichés into honor and respect, and coldness into warmth. It enriches the generations that had the privilege to diminishingly follow.

While the roots of rock 'n' roll harken back to plantations, share-croppers' porches, seedy dives, and urban Chicago honky-tonks, the roots of American climbing started in the European Alps. Since this story involves both American and European relationships, it becomes intertwined with the social dynamics between cultures. For a long time, especially in the world of art and culture, Europeans looked down their noses at the primitive and uncouth Americans—anything coming from the primitive "Daniel Boones" and living on the roguish frontier paled in comparison to the land of Mozart and DaVinci. So, naturally, when it came to climbing, the Europeans, with their wondrous Alps, were amused by Americans and their silly notion that they played in the same league.

For the longest time, American climbers bought into this inferiority complex. American climbers might learn to climb or ski on American bunny slopes, but to be *real* climbers, they must make pilgrimages to the hallowed Alps.

With a fixation on the Alps and the perceived superiority of European climbers, Californians began noticing that while they might not have alpine mountains comparable to the Alps, Yosemite Valley's monstrously steep cliffs provided a different type of climbing—one in which the Californians could make their own distinct mark. They soon discovered that for this type of climbing, nowhere else in the Milky Way compares with Yosemite.

For too long, American climbers endured European derision, much like the taunting Frenchman in *Monty Python and the Holy Grail.* However, after the golden years of Yosemite climbing, Californians could finally spit and fart back in the general direction of their taunting European brethren. After the ascendency of Yosemite climbing, California climbers could then stand in arrogant contempt of other American climbers. Except for hapless Kansas climbers, the Yosemite hotshots ridiculed perhaps no other region as much as the Pacific Northwest.

The Californian climate allowed nearly year-round refinement of climbers' technical skills and muscle tone, compared with the typical flannel-clad Pacific Northwest climber's season, running from July 16 to August 9. Outside those dates, climbers hunker down from the onslaught brought on by rain, snow, avalanches, sodden moss, bare ice, rockfall, exposed crevasses, or snow-free tangles of jungle vegetation. Pale and clammy-skinned scramblers wait for the clouds to part and the drips to go into remission. To say weather limitations hamper technical climbing development would be putting it mildly.

When Northwest climbers traveled to sunny California, they felt ill-prepared for the intimidating and dizzying walls of Yosemite. They returned humbled. And the Californians further mocked the Northwest's snow-sloggers.

This changed the moment Jim Madsen stepped into Yosemite. Instead of being intimidated, he headbutted Yosemite challenges with an energy and fearless intensity the Californians had never seen before—from anywhere. Even more startling, unlike Fred Beckey, who climbed impressive Yosemite walls using old-school techniques and attitudes, the moment the young and bold Jim Madsen stepped into the Valley, a Northwesterner met the Californians on their own terms, on their home turf. And he held his own.

The Yosemite sun gods took notice, not like the old-school musicians who ignored young Jimi Hendrix when his distorted guitar burst upon the scene at the Monterey Pop Festival. At nearly the same time Jimi Hendrix wowed at Monterey and burned his Stratocaster, Jim Madsen burned up Yosemite's hardest classics, spat flaming residue, and immediately went back for more.

When Jim returned to the rain-drenched Pacific Northwest, he and his like-minded climbing partners unleashed their combined fury upon the rocks, cliffs, and alpine walls throughout the Northwest. The Northwest climbing scene's conflagration began just a few months later, with the epicenter squarely at the University of Washington.

Many leading climbers of the day began climbing, and met each other, at the University of Washington and its Climbing Club. Many were students, while some had looser university connections. Regardless, the Climbing Club became the catalyst for great things to come. The Climbing Club's membership and instructors became a who's who of the Creedence climbers, such as Jim Madsen, John

"Mead" Hargis, Al Givler, John Marts, Mark Weigelt, Julie Brugger, Don McPherson, Jay Ossiander, and Ron Burgner. Whether they liked each other or not, they all became close, and all knew everyone else. Several individuals within this tight bunch lived together in the same off-campus house affectionately called The Wilbur House.

Ron Burgner recalls that he first met Jim Madsen on a summit in the Snoqualmie Pass area. The two soon teamed up on many climbs and instructed climbing courses together at the university. Jim Madsen stood out above them all, not just because of his technical ability but also for his singular intensity and drive. This drive extended to all aspects of his life, including moral outrage.

Jim's friends recall a party at which they were all having a good time. An unknown drunk started bad-talking a young woman partygoer. Jim would have nothing of this. That is *not* how you treat a lady. He attempted to overcome the rude problem in much the same way he overcame difficult climbing problems—he worked himself into a rage. Friends had to pull Jim away to keep him from teaching the sod a lesson and getting everyone, including himself, into trouble. Jim filled everything he did with full intensity, passion, and energy.

Jim Madsen studied to become an engineer. As his thermodynamics courses likely taught him, heat and energy need an outlet to keep any system functioning. To dissipate his boredom and pent-up energy, on many occasions, when upstairs library studies lost his interest, Jim and Ron Burgner opened the window, climbed out, and ascended campus buildings and ramparts.

When I went to the University of Washington fifteen years later, Jim's clandestine building ascents were legendary. I have no idea which were true or which were highly embellished. One memorable story had the dean looking out his third-story window and, instead of seeing the typical distant manicured lawn, he saw a close-up of Jim Madsen splayed across the window frame in a wide stemming move. The story goes that the dean hauled Jim off for disciplinary actions. However, in 2020, I asked Ron Burgner about his and Jim's campus building climbing. Ron said he, Jim, and others frequently climbed the buildings out of boredom, but he claimed no one ever caught them and that they never worried about legal or academic consequences.

I have a fading mimeographed copy of the original University of Washington building climbing guide written circa 1970 and the revised version that came out in 1972. The guides provide ratings not only for climbing difficulty but also PI, or police interference. The implication is that campus police had expelled many students over building climbing, so there may be more to the Jim Madsen legends than Ron preferred to admit.

Many young and hot Pacific Northwest climbers weren't content to climb only campus buildings. They took their technique, boldness, and attitudes to Northwest walls and mountains. Stories of the new climbing standard in Yosemite made their way across the nation. The new Seattle crowd took notice. No longer content with climbing buildings and lower Northwest crags, the climbers, in various waves, made pilgrimages to Yosemite. Some, like Jim, stayed in Camp 4 for extended periods, while others returned to the Northwest and their studies.

When Jim Madsen, Tom Hargis, and others returned from Yosemite, they imported the Californian attitude and technical mastery to the Northwest. They demonstrated advanced climbing skills to the wide-eyed Northwest climber. It was as if an oil painter had come back from a sojourn with a European painting master to tell his students back home that all along, the American painters had been holding the brush by the wrong end—that they could generate better brushstrokes if they dipped the brushy end in the paint, not the wooden end. A heavenly light shone down and turned a switch: painting with the camel hair end *did* seem much better. Who would have thought?

The tight-knit group soon began developing as an entity beyond just a collection of individual members. They no longer were John, Paul, George, and Ringo. They were the Beatles. Or, rather, in their terms, they were no longer Jim Madsen, Kim Schmitz, Paul Boving, Bruce Albert, Carla Firey, Mead Hargis, Mark Weigelt, Don McPherson, Julie Brugger, and Al Givler. They were the group that coalesced into the Pacific Northwest climbing scene of the late 1960s.

At a furious pace, the University of Washington Creedence crowd put up new routes on the Index Town Wall, the Leavenworth area, Liberty Bell, and the Mount Stuart region. They took the technical Yosemite climbing skills and attitudes onto the big walls and ramparts in the Northwest. Their climbs set a new standard for the Northwest, and they inspired later climbers, even spuds who flailed in their footsteps, wandered in their shadows, and felt the loss created by the eventual vacuum they left behind. For those who penetrated beyond the sunless cleft, we're but lighted fools. And life is but a walking shadow. But oh, what a cleft and shadow they laid.

By the time I came around, many of the previous crowd had moved on or were operating in different orbits than my electrons. I heard stories of the Creedence climbers, but I didn't know any of the individuals personally. I also didn't know the specifics of their growing legends, so my mind freely filled in the details. However, given the nature of their times and troubles, I imagine many were having their own Holden Caulfield moments. They all had to contend with the realities of the growing war, the draft, and understanding life's purpose and how climbing fit into everything.

I imagined the Creedence climbers, like Holden Caufield, saw much pretentiousness, hollowness, alienation, and superficiality in "normal" society and expectations. Like many climbers and spuds who followed, I imagined the Creedence climbers found solace, answers, purpose, and authenticity only in the wilds and during the intensity of life on the edge. For the Creedence climbers, that edge turned into rocks, fins, arêtes, jam cracks, faces, walls, ice flows, and alpine big walls of ice and rock. Unlike the turbulent storms blowing in the lowlands, political theater, and distant jungles, rock-climbing challenges could be overcome. Even alpine storms can be weathered with endurance, commitment, and personal fortitude. The storms brewing down valley and overseas were a different story.

My young mind wandered and filled in their stories. I somehow— without any knowledge—believed Donn Heller and Don Harder, like Lionel Terray and Louis Lachenal, epitomized the perfect climbing partnership. I had a feeling. Mark Weigelt epitomized a carefree spirit seeking hidden gems nestled next to or behind what should have been obvious. Paul Boving became the intensity-driven problem solver; Jim Madsen the driven climbing machine; and Ron Burgner the master artist on elegant rock lines. Carla Firey and her extended family represented the ego-free spirit, wilderness adventurer, and generational continuity. I imagined Reese Martin as the young zen master apprentice, and Julie Brugger the pioneer convention-bending rock master and solid climbing partner, regardless of problems at hand.

For reasons I can't explain, the Creedence climber I most wanted to climb with was Mead Hargis.

Regardless of my uninformed imagery, together, they spawned an entity bigger than each individual. Perceptions might not have been true, but for me, it didn't matter. The legend mattered—and the legend inspired me to endure my own storms, setbacks, and challenges. I almost didn't want to better understand the person behind the façade. I drew imagery and inspiration from the legend. So, discovering whatever individual flaws lay behind drawn curtains would only serve to disappoint.

My Pacific Northwest climbing age, after the tumultuous Vietnam years, came from an entirely different dimension, one that overlapped the transitional arc between Carter and Reagan. In other words, the lost years—lost in purpose, lost in identity, and lost after the chaos and disillusionment of the Vietnam War and the failing of youthful idealism. The Age of Aquarius never came—or never existed. The loss and disillusionment that resulted from Creedence climbers' deaths, and the subsequent vacuum, hung in the air and consumed much-needed oxygen.

I formed images of Creedence climbers based on what few stories I heard, coupled with the nature of their art, and mashed them through my own unique worldview and understanding. Therefore, from the enchanting loveliness of the Prusik Peak's west ridge, I gazed upon the stupendous south face. Few images not containing ice could be as lovely. Although lovely and wonderful, my moderate finger painting on the well-worn western canvas paled in comparison to the south face's art. I imagined the south-face master artisans, Ron Burgner and Fred Stanley, to be masters not only in climbing technique but also in climbing class, beauty, and style.

Farther into the icy realm, the Picket Range formed the epitome of alpine ice beauty and elegance. Even the names drew my breath short—the northern Pickets held Fury and Phantom, and the southern beauty bastion held Inspiration and Terror. Draped in ice, rock, lore, and legend, how could any peak be as glorious and awe-inspiring as

Mount Terror? The Pickets were wilderness and art in the purest and most primitive form.

Primitive it was. The grueling feat to even get there became a climbing and endurance epic all by itself, considering the peaks were guarded by wayward walls, tangly jungles, blind alleys, waterfalls and water-slicks, rain, storm, and fog so mysterious it rearranged landscapes before your eyes. There was also the ever-present, endless uphill march into the heavens. While in such remote and rescue-proof loneliness, who would dare put their neck out on unknown new routes?

The bold, the beautiful, and the legends. In other words, the Fireys.

The Fireys aren't just an attitude and symbol of wilderness purity. It's also a name—led by husband and wife Joe and Joan Firey. When she was old enough, they occasionally took their daughter Carla into the primitive wilds. While my teenage years were marked by exploring the streets of South Seattle by bicycle, Carla Firey explored the North Cascades' forested, meadowed, alped, rocked, and iced wilderness wilds.

Many of the remote Picket Range summits were climbed, firsted, or seconded by one or more Fireys. In 1970, Joan and Carla, accompanied by frequent wilderness patrons David Knudson and Peter Renz, first climbed Mount Terror's exquisitely beautiful east ridge. I know beauty when I encounter it, even if I've never seen it firsthand. I've never climbed Mount Terror, but I've gazed at it from afar for so long and read about it so intensely that I feel I almost know it by feel, and I intuitively know that our hearts and souls are somehow connected.

At times, I try hard to visualize myself looking at the scene through the eyes of master alpinists as they released their art onto the world. I can imagine the Fireys' eyes panning from the jungle wilds of the McMillan Creek cirque, past the Pickets' spine, across the horn-like Mount Triumph, continuing past Eldorado Peak's lovely snow crest, and then slowly returning to the point of origin. I imagine this to be the center of the world. And after attaining its lofty summit, I found the center of life, and I found home.

The Fireys lived in the Pickets and everywhere in the Northwest where existed unexplored wildness, graceful snow and glaciers, and alpine spiritual pursuits. They spent a lot of time in the ice fields draping Eldorado Peak's northern side—the most extensive glaciated area in the United States outside Alaska. Peter Renz and Dave Knudson weren't the only explorers who accompanied the Fireys into these icy realms. They were joined by another climbing family: the Meulemanses—John and Irene.

⚹

Once on the cusp of Eldorado Peak's remoteness, on the fringe of sublimity in the twilight between winter and spring, on one fine morning, I found myself waking to a beautiful soft orange sunrise glow upon the near and far glaciers and ice fields. I threw open the tent flap and was suddenly blasted with a sight of a sea of peaks and their tumultuous, upheaved ice flows. I lay motionless, marveling that such serene enchantments can, and still do, exist.

Just then, Andrew, one of my three companions, remarked, "Look up at the Meulemanses."

Apparently, while I remained groggy and bundled in my sleeping bag, the Meulemanses had quietly skied past our camp and were now enjoying telemarking upon the sunrise's reflection on pristine powder snow.

I watched in awe as their graceful strokes painted a masterpiece on the glistening virgin-white canvas. Watching involved both contentment and aggravation. Contentment in witnessing such masterful and graceful brushstrokes, but aggravation in wondering why I was still in my sleeping bag while they'd obviously had the motivation to rise much earlier. Clearly, this may have a bearing upon why some people are masters, some are apprentices, and some are spuds.

Their inspiration became motivation enough to get me to brave the cold and stiffness of the morning, don wintery and frozen clothing, and plod up the slope in snowshoes. Placing my chunky snowshoe footprints across the Meulemanses' masterful canvas and brushstrokes felt sacrilegious. I carefully stepped over the most artful and graceful of the curves as we continued to the summit of snow and ice—and the summit of dreams, art, and serenity. Why had I ever questioned the purpose of life?

My Eldorado enchantment was far removed in time and place from the concerns and challenges the Creedence climbers must have felt and endured. The height of their Holden Caulfield loss and alienation years coincided with the beginning throes of the Vietnam years. For passionate people, the prospect, fear, and apprehension of being drafted and having to fight in a war and for a cause they had no passion for became palpable. This was also a time of freedom, purity, and togetherness, and what better place for freedom, purity, and togetherness than linked by mind and linked by rope on a challenging new climbing route that pushed the mind and pushed the body? For some, climbing became an escape from the artificial and shallow world held tight below the smog-encrusted Puget Sound inversion layer. When given a choice, like a salmon following an unexplained yearning to return to natal streams, where else would one return?

Not all the Creedence climbers found solace in the mountains' wildness. Ron Burgner found grace and beauty and peace on challenging new rock routes—the harder and the bigger, the better. He longed for new routes and new art. Why copy someone else's art when you can create something entirely new?

Other Creedence climbers found school and career pursuits less to their liking. Mark Weigelt perfected not only climbing skills but also the ability to live without a job or income. He represented the quintessential climbing bum. He and fellow Creedence climber Julie Brugger wandered wherever alpine wanderlust took them. They were more into alpine mountains than Ron or Jim, but they likely couldn't define why or where the winds blew them. They only knew they wanted to climb, wander, and search for the ultimate experience.

As is the case with many quests, youthful energy is rarely sustained. The laws of physics rule in the end. For Jim Madsen, the energy master, we'll never know where this force could have led or how and when it would have dissipated, since circumstances took that decision from Jim Madsen. Fate decided for him.

Jim's energy might have burned the brightest, but it was short-lived. While in Yosemite, he heard that a couple of friends were stranded in a storm near the top of El Capitan's Dihedral Wall. Jim and others hopped in a helicopter, which rushed them to the top. Jim threw a rope over the edge and began rappelling the three-thousand-foot face to take supplies and good cheer to his stranded friends.

Rappelling off a three-thousand-foot vertical cliff may daunt some people, but not Jim Madsen. His friends were in need. Perhaps he should have had less confidence. Jim only tied a single-hand knot at the end of the rope. It's not wise to trust a single overhand knot as a backup precaution to stop a rappel if it should run amok. He should have known better. In this instance, the single knot proved insufficient. Perhaps his mind centered on helping friends and not on the approaching end of the rope. As the knot hit his rappel device, it quickly slipped through. His "Oh shit!" was the last anyone heard from the Pacific Northwest climbing scene's spiritual leader.

The sixties' youthful idealism and the counterculture's belief that they were indestructible as they transformed society into a utopian Age of Aquarius died when Jimi Hendrix, Janis Joplin, and Jim Morrison died. It marked the end of an era. Similarly, youthful Northwest climbers were stunned upon the loss of their indestructible Jim. They'd assumed he had no limits and that nothing could stop him if he set his sight and rage upon it. The air had been taken out of the sunny Seattle climbing scene. Climbers were once again lost below swirling clouds.

Even Jim Madsen confessed just days before his fateful rappel that he'd tired of Yosemite. He was looking forward to returning to the University of Washington and finishing his long-on-hold engineering degree. He must have thought he couldn't sustain the life he'd been leading. So, too, had others. Several of Jim's inner circle quit climbing after losing Jim.

Ron quit climbing. It wasn't just the emptiness of losing such a charismatic climbing partner and friend. All of Jim's friends began thinking of their own mortality. If someone as driven and talented as Jim could go, where did that leave everyone else?

The Vietnam draft also got in the way. While some climbers quit after Jim's death, others graduated college and went on to other life pursuits. Still others changed their lives in substantive ways because of the war. The wave of forty thousand souls who migrated to Canada to avoid the draft and avoid killing and dying in a war they didn't believe in also claimed some of Ron's climbing partners.

The brilliant, focused, and determined Mead Hargis settled into a quieter life. He didn't do so willingly. His passion for mountains still burned bright. Arthritis pain became too debilitating for him to continue climbing at the same level as he once had, so he painted many fewer masterpieces. His hands could no longer hold the brush as deftly. Instead, he married, had kids, and moved to Yosemite to work as a park ranger. He led rock and mountain high-angle technical rescues.

Back at home in the Cascades, according to surviving friends, a few others, such as Mark Weigelt, Al Givler, and Paul Boving, subconsciously did their best to keep the momentum rolling in light of a noticeable vacuum within the Pacific Northwest.

Almost four years to the day after Jim Madsen rappelled to his death in Yosemite, Mark Weigelt died in his beloved mountains in an unexpected ice fall and rock avalanche on Mount Stuart. The mountain gods also took this free soul before he could decide his fate for himself.

Two years later, Donn Heller and his climbing partner had just completed a challenging new winter ascent one mountain over from where Mark died. Unlike Mark, Donn made the summit on this fateful day; however, he never returned. While descending the steep gully from Aasgard Pass—the same steep access route that leads into the Enchantments and Prusik Peak—Donn took the crampons off his boots. He might have believed more snow covered the ground than ice. Crampons don't work well on snow. It must have been icier than he anticipated because he slipped on ice and took a long fall. He died a short time later.

A few months later, Bruce Carson died while climbing in the Himalayas when a fragile cornice that he unknowingly stepped on gave way. In a few short years, many of the leading young Pacific Northwest climbers who'd defined the Creedence era had suddenly died. The remaining climbers back in the Northwest were once again lost and demoralized. Reese Martin, one of the young climbers coming up within the ranks at the time, looked up to Paul Boving as the spiritual leader. Paul's climbs, friendliness, and climbing talents did more than anyone else to keep what used to be a tight-knit group intact, according to Reese. Other climbers of the period cite Al Givler as the motivational force, although at the time, Al increasingly climbed in distant ranges far from the Cascades.

To those who knew him, Al Givler seemed larger than life and, like Jim Madsen, larger than death. Al developed a reputation for being unstoppable in the mountains no matter how technical the obstacle and how grim the conditions. All the while, he had an infectious smile and an enduring sense of hope that just drew people in regardless of their walk of life. These qualities make a great expedition climber.

An expedition climber is one who often spends months on an almost military siege-style ascent, often in the world's highest mountains in the borderlands between Nepal, India, and Tibet. Expedition climbers often place a succession of camps and supply depots up the mountain's flank. When the combination of time, supplies, and weather is right, whatever team members are in position in the highest camp make the final dash for the summit. Such tactics require technical climbing skills *and* the single-minded drive to relentlessly make incremental progress despite weariness and the mountain's inhospitality. Most of all, expedition climbing requires the personality to endure days-long or weeks-long storms, live cramped in small tents, *and* avoid getting on other's nerves. Team infighting in such desperate, cold, dangerous, and lonely places is not a recipe for success or a long life.

Understanding the qualities that make an ideal expedition climber, expedition leaders began assembling a team to tackle the most coveted climbing goal of the mid-1970s—the summit of K2.

While K2 is slightly lower in elevation than Mount Everest—the world's highest mountain—K2 is a much more challenging quest. No American had ever stood on its summit despite decades of trying. Naturally, the expedition planners invited Al Givler to this coveted team. Al accepted.

To train for the 1978 climb, expedition members Jim Wickwire, Dusan Jagersky, Steve Marts, and Al Givler—all Pacific Northwest mountaineers—went to Alaska in the summer of 1977 to ascend unclimbed and mostly unnamed mountains recently discovered in a remote corner of Southeast Alaska. This signified pure exploratory alpine climbing in a remote range. It would have been a fitting preparation for K2; however, something went wrong. Al and Dusan fell to their deaths. Another two beloved Creedence climbers lost. Three months later, we lost another Northwest climbing master when Paul Boving also never returned.

One of the hallmarks of rock climbing in the new era is the potential need to persistently work on a particular climbing move, over and over, until the climber has the specific combination of moves wired so they can reach, and ponder, the next set of moves. Eventually, if skill, luck, conditioning, determination, weather, and other factors are all favorable, then the climber may reach the top and claim a first ascent. Paul Boving's single-minded determination certainly helped when he ushered in the 5.11 climbing standard on Index Town Wall's Thin Fingers.

As the name implies, Thin Fingers is a thin crack that demands skill at ascending vertical rock by pulling on painful fingertips jammed into thin cracks. Paul Boving relentlessly worked on Thin Fingers problems until he finally succeeded in 1976. His new climb set a new rock-climbing standard for Washington.

A few months later, he climbed the route again. He loved the graceful look of the crack and chose to climb it for the third time in October 1977. He got partway up and fell. Some of his protection pieces pulled. During the fall, he hit his head. He died a few hours later.

Paul's death was not only a sad loss to family and friends. It also caused a severe blow to the psyche and spirit of the Washington climbing scene. It had only been eight years since Jim Madsen's death. Then Mark Weigelt and Donn Harder died. Their deaths, and Al Givler's the previous year, took the air out of any sail, even those propelled by the Creedence climbers.

A new day had come to the Pacific Northwest climbing scene. It seemed climbers left the scene in droves to pursue careers, families, and other aspects of life. A stillness and chill settled on the rock walls throughout the state.

☙❧

I attained my first summit one year before Al's and Paul's deaths. My rise into climbing perfectly aligned with the pall and vacuum left by the loss of the Creedence climbers. This didn't stop me, but it helped shape my climbing worldviews and perspective—not only in climbing. I also enrolled in the University of Washington and its Climbing Club.

While I was at the University of Washington, when not holed up in the basement archives researching Hermann Ulrichs's climbs and everything on the North Cascades, I occasionally wandered to the other Forestry College's buildings to chat with Reese Martin. I can't recall how I met Reese, other than not through climbing. It must have been through my forestry curriculum.

Reese had once been a University of Washington student, but now he was staff. He was working on a forestry research project. Our first conversations centered on forestry matters, but they later turned solely to climbing. During one chat, I must have said something about my many climbing spud weekends, because he casually said, "I climb a little myself." I assumed he was a fellow spud, but later, he slowly began telling stories that hinted that he was anything but a spud. It turns out he was a talented climber who'd climbed with some of the leading Creedence climbers. It took many such talks to pull details out from him—not because he wouldn't open up but because he was understated and humble.

Although Reese had only six years on me, so much happened in the Pacific Northwest climbing scene within those few short years that his stories of the earlier generation opened my eyes to the Creedence crowd and piqued my interest to an even higher degree. He was too young to have climbed with Jim Madsen, but he'd fallen under Paul Boving's spell. Upon Paul's death, Reese began to rethink bold adventures. However, unlike many others, Reese never gave up climbing.

Regretfully, I never kept in touch with Reese after I moved away. Years later, I chanced upon his obituary. He died in 2004 while participating in a paragliding competition. Fate and the gods took him too.

What is it about the Creedence crowd? While they lived life fully, they had their fair share of having dark shadows hovering over them. Just a few years before Reese Martin's paragliding accident, Creedence climber Dave Anderson was involved in a skiing accident. While he was enjoying the wondrous powder snow of Wasatch Range's Snowbird ski resort, an avalanche slammed into him and broke both legs and a hip. He might have thought, *It could be worse. I'm still alive.* The rescue crew bundled and secured him in the helicopter so they could fly to the emergency room. Shortly after take-off, the helicopter crashed, killing all on board.

It takes surviving dozens of stupid mistakes to gain experience, but it takes only one to become a statistic. Often, such matters are influenced by forces beyond our control. It's a high-stakes game of chance, and anyone would be a fool not to recognize that in the long term, the odds are with the house. From the perspective of the house, humans don't even enter the equation since they're not even a rounding error. The experienced are wise, but the experienced are also lucky. Those who don't heed this dictum may pay the house a heavy price.

Non-climbers repeatedly ask climbers, "Why do you climb?" Are skiers asked why they ski? Climbers aren't the only ones hit with avalanches. Why do artists perform their art? Are automobile drivers constantly asked, "Why do you drive?" Drivers may have a higher rate of accidents than people who climb.

Besides glaring inconsistencies and biases, clearly, there are inner demons that continue to drive afflicted climbers. Perhaps there are as many reasons to climb as there are climbers, since no group, let alone climbers, is monolithic. What gets a climber up the physically draining, dangerous, but technically easy Everest South Col route likely isn't the same drive that pushes a person to establish a punishing new route up a blank alpine wall. The Yosemite big wall bug bit Jim Madsen differently than it did many of his Northwest friends. Some partners wanted to combine climbing with a job, settled life, family, and other such normal functions, while people like Mark Weigelt preferred wanderlust alpine adventures.

The Pacific Northwest Creedence climbers consisted of a collection of unique individuals. Each had their own personality, idiosyncrasies, and even flaws, just like the rest of us. However, within a few short years, they helped us see the potential for unlimited possibilities, and they left testaments and monuments to their inspired passing.

Despite many differences, there are a few commonalities shared by most of the Creedence climbers. During their climbing days, they each threw themselves into climbing in a way that could be described as an intense religious experience. Many felt ill at ease with mundane, colloquial life before they began pushing their climbing limits.

The transition between adolescence and working adult during college years is never easy for any generation, but it was perhaps even more difficult during the height of the Vietnam War and home-front social unrest. Youth at the time were shedding the shackles of societal conformities in more ways than previous generations. For those who felt lost and found some solace or meaning in life through climbing, it would have been hard to give it up. For what would be the alternative?

The reasons why people climb are only casually interesting to me. Instead, I'm much more interested in what sustains their passion and what precipitates its demise. Is it as Neil Young sings in his song "Hey Hey, My My," when he claims it's better to burn out than it is to rust? To get up each day and persevere during long climbs is hard enough. But to keep at it month after month, year after year, and decade after decade requires a level of commitment, passion, endurance, and mental fortitude that's a noteworthy story in of and by itself.

It's easy to understand that a climber's biggest challenge is often not falls, technical difficulties, avalanches, storms, or inclement weather. Instead, it's time, life, and transitions. To climb at such high levels requires a commitment of time, attention and money. It demands that the climber forgo creature comforts, traditional relationships, and families. As age sets in, they also must accept the cold realities of a fading physique and the wariness that comes from the thought of having to face yet another harsh bivouac. People change over time, and such changes naturally affect a person's inner demons and drive. There's no graceful exit strategy or transition plan for artists who live on the edge. There may come a time when they look upward into splayed skies and, where once they saw stars, see only sky and an approaching storm.

While Donn, Jim, Paul, and Mark left their vibrant life too soon for us to get a glimmer of their future fates and life decisions, the remaining class scattered in all directions. Ron Burgner found religion. Ron quit climbing after Jim Madsen's death; however, over time, he came back in fits and starts. Some quits were for safety concerns—life's worries—but others went deeper and even invaded his dreams.

In one of Ron Burgner's poignant and fitful dreams, after witnessing a long and intricate tale, he felt a disturbing presence and heard a singular voice. The voice spoke with a command, depth, power, and resonance that only a god could command. The voice simply said, "No!"

Ron took this as a sign that he had to make life changes, that he'd wandered upon the wrong path. That he, too, was off route. He took this as a personal connection with God. His destiny no longer focused on climbing, and certainly no longer in the lifestyle inherent in climbing in the Creedence era. He decided then and there he would commit his life to God. Regarding climbing, he couldn't serve two masters.

Ron found it hard to break from old habits while still immersed in his old friends and old, comfortable ways. So he made a bold break. He packed his few belongings and moved to Spokane—on the drier, east side of the state, not far from Idaho. One by one, the Creedence climbers dissipated into their own separate Idahos.

This is the void I experienced when I began climbing in the Pacific Northwest.

In many ways, my climbing journey has also ended, at least compared to the level at which it once burned. Do I miss those times and wish to relive my active days? Or do I regret today's reality?

No, not really.

Grace Slick of the classic rock band Jefferson Airplane, a band that epitomized the San Francisco hippie era, was asked if she missed the Haight-Ashbury hippie and youth counterculture scene of the sixties. She said, "No, it's like elementary school. I may have enjoyed second grade, but I don't want to go back and remain in the same grade forever."

I began drifting away from climbing because I saw diminishing purpose. Why would society care if I climbed Hard Very Extreme level on the British scale, Cliffs of Insanity level on the Vizzini scale, or Zero dot Meh on the Spud scale? What does nature or wilderness care if I climbed rock, ice, ridge, or couloir, or if I stayed at home? Is nature better preserved or species protected by my personal and egocentric pursuits? I wanted the world to be a better place upon my passage.

Ye of lesser climbing skills and boldness, I'm never climbing into the heights of a Madsen, Burgner, or Boving. Perhaps I could make my mark somewhere else. In this, it's not unlike Ian Anderson of Jethro Tull when he realized he would never leave his mark as a mid-rate guitar player, so he switched to flute. That decision led him to board the locomotive to distinctiveness.

This is one reason I gravitated to caves. Cavers also seemed to be an even closer-knit community than the fragmented climbers of the Northwest's lost years. Community is important to me. This may be one reason I felt such an affinity for the Creedence climbers. They had such a strong sense of community. Not just a group of dedicated climbers, together, the Creedence climbers were, by every mark and every metric, a family.

After Birth ~ Premortem

*Y*oung mountaineers today climb at a much higher technical standard than anyone did in my generation—at least in my sphere. I started technical rock climbing on easy and low-angle routes that deserve few, if any, intimidation stars or accolades. It took me years to work up to the moderate-level standard. Ten years later, at my technically fittest self, I broached the ceiling of what's now the starting floor for the many twelve-year-olds I've seen at the Vertical Rock Climbing and Fitness Center indoor rock-climbing gym located in Manassas, Virginia. Watching young climbers at home on Vertical Rock's walls and overhangs is like witnessing the reincarnation of Jim Madsen—minus the rage. Such sights only serve to highlight my spud factor.

If these trends continue, I can imagine witnessing a young woman giving birth on a Hard Very Severe, Cliffs of Insanity-level stemming move as her newborn emerges, takes over the lead, and breaks out an entirely new climbing standard, Ultra Hard Extremely Insane level, belayed only by its umbilical cord as it ascends to the Vertical Rock's top rung in impeccable style and grace—all while witnessing spuds remain gape-jawed as they retreat further into the depths of their spudly mediocrity.

⚶

I have no doubt that young climbers born to indoor rock-climbing gyms will likely go far. However, there are many more pressing issues and concerns out there in the real outdoor world affecting mountains, caves, and wild habitats that go well beyond the mere self-absorption of an individual's technical mastery.

Climbing access remains an ongoing challenge for many cliffs and routes. The cost of rescues and the question of who should pay are also key points of conversation, as is how best to share the rocks and mountains with other user groups.

Within the world of caves, closures remain a constant threat affecting future access. The need for preservation and conservation-oriented laws to transition from a site-specific cave perspective into ones focusing on the holistic karst system is also sorely needed. In addition, new threats, including a mysterious disease—white-nose syndrome—have crept upon the scene and killed millions of cave-inhabiting bats. Some believe cavers who haven't decontaminated their gear may contribute to spreading this deadly bat disease.

In addition to new impacts, old threats continue to affect caves and their habitat. While caves can effectively transport cave and vadose waters, they can also, unfortunately, effectively transport water pollutants, ranging from sewage spills, petroleum leaks, and fracking fluid wastes to all the myriad water quality problems that their cousin, surface waters, suffer from. Well, not cousin, per se. Instead, identical twin.

Despite the sameness of water being water, water protection laws in many states dramatically change, or entirely disappear, as water plunges from the surface into a cave—much like a spud rappelling into Green's Well may suddenly disappear from a surface-bound observer's perspective. However, knowledgeable people understand that neither the spud nor the plunging water truly disappears. Also, the cave scientist who performed dye-tracing studies may know which spring the water will reemerge from upon the surface. Springs are nothing more than groundwater reemerging onto the surface—much like Mammoth Cave's Echo River reemerges at Echo River Spring.

Waters in many cave and karst regions may plummet into caves and then reemerge again multiple times as they descend to base level. Many state lawmakers haven't yet wrapped their heads around the fact that surface water, cave water, and groundwater are often the same water. Consequently, many state water laws apply only when water flows on the surface—as if a person's constitutional protections end the moment a TAG caver leaves the surface anchor and rappels into the subsurface. As such, a dry region may have restricted all additional new surface water withdrawals due to an active drought. But at the same time, it doesn't regulate water withdrawals from groundwater sources. And then regulators may wonder why surface streams and springs are drying up.

Preservation thoughts often run deep through the ranks of those who traipse through impacted wildlands. It's one thing to read about threats to mountains, caves, cliffs, and canyons, but it hits closer to home upon seeing the challenges, and losses, firsthand.

In the caving world, some cavers join conservancies, such as the regional Cave Conservancy of the Virginias. Cave conservancies work to save, conserve, and manage caves and cave access. Some organizations, such as the National Speleological Society, promote caves and the caving public more broadly.

Other cavers wanting to help thwart unneeded negative impacts to caves take a volunteer data-gathering approach, such as the Tongass Cave Project in Alaska. Educational approaches have long been a cherished tradition within the caving community. The American Cave Museum in Horse Cave, Kentucky, and the Virginia Cave and Karst Trail are noted examples.

In the mountaineering world, some climbers, like Reese Martin had, devote time and effort to organizations, such as the Access Fund, that secure access to threatened climbing areas.

A small fraction of climbers may pursue their wildland preservation interests by taking a more direct approach. And some have utilized specialized climbing techniques to further their conservation message.

❦

Two years after our Mount Triumph climb, Derek became involved with the Earth First! movement. His notoriety ratcheted up when he combined environmental activism with his climbing skills and equipment.

Earth First! planned a demonstration over the Forest Service's proposed harvesting of a unique stand of old-growth conifers. Derek had witnessed all too often the ineffectiveness of surface demonstrations because the local sheriff could easily arrest the demonstrators, only to have the wanton destruction continue with little to no delay. This observation inspired Derek to take a different approach for his demonstrations. While surface and subsurface waters are all effectively the same water, Derek knew the distinct disadvantages surface demonstrators have compared with a climber taking the demonstration to a different level—one that doesn't so easily disappear. Derek's demonstration inspiration took him higher and into the trees—a place where he knew the sheriff would have problems affecting an arrest.

Derek's inspiration drew upon the use of ropes, climbing equipment, and, especially, a climber's portaledge, a framed hammock that Yosemite big-wall climbers often use to sleep on the vertical and overhanging rock in Yosemite Valley—and, apparently, the first ascent of Mount Triumph's east face.

After choosing a suitable tree in Oregon, Derek hauled up ropes, rappelling equipment, several days' supply of food, and a large banner that read, "Don't Cut Us Down!"

After Derek unfurled his portaledge banner, he waited. Forest Service and law enforcement officers eventually responded. With a megaphone, they ordered him down. Derek remained tree-bound. The officers had no reasonable means to remove him. However, a few hours later, when it looked like people had left, Derek rappelled from his portaledge to check out the climbing potential of nearby rocks. Unbeknownst to Derek, the officers also had been waiting. A federal officer quickly arrested him and took him away.

Tree sitting has now become a much more common tactic for forest demonstrations. Over ten years after Derek's Oregon tree sitting, Julia Lorraine Hill employed the same technique in the California redwoods. Her demonstration lasted 738 days and resulted in national and international attention, the writing of a popular book, and an interest in securing the Hollywood movie rights. Julia might have taken some inspiration from Derek's tree sitting, since he's often cited as the father of American tree sitting. Julia's tree sitting lasted much longer than Derek's relatively short-lived effort. However, Julia didn't have to contend with Derek's insatiable passion for rock climbing and the lure of new routes.

As you could imagine, Derek wasn't popular within the timber-dependent logging communities of the Pacific Northwest or within dam management circles after they found mysterious anti-dam slogans spray-painted on the dam's façade (apparently on rappel). A few years later, Derek left Earth First! and tree activism and took up residence not in a tree but in a timber-dependent logging community. He still felt the passion to save rivers, forests, and mountains from abuse, but he increasingly grew to believe that activism alone is insufficient to bring about change. He believed society must also provide reasonable alternative economies to resource-based towns rather than just having outsiders descend upon them and scream, "No!" Consequently, he explored means to offer more sustainable alternatives but couldn't effectively do that using his real name, which had been printed in local papers throughout Pacific Northwest timber communities.

A few years later, I was driving through where I thought he was living at the time, but I only had vague directions. I went looking for him, but I didn't know until later that he'd been using a different name to maintain harmonious relations with his neighbors and new forestry friends. So, when I began asking around for him, using his real name, it didn't sit very well with him. I almost ruined his anonymity. (This is why throughout this book I have not used his real name and many place names have been altered within the "Mount Bad" chapter.)

In the end, it worked out well for him. He continued pursuing his endeavors, and I mine. We each chose different paths, and over time, we drifted apart. We never climbed together again. Although I greatly enjoyed our climbs together, mountaineers' paths often come and go with the passage of time. Not unlike how my knowledge of pioneering climbers' adventures enriched my climbing experience, recollections of now distant climbing partners have become an integral layer in my overflowing tapestry of mountain memories and the birth of a quality life—whether indoors or outdoors, or inside or outside the mountains.

⊙╎⊙

Oftentimes, legal intrigue and subterfuge get in the way of career growth within a federal land management agency, but this isn't always the case. The Carlsbad Caverns National Park cave specialist who hired me as a cave specialist got his career start specifically *because* of former clandestine activities. Well, clandestine as it relates to the backward-leaning cave access regulations at the time.

Charlie, who'd been managing the park's caves through its fire program, planned to retire. His supervisor asked him for suggestions for who should take over managing the park's many caves. Always a progressive thinker, Charlie suggested Ronal.

"Who's Ronal?" the supervisor asked.

"He's the local unemployed oil roustabout who keeps illegally entering the park's caves," Charlie replied.

"Why would we hire a person who's always breaking the law and trespassing into the park's caves without a permit?" the bewildered supervisor chortled.

"He's the only one around here who knows where the caves are located."

"That's a good point," the newly minted progressive supervisor said.

"Besides," Charlie added, "if a guy's going to constantly enter park caves whether we want him to or not, regardless of how many laws we put on the books, wouldn't you rather have the guy working *for* us rather than *against* us?"

That logical reasoning won in the end, and that newly minted cave specialist—the former unemployed oil field roustabout—forever changed the nature of cave management, since he's now highly regarded as the father of modern federal cave management and the person responsible for bringing caves into the minds and attention of land managers throughout the nation. He no longer allowed the federal agency to ignore or abuse caves.

However, in modern times, many problems facing mountains, caves, cliffs, and canyons go well beyond that which local progressive managers can solve on their own—even the Ronals of the world. Some are broader and infused with challenging social, environmental, and political entanglements more than those wrought by a single federal agency.

❦

In the wet Pacific Northwest, it's hard to imagine droughts and water restrictions. For too long, rainy and wet had become the region's defining characteristics. David Laskin, in his little gem, *Rains All the Time*, agreed. For me, that defining characteristic continued vertically beyond the rain-soaked emerald valleys, past the white cloud-shrouded hillsides, to finally land upon the crowning jewel—the hundreds of glaciers that bound and held together the world of mountain, forest, water, and sky. For someone who spent his youth traipsing through the North Cascades' hills and dales, the loss of the region's iconic alpine glaciers had become unbelievable—a poignant harbinger of a wildly different future in trying times ahead.

Eminent glaciologist Austin Post, in his 1971 publication, "Inventory of Glaciers in the North Cascades, Washington," listed 756 glaciers within Washington's Cascade Range. In this same publication, he highlighted the important role glaciers play in sustaining summertime river flows and water supply. Other researchers, including North Cascades National Park glaciologist Jon Riedel, also recognized the region's reliance upon glaciers in the otherwise dry late summer. Despite rumors to the contrary and David Laskin's book title, it does not rain all the time in the Pacific Northwest. In late summer, the region relies upon ice melt from its abundant glaciers. Well, to put things in the proper tense—*used* to rely upon. Climate change, including the human-induced variety, has thrust this change upon us, and it's happening faster than anticipated.

In countless teenage and young adult rambles on Mount Rainier's slopes, I never entered the Paradise Ice Caves. I felt no rush. They would always be there.

They were not.

Snow and ice melt permanently took them from us by the 1980s. I also missed the opportunity to experience the dangers of Snohomish County's Big Four Ice Caves. That ice has melted too.

The 1990s saw the loss of the Lewis Glacier, Milk Lake Glacier, Lyall Glacier, and West Lynch Glacier. The aughts saw the demise of the Spider Glacier within the once aptly named Glacier Peak Wilderness Area. The 2010s witnessed the loss of additional cherished and storied glaciers within the once-wet North Cascades. A fact sheet produced by the Washington State Department of Ecology stated that the range lost fifty-three of its glaciers from the 1950s to the 2010s. Mauri Pelto, of the North Cascades Glacier Climate Project, highlighted at least sixteen Cascade Range glaciers that are imminently headed toward evaporation—and to eventually reside in memory only. In February 2023, my computer-generated news update brought tremendous sadness to my Virginia morning hours. The news greeted me with a notice of the loss of the gentle giant Hinman Glacier—once the largest glacier between Mount Rainier and the now much diminishingly glaciated Glacier Peak.

The Hinman Glacier once fed the Skykomish River as it flowed past strawberry and tulip fields. The river wetted parched riverbanks and thirsty throats on its way into Monroe and then Everett. It sustained salmon runs, boaters, and more.

Now, with the loss of this gentle giant, the region's already existing droughts will become even more severe and intolerable. It's a drying punishment for how we treated our climate, our Earth, our glaciers, and our water supply. This, too, wilts our psyche, culture, and self-identity as we head into our uncertain future and our ever-warming and drying times with fewer and fewer glaciers.

In the winter of 2018-19, Canary - A Literary Journal of the Environmental Crisis published my short story, "Ice Remembered." This nonfictional piece lamented the loss of polar ice and highlighted ice's global importance. At that time, credible climate scientists knew global warming was happening faster than originally calculated. However, with the loss of the Hinman Glacier and the likely additional glacier loss in the next few years, suddenly, this loss landed remarkably close to home.

Shall We Meet Again in Thunder, Lightning, and Rain?

The white clouds rose above the mountaintop, and as I stood below, I understood a simple story with a counterplot. Man builds of evil ... God creates but good ... and all the tearful beauty of the sky could never be contained in man-made things, while every mountain breeze can softly sigh a tender note that only heaven brings. And as I gazed, I somehow seemed to know I'd never rest until I climbed its peak, much as the salmon in the stream below, would fight my way to reach the goal I seek. One cannot quiet souls where sunsets burn, nor visit heaven once and not return.

—Virginia Pennock

O n April 18, 1906, a 296-mile segment of the San Andreas Fault ruptured and initiated calamity and mayhem throughout the San Francisco Bay region. As if a major earthquake had not shaken nerves enough, the rupture set off fires that swept through the city.

The great fire spread no farther than San Francisco proper, but helpless spectators could easily see the conflagration from across the bay along the Alameda shoreline, where three-year-old Hermann Ulrichs and his parents shook, watched, and worried.

Despite living through the infamous 1906 San Francisco Earthquake, young Hermann suffered an even greater traumatic event just seven years later. On May 31, 1913, doctors noted complications in his mother's delivery of her second child. The complications became too much for the newborn to endure, and the child died later that day. There's no known surviving evidence to support this claim, but those same childbirth complications, combined with the trauma of losing her child, might also have been too much for Hermann's mother to endure, since she died three weeks later.

Losing his mother at the tender age of eleven impacted Hermann greatly. So much so, he refused to talk about it throughout his entire adult life. After his mother died, Hermann's father rarely came home from his overseas business trips or took any interest in his son, even when stateside. This abandonment forced Hermann to move into his wealthy and aristocratic grandparents' Alameda home.

Hermann's extended family lived under the same roof and raised and cared for Hermann as if he were their own. His grandmother, wealthy socialite Sophia Siegfried, took a special liking to young Hermann, and she, more than anyone else, raised Hermann and provided him with much-needed stability. This included taking walks together. Hermann's grandmother used to frequently take him to Mount Tamalpais to stroll, breathe fresh air, and steal an opportunity to get away from their normal, albeit well-to-do, lifestyle.

Due to its proximity to San Francisco, Mount Tamalpais provided countless outdoor experiences for San Francisco Bay-area residents, and even an occasional inspiration. The poet Edward Rowland Sill lived on its slopes and communed with nature for most of the summer of 1865.

> *I sat last night on yonder ridge of rocks to see the sunset over Tamalpais, whose tinted peak, suffused with rosy mist, blended the colors of the sea and sky, and made the mountain one great amethyst ranging against the sunset.*
>
> —"The Hermitage," by Edward Rowland Sill

Although it supplied exercise to many, and poetic solace to a few, Mount Tamalpais offered a spectacular view of the San Francisco Bay region, nearby coastal communities, and east toward the Sierra Nevada crest. For over a hundred years, Mount Tamalpais, known locally as Mount Tam, provided a welcoming outdoor outing for Bay Area residents. However, it was no wilderness.

In the first decade or two of the twentieth century, farmers used Mount Tamalpais's lower slopes for cattle grazing. Conflicts between private landowners and recreationalists were frequent. Visitors left farmers' gates open, and cattle often escaped and wandered off. Visitors left prolific litter everywhere, which prompted even more landowner agitation. Eventually, conservationists secured funds to buy the properties and have the public run it as a state park. However, during Sophia Siegfried and Hermann Ulrichs' strolls, a trip up Mount Tamalpais neither offered wilderness nor conserved and protected land. At the time, a trip up the mountain offered what people today call greenspace. Greenspaces near urban centers provide an exposure to nature that generates interest in exploring more primitive wilderness environments later.

Reaching Mount Tam then required only a short ferry ride from Hermann's family's Alameda home, followed by a trail that wound through redwood and oak groves to the 2,571-foot summit. Back then, instead of using a trail, visitors could also take the Mill Valley and Mount Tamalpais Scenic Railroad all the way to the summit.

On a clear day, a person standing on the summit could see the entire Bay Area and gaze upon the distance lofty and enticing Sierra Nevada. In my mind's eye, I can visualize young Hermann staring at an expansive view while fresh with the excitement of standing on his first summit. In this mind image, Hermann's young eyes slowly traverse past ocean, bay, Alameda shipyard, and downtown San Francisco, and then slowly rise past coastal foothills to eventually stop, transfixed, on a wondrous sight in the distance: the rugged beauty of the Sierra Nevada—the tallest mountain range in the contiguous United States.

Hermann needed only one gaze to have a moment of clarity, an epiphany, a point at which he saw purpose and meaning in life. His epiphany became something tangible and animated, not unlike Pinocchio rising from Geppetto's lifeless wooden carving. Hermann knew something of importance had just been given birth. His High Sierra gaze instantaneously formed his lifelong bond with and passion for mountains, adventure, and the wild unknown. His pulse quickened as he yearned to explore the magical secrets of the Sierras.

Millions have experienced the same view from Mount Tamalpais. What is it about the human heart and spirit that allows similar experiences to produce radically different emotional responses—spark or no spark? Where Hermann saw mystery, excitement, adventure, and inspiration, perhaps others gazing at the identical sight simply saw a picturesque view.

Decades later, in what seemed to be a world apart, I stopped to people-watch on a warm spring day—the day I strolled up Mount Tamalpais. At first, the summit and I were alone. Sitting off to the side, I discreetly watched various groups reach their summit, talk, eat a snack, picnic, gaze at the view, and then descend. Although there were no clouds, haze and air pollution obscured the Sierra view. From the summit, you could still get a decent view, particularly of the San Francisco Bay and surrounding foothills. Despite the scenery and the summit-like feel, few people appeared to notice they were on a mountain. The principal comment I overheard concerning the view came from those who pointed and excitedly exclaimed, "I can see our house!" All conversations that day on the summit were ordinary and lacked deep emotional connection. The obscured mountains inspired no one that day.

Despite the ninety years separating our Mount Tamalpais experiences, I sat on the summit and tried to imagine Hermann's thoughts while gazing at the same view. Time, experience, emotional maturity, and life's burdensome encumbrances altered my frame of reference. I could look at the same scene, but I couldn't see the same view. I'd already formed my connection to mountains through alternate pathways. For me and other people who visited Mount Tam that day, it simply became an outing. Besides, the scene was *not* the same. Urban haze and smog obscured the Sierras. The view that set the course for the rest of Hermann's life is no longer physically possible due to air pollution. Both tangible and intangible obstacles prevented a replication of Hermann's experience. Life is like a river—it flows only in one direction.

When Hermann Ulrichs stood on the summit of Mount Tamalpais as a young teenager and gazed at the Sierra Nevada skyline, he saw a boundless horizon. Perhaps he saw something only he could see. Mountain forces chose to connect with only Hermann on that day. This connection enabled him to view this vantage point as an unresolved mystery. What are these mountains like? What sort of potential adventures are available in the hitherto unknown mountain valleys and clouded, windswept summits?

Toward the end of Hermann's mountaineering adventures, did he still retain his Mount Tam view and understanding? His first wild and largely unexplored North Cascades experience made the Sierra Nevada seem tame and less mysterious by comparison. Similarly, after exploring much of the North Cascades and then leaving for World War II and life at sea for six years, the North Cascades also seemed different when he returned. For one, others had drifted in, explored, mapped, and climbed its summits. Hermann also had changed. His job and life were then in California. It became logistically problematic to make exploratory trips to the Cascades, especially the impromptu ones he preferred. For Hermann, life wasn't scripted. He preferred to follow where his inspiration led. Eventually, even the North Cascades and Canada lost some of their mystery and luster. Increasingly, to fulfill these same longings, Hermann turned more and more to other passions, like music.

In *Climbing in North America*, Chris Jones, in comparing alpine climbing with rock climbing, said, "The rock climber has reduced the overall difficulties in order to concentrate on the technical problems with rock." This is also true with the evolution of alpine climbing. The pioneers in the Cascades resolved many of the range's mysteries that enabled increasingly technical climbs to follow. Pioneering climbing in the North Cascades began in earnest in the 1930s by Hermann Ulrichs and other pioneer explorers. Although he had a short climbing career in the North Cascades, those few years were instrumental in developing Cascade climbing into what it is today. Hermann exemplifies the notion that not even the solo climber truly climbs alone, for we all climb upon the shoulders of giants. In the case of the few remaining Winkettes, we climb shoulder to shoulder with them as they show us the way.

Hermann also unconsciously helped break down the strict and rigid climbing protocols of the pre-war old guard, not only in the Cascades but also in the Canadian Rockies and the Sierra Nevada. Similarly, the Creedence new-guard climbers broke other barriers and ascended even higher because, after all, we all stand on the shoulders of giants. It's the great arc and continuum.

In land-management jobs I've held, I occasionally reflected on what climbing and wilderness must have been like during Hermann's day, for I've been one of the "recreational experts" Hermann once derisively commented upon when speaking about causes of the loss of wilderness. Due to mounting impacts from increasing numbers of people wanting to enjoy wilderness, more and more land managers saw the need to manage use and keep resource impacts at acceptable levels. This management structure keeps the resources in better shape and keeps the crowds dispersed; however, there's little doubt that there's a cost to such an approach. Wilderness is less wild now than in Hermann's day.

Hermann Ulrichs never developed refined technical climbing abilities. His skills belonged less to the gymnastic rock climber, like Ron Burgner, and more to the solid, determined, and persistent mountaineer. If he could have put up with the rigid organizational and social structure, he probably would have made an excellent expedition climber. However, he never liked the confines that expeditions required.

Chris Jones said in *Climbing in North America* that the small and compact nature of the Teton Range, insomuch that we can see nearly the entire range from one valley location, helped climbers advance their technical skills. The range's compactness allowed climbers to spend time advancing technical skills by putting up new and harder routes rather than "fritter away [their] time looking for untrod summits." Hermann Ulrichs, without a doubt, if given the choice, would have preferred to fritter away time looking for untrammeled summits, not because of a rigid and outdated viewpoint but due to the sense of wonder and excitement that untrod summits offered his restless soul.

Where's the excitement and wonder of putting up a new route on a popular mountain when there are unclimbed mountains on distant, mysterious blank regions on the map? In the case of Ron Burgner, what's the point of burdening a climber with exploring blank unknown map spaces when there's a classic crack running up the majestic wall staring down on the trailhead parking lot? Both perspectives push standards to new heights.

In *Challenge of the North Cascades*, Fred Beckey says the following about Hermann:

> Ulrichs ranks high among the pioneers of western mountains not because of climbing abilities, but because of a vigorous pursuit of unexplored problems. Many more severe climbs than his have now been made but his spirit and courage have not been surpassed.

Many climbers today—with their lightweight gear, topographic maps, communication equipment, route descriptions, and good road and trail systems—often don't realize how much hard work it involved to even approach the mountains in the 1920s and 1930s. It took dedication and a high spirit of adventure to climb in those days, with no chance of rescue or help. Hermann once commented about his North Cascades climbs:

As is always the case with pioneering, a good deal of effort and time was spent in finding out what was *not* the best approach, but that all has to be charged to reconnaissance. Then, there was the occasional handicap of bad weather. But notwithstanding, some twenty-one first ascents crowned the struggle. Nothing in the Canadian Rockies or the Alps has given me quite the same thrill or inspiration as that which came from penetrating these lonely valleys with eager curiosity to see what lay at the head of them, or as I pulled myself over the final ridge with beating heart to see what unknown wonder might lie beyond. There is an indefinable bloom, a mysterious and haunting loveliness that lies in all country that has not known the hands and hoofs of the despoilers. How quickly it disappears before the loggers, the miners, the hunters, the sheepmen, and the recreational experts!

Back in my college years, while holed up in the University of Washington's archives in the basement of Suzzallo Library, I increasingly read about Hermann Ulrichs and his climbs and explorations. I kept coming back to the same archives and the same climber. This prompted me to write a paper summarizing Hermann's Cascades climbs. I then expanded the writings to include the North Cascades' fascinating and pivotal 1930s-era climbing history. As part of this project, I wrote Hermann Ulrichs a letter. I assumed I would receive no response, since he would likely view a letter from a spud as an intrusion or annoyance. To my amazement, not only did Hermann answer my questions, but he also elaborated on them to a greater extent than I could ever have hoped for.

He said my letter "Awakened a great many pretty well buried memories of the North Cascades and has sparked a reawakening interest ..."

It seemed he, too, felt the same emotional pull of the wild. Later, I received other correspondence from Hermann. A couple of months later, shortly after getting out of bed, I received a call from Hermann, asking if he could meet me. In a couple of weeks, he planned to be in Seattle for a day, and he asked me if I could stop by and meet face-to-face to discuss mountains.

"Yes, of course!" I replied faster than a young spud can fall from a tree while imitating a leader's fall.

I met with him and spent the better part of the afternoon reminiscing. Hermann represented a connection with the past, a spirit relevant to any generation—even a century earlier. I saw the glimmer in his eyes as he spoke with soft and reverent tones of his adventures. I could relate, but I felt feeble in content, scope, and depth. At the time I awakened his deeply buried memories of our mountains and his early passions and energy, I'd only begun to forge my own. I witnessed firsthand his reawakening. While I felt privileged to witness the intensity of his emotional recollection, at the same time, I felt intrusive, as if I'd rattled his sense of calm and contentment.

Out of respect, someday, I had to put his thoughts and my experiences on paper. I thought to myself, *How many fascinating and wonderful things did this person see and experience?* During the conversation, his passion for the North Cascades showed not only by cheek quivers and the crackling in his voice but, especially, in his eyes. The eyes hinted at intense emotions behind the words. I hoped and imagined that despite my youth, he saw in me a shared connection with the North Cascades. I absorbed Hermann's stories and recollections. I meant to take notes, but I found I'd just listened.

I continued my 1930s North Cascades climbing history research by studying archived collections and interviewing Lloyd Anderson.

I completed my Hermann Ulrichs paper; it consisted of a detailed list of Hermann's North Cascades climbs with a summary and a few highlights. The finished article clocked in at twelve pages in length, single spaced—much too long for a typical magazine piece. Besides, I felt a magazine article didn't have the permanency I looked for. I hated the idea of my paper relegated to lining a birdcage or used as tinder for a fire. I preferred the journal format.

I sent my paper to Seattle's The Mountaineers with the hope they would print it in their annual journal since I was a member of The Mountaineers at the time. However, this was the first year since World War II that they didn't print a journal, so my paper remained unprinted. I mentioned this publication attempt to Hermann, and he replied, "The Mountaineers never really liked me; they probably wouldn't be interested in printing anything on my North Cascades climbs."

While attending my first and only annual meeting of the American Alpine Club, I went into the bathroom during a break. To my amazement, Alex Bertulis, a famous climber, began using the urinal to my right. Shortly after, Jim Wickwire, another famous climber, began using the urinal to my left. Looking past me as if I weren't there, Alex Bertulis mentioned to Jim Wickwire, from one urinal to the next (and I paraphrase), "We really need to interview some of the old-timers before they all die off. For instance, we really should interview Hermann Ulrichs. You know he still is living somewhere in California!" The urinal conversation continued with someone mentioning that later that evening, the club's president, Price Zimmerman, planned to hold a meeting on this very topic.

Sensing a lull in their urinal talk, I shyly interrupted and said, "I interviewed Hermann Ulrichs."

Alex replied as if he'd just seen a bush mysteriously burst into flame and a shy spud miraculously appear out of thin air.

"Who? *You?*"

Even more feebly, I replied, "Yes, sir. I interviewed Hermann Ulrichs and wrote a paper on his North Cascades climbs."

By then, our three porcelain receptacles had long ceased to be mere urinals. I saw them as podiums that just happened to be in a Seattle DoubleTree Plaza Hotel's restroom. Alex, from his lofty, stout, and gleaming, refined lectern, spoke down to what felt like my measly particle-board podium to inform me that he and others would be meeting Price Zimmerman soon—as if I hadn't just heard it moments earlier at the urinal. He then invited me up to the clouds for the official American Alpine Club board meeting and follow-up discussion. Suddenly, another bush burst into flames and consumed all available urinal oxygen. I lacked the necessary air needed for an intelligent and lengthy reply.

"Yes," I choked.

I had a couple of hours to wait and prepare for the meeting in Price Zimmerman's room. I carried with me no supplemental oxygen to sustain me in the rarified heights needed for an Alex Bertulis and Jim Wickwire conversation, but I forged on regardless. Who would have thought my walk into the DoubleTree Plaza's bathroom on that fateful day at that fateful minute would have sent me on such an illustrious oxygen-free ascent into the alpine heavens.

During the long wait, I rushed to my car and retrieved my Hermann Ulrichs paper. I have no idea what had prompted me to throw it in the car at the last moment. Although I, in those days, never let Hermann get far from my sight or mind.

The meeting started as a typical administrative meeting, but then Alex Bertulis began talking about the need for a project to interview old-time climbers. While talking with Price Zimmerman, he pointed to me and said, "This young person— What was your name again?" He continued, "He says he interviewed Hermann Ulrichs."

Price asked me if he could read my paper someday. As I sheepishly handed it to him, he seemed surprised I had it with me. Price read my paper immediately after the meeting. He turned to me and said the American Alpine Club would publish it in the *American Alpine Journal* if, and only if, I added Hermann's Sierra and Canadian climbs. He said Hermann's significance extended far beyond just the North Cascades, and the journal, after all, was national in scope.

I succeeded in my oxygen-free quest: I'd reached the summit. I now stood high above all else, looking down to the gray spudland below. My paper would soon be in bold black and white in the country's premier climbing and mountaineering journal. However, as my euphoria subsided, I spoiled the moment with nagging doubts. Hermann loathed giving up valuable elevation. And I realized that I loathed changing *my* paper. I politely explained to Price that the reason it had a North Cascades focus was because I wanted it that way.

Did anyone ask Paul McCartney to change his song "Penny Lane" to include Mossley Hill and Smithdown Road neighborhoods? I wanted to write about Hermann's North Cascades climbs. I didn't want to turn away from Penny Lane and head down Smithdown or Greenbank Road. I politely refused, telling Price of my interest in keeping the North Cascades as the paper's focus.

He said if I ever reconsidered, to give him a call. He handed me his business card and then left.

Even at the time, I knew that my idealistic, naïve, and sophomoric notions had taken over logical reasoning. (Well, you can't blame a sophomore in college for acting sophomoric.) I acted like a young, unknown musician telling a record producer with a worldwide record distribution that he would only record songs that *he* wrote, only for the producer to show the naïve musician the door. Then, that naïve musician slowly faded into just another unrecorded bum with lost dreams. Nonetheless, I needed, I thought, to stick to my principles.

I sent my paper to The Mountaineers the following year. But, once again, they decided to go another year without printing a journal. Not knowing where to try next, and with my busy efforts to start my career and find a life outside the North Cascades (if there was such a thing), I filed my paper away. I always maintained a strong desire to have the paper published while Hermann still lived. However, I never changed the paper's focus, and it remained unprinted.

On February 17, 1988, Hermann F. Ulrichs passed away quietly in his home in San Anselmo, California. I was saddened at the loss and sad that Hermann never saw the paper in print. It remained in one of my many boxes that I carried across the country from one work assignment to the next.

Years later, I reflected more and more upon my Hermann interviews and conversations. I remember most his intense personal connection with the North Cascades and how these deeply buried thoughts and emotions burst forth after my questions had disturbed his surface tranquility. The stark realization hit me—my draft paper didn't do Hermann justice. It read merely as a list of climbs and an emotionless description of his adventures. It lacked passion, intensity, and depth—the core and essence of Hermann, the climber and the person.

Today, as I gaze at my photographs of Mount Formidable, Snowking Mountain, the Ptarmigan Traverse, Buck Creek Pass, Whatcom Pass, and other alpine regions of the North Cascades, or as I hike along the Sierra's Evolution Basin, I often reminisce and reflect on Hermann's adventures. I occasionally reflect upon our conversations and his comment that my letter awakened deeply buried, intense memories of the North Cascades. Early in my climbing career, Hermann Ulrichs helped inspire and awaken my adventuresome spirit and form my emotional bond with the North Cascades. It's ironic, then, that at the end of Hermann Ulrichs's climbing career, I, in a small way, awakened a similar deeply buried emotional bond in him.

Such is the magical power that mountains have over all wilderness souls.

Distant Reflections and Deep Awakenings

Last campfires never die and you and I on separate ways to life's December, will always dream by this last fire and have this mountain to remember.

—Clark E. Schurman

For me, difficult and challenging mountaineering is in the past. I fully understand and accept that my better summits are behind me. I followed Hermann's and the Creedence climbers' footsteps, and others will follow mine. This is the great continuum of mountain adventures. Each successive generation may view the mountain experience diminished as time progresses, but this is only a state of mind. The newer generation knows no difference, and for them, each adventure is fresh and new. In addition, perhaps value systems change, thereby rendering previous viewpoints antiquated.

This is another reason that no climb can be repeated. No matter the number of ascents, the equipment, individual viewpoint, historical context, and weather and mountain conditions are never the same. I could never experience a Hermann Ulrichs adventure, and modern-day

315

climbers can't repeat my climbs. This is what Heraclitus meant when he claimed every river crossing is a unique experience. By the time the second person in line attempts to cross, the specific water the first person crossed is now downstream. Therefore, every experience has its place, time, and unique perspective in the world.

Although no two water crossings are comparable, there may still be some relatable experiences between those travelers who dare cross uncharted water versus those who remain on near and comfortable shores. Intense mountain experiences forge intertwined histories linking the past with the present. No starlight smells as sweet as that which shines down on us all. For some, this is the recipe for unlocking the human spirit. The past forms the foundation narrative that present and future experiences augment and enrich.

Why do people climb? Many people have attempted to answer this deep and philosophical question. Perhaps Sir Edmund Hillary's terse response, "Because it's there," while being a quick brush-off, might have been the closest to an answer. "Because it's there" succinctly captures the inward drive buried deep within a soul and leads that person to search for answers, challenge the unknown, and probe hidden longings and deep philosophical mysteries, such as the meaning and purpose of life.

Most climbers would find it hard or even impossible to answer the real reason why they climb, even if they knew themselves. Perhaps it's a similar dilemma for other people who share a deep connection and passion for their avocation, such as musicians. Why do they play music? Would someone truly understand if they weren't a musician? Would someone who asked such a question be capable of understanding any meaningful answer? Do musicians get these questions, or is it only climbers? Why land a person on the Moon?

Why did eighteenth- and nineteenth-century Americans explore the western frontier? President Jefferson presented economic justifications and practical reasons for why he wanted to send Lewis and Clark to explore the American West, but deep down, he had a deep, burning need to understand unsolved mysteries. The mystery simply needed to be solved—because it was there.

Whether immersed in his mountains or his music, Hermann constantly sought lonely places—geographically, metaphysically, and metaphorically; however, across generations, his spirit had company. He sought the unattainable—a deeper spiritual and emotional connection with and meaning to the world around him. Over time, the bond becomes prolific, since it not only connects Hermann and me. It also connects Cucamonga Dan, a particular Coloradoan introvert, cave-connecting denizens, TAG pitters, green-book aspirants, and the combined spirit of the Creedence climber collective.

Through these connections, I began to understand the timelessness of the human spirit. This interconnectedness of human spirits across generations would never have been possible if it weren't for the shared and enduring experiences that wild places provide. I now see with greater clarity that a summit, the cave's lowest depth, or any other destination doesn't, in the end, matter that much. I now see that our journeys had no real or attainable physical destination. For the Lakota at Bear Lodge were right. It's all about the journey.

It's the search that binds us as one. I see Julia's search for purity of experience as something not unlike Hermann Ulrichs's. Don searched for the perfect synthesis of body and mind while solving the ultimate technical challenge. Regardless of the generation, there are always people who search for the perfect expression of their heightened experiences, including the Meulemanses' ski expressiveness; Larry's search for the perfect rappel; Harry's, Gill's, and Diana's search for answers to universal scientific riddles; and Saul's search for a means to give back to the mountains and preserve what's left of the world's diminishing landscapes.

For many of us, in a sea of meaningless distractions, we may also be searching for like-minded souls—those who could form the perfect climbing team or partnerships. This search can take forms ranging from the individual to the community. A sense of community seems to permeate many searches, such as The Wilbur House, Icicle Canyon, Camp 4, National Speleological Society club membership, and Flint Ridge cavers' sense of identity. This may explain concerns over connecting disparate cave segments. Maybe, as Mammoth Ridge cavers searched for connections to form the ultimate cave in length, the Flint Ridge cavers feared it could diminish the connections most meaningful to them—that of the local Flint Ridge sense of community.

While we all may search for different things, as long as there remain mountains, caves, canyons, and challenging wildness, then there can be this continuity and sense of expanded community that for many of us may be our ultimate goal. If so, then maybe we're approaching the cusp of why we climb, cave, and adventure despite all the pain, suffering, dry heaves, and sorrow that come along with wild landscapes.

Upon reflection, while the journey may have no physical destination, it would be inaccurate to say it's bound for nowhere.

About the Author

David Ek held a successful and award-winning career with the National Park Service, where he led science and natural resources teams throughout the country. His resource management work often tackled complex issues of regional and national scope. David's extensive natural resource-related writings have appeared in dozens of science and management publications—and in countless forms intended for general audiences of all ages.

On the literary side, David writes both fiction and nonfiction. Editors for literary journals have found his writing "strong" with "much to admire." His short stories and essays have appeared in *Canary, Weber: The Contemporary West*, and elsewhere. *Pedro's Pickles and the American Dream* was his debut novel. He is a member of the Virginia Writers Club, the Independent Author Network, and the Pacific Northwest Writers Association.

When not sciencing or writing, David has been an active rock and mountain climber, caver, and explorer of the American wilds. A native of Seattle, Washington, he currently lives with his wife, children, cat, and dogs in rural northern Virginia. To learn more about David's writings, please visit him online at https://EkDavidAuthor.com.